EXPLAINING ENVIRONMENTALISM

For Patricia

Explaining Environmentalism

In search of a new social movement

PHILIP W. SUTTON
University of Leeds

Ashgate

Aldershot • Burlington USA • Singapore • Sydney

Published by
Ashgate Publishing Limited
Gower House
Croft Road
Aldershot
Hampshire GU11 3HR
England

Ashgate Publishing Company
131 Main Street
Burlington
Vermont 05401
USA

Ashgate website: http://www.ashgate.com

British Library Cataloguing in Publication Data
Sutton, Philip W.
    Explaining environmentalism : in search of a new social
    movement
    1. Environmentalism - Great Britain 2. Environmentalism -
    Political aspects - Great Britain 3. Social movements -
    Great Britain
    I. Title
    333.7'0941

Library of Congress Catalog Card Number: 00-130584

ISBN 0 7546 1312 7

Printed and bound by Athenaeum Press, Ltd.,
Gateshead, Tyne & Wear.

Contents

List of Figures   viii
List of Tables   ix
Acknowledgements   x

1 Environmentalism and Radical Ecology   1
   Introduction: The Basic Divide   1
   Environmentalism   2
   Radical Ecology   4
   Post-Industrialism and the New Social Movements   8
   Notes   12

2 Theories of Old and New Social Movements   13
   Introduction   13
   Definitions of 'Social Movement'   14
   Approaches to New Social Movements   18
   Distinctiveness of the New Social Movements   19
   Social Movements in Programmed Societies: Alain Touraine   27
   Social Movements as Signs: Alberto Melucci   33
   Revising New Social Movement Theory   37
   Notes   40

3 The Rise of Environmentalism and Radical Ecology   43
   Contemporary Environmentalism and Radical Ecology   43
   Contemporaneous Explanations   43
   Historical Explanatory Frameworks   51
   Cyclical Approaches and Political Opportunities   51
   Critical Remarks   55
   Karl Werner Brand: A Cyclical Phenomenon?   56
   Klaus Eder: The Emergence of a Submerged Counter-Culture   61
   Ulrich Beck: Reflexive Modernization and the Risk Society   69
   Back to Society: The End of Nature   72
   Conclusion   76
   Notes   78

4   The Origins of Organised Environmentalism   83
     Introduction   83
     A Background of Changing Sensibilities   85
     Origins of the Organised Environmental Movement   89
     Organisational Forms and Campaigning Styles   100
     'Green' Ideas in Socialist and Anarchist Thought   107
     Conclusion   112
     Notes   113

5   Twentieth Century Environmentalism   117
     The Organisation of Twentieth Century Concern for Nature   117
     Creation of a Mass Movement   120
     Globalising the Environmental Movement   124
     Precursors of Contemporary Ecocentrism   128
     Ecocentrism: The Deep Ecological Ideological Bond   137
     Ecocentrism in the Green Party   145
     The Green Party   148
     Development or Disjuncture?   156
     Notes   158

6   Industrialisation and Nature Politics   163
     Introduction   163
     Industrialisation in Historical Perspective   164
     Structural Bases of Environmentalism and Radical Ecology   168
     Institutional Dimensions of Modernity   171
     The Creation of an Industrial Society in Britain   176
     Conclusion   186
     Notes   187

7   Towards a Socio-Historical Explanation of British   189
     Environmentalism
     Environmentalism and Radical Ecology: A Conceptual   189
     Distinction
     Phase Models and Social Process   194
     The Reformism/Radicalism Axis   199
     The Problem Identification/Practical Implementation Spiral   200
     State Involvement: Established/Outsider Relations   201
     The Long-Term Development of Environmentalism   202

Conclusion 210

Notes 211

Bibliography *215*

Index *237*

vii

List of Figures

Figure 7.1   Environmentalism   190

Figure 7.2   Radical ecology   191

Figure 7.3   The expansion of nature conservation: open spaces   207
               to National Parks

Figure 7.4   Man/environment relationship   211

Figure 7.5   Social construction of nature   212

List of Tables

Table 1.1   Shallow versus deep ecological perspectives   7

Table 4.1   Dates of formation of selected nineteenth century   90
            environmental organisations

Table 4.2   Examples of the extent of early memberships   98

Table 5.1   Twentieth century environmental organisations   119

Table 5.2   Summary of Green Party performance in British General   151
            Election 1992

Table 5.3   Green Party performance in national elections 1974-92   152

Table 6.1   Urban population in England and Wales 1841-81   181

Table 7.1   Phases in the long-term development of British   203
            environmentalism

Acknowledgements

This book is a revised version of my doctoral dissertation and has benefited enormously from several disparate sources. I would like to thank my thoughtful colleagues and friends, particularly Stephen Vertigans and Steve Clarke for taking the time to read the entire manuscript at moments more crucial for the project than perhaps they realise, and for their constructive (and destructive!) comments which forced me to re-think some of the arguments. Ian Varcoe and Richard Kilminster were continuous sources of support, encouragement and sociological good sense over a number of years, and I have been fortunate to be able to discuss important theoretical issues with Chris Drinkwater and Conrad Russell. Paul Bagguley and Steven Yearley provided thoughtful and insightful critical comments on the thesis and I have tried to pay them heed.

Participation in Cultural Studies Workshops at the University of Leeds brought me into contact with different departments and specialisms and helped to convince me of the need for a sober sociological assessment of recent social change. I must also take this opportunity to express personal thanks to Judith Graves and Lynn Towell for their infectious enthusiasm during the book's pre-history, and for which I am ever grateful.

Thanks to all the Editorial staff at Ashgate for their efficient work on bringing the book to completion which has undoubtedly improved the final version, and special thanks to Rosalind Ebdon for her keen-eyed checking of the whole manuscript. The anonymous reviewer at Ashgate also provided positive comments and very helpful suggestions for improving Chapter Three, and deserves to be mentioned. You know who you are! As usual, all the book's failings are mine alone, though I cannot claim the credit for all of its virtues.

Finally, special thanks must go to Kevin and all of those who shared in the practical seminar on perseverance and self-belief in Barcelona on the evening of May 26th 1999, where we learned so much, and heartfelt thanks to Pat, without who this book simply would not have been possible.

1 Environmentalism and Radical Ecology

Introduction: The Basic Divide

In the literature on varieties of environmental or Green thought, a basic distinction exists between 'reformist' and 'radical' approaches to the defence of the natural world from human interference. Unfortunately there is no consensus on the use of terms in this literature, so that whilst some writers use 'environmentalism' to describe a managerial reformist approach to the conservation of nature, others use the same term to refer to radical ecology or 'Green' politics which rejects reformism, arguing for major transformations in the Western way of life.

The basic dichotomy goes back to Arne Naess's (1973) use of the distinction between 'shallow' and 'deep' ecology as philosophical approaches to society/nature relations, but since then a range of other terms have entered the discourse. Andrew Dobson (1990), uses 'green' (reformist) and 'Green' (capital G) (radical), Eckersley (1992) defines 'ecologism' (radical) in contrast to several other forms such as 'conservationism' (reformist), while Jonathon Porritt makes a distinction between 'light' (reformist) and 'dark' (radical) Greens (1984). What all the above writers are attempting to do is to show that the earlier ideas and practices of nature conservation, preservationism, and arguments for public access to natural areas only produced strictly limited analyses of the human/nature relationship, and do not call for urgent action and social change, whilst the newer Green, ecological perspective goes beyond these, to demonstrate that solving contemporary environmental problems will require a radical restructuring of the ways of life currently enjoyed in modern societies. It is this political message which seems to set 'ecologism' apart from 'environmentalism.'

Throughout this study I will characterise the basic distinction between reformist and radical approaches as that between 'environmentalism' and 'radical ecology' respectively, though for grammatical purposes I will sometimes refer to the latter as 'Green'. Part of my argument is that the two approaches are distinct enough to justify the separation, but also because the

1

historical development of reform environmentalism and radical ecology are substantially divergent. What Dobson calls 'ecologism' and Eckersley calls 'ecocentrism' *do*, I believe, ask questions of existing political ideologies and worldviews respectively, but these questions are not wholly new ones. The kinds of questions asked by radical ecology, and many of the answers offered have a familiar ring, but what seems to have changed is the context in which these questions are raised. First though, we must establish the terms of the discussion.

Environmentalism

The term 'environmentalism' is often used in Green circles, to describe an earlier form of nature concern which is now superseded by a deeper, 'ecocentric' analysis of the relationship between human societies and the natural world. As I use the term in this study, environmentalism refers to those approaches to society/nature relations which emphasise the benefits to human beings of natural objects, and to attempts to rectify problems of environmental damage and pollution through technological means. For environmentalists, interest in and contact with the natural world are seen as part of an enlightened view of human well-being. Humans can benefit in several ways from this interest. Nature study offers pleasures of aesthetic or scientific kinds, leisure pursuits can help humans to lead healthier lives, society can benefit from the preservation of endangered species as this maintains genetic diversity and can be useful in developing new medical treatments (an argument often advanced in support of protecting tropical rainforests), and so on. This perspective is human-welfarist in so far as its main arguments rest on the value of nature conservation *for* society and where no benefit can be gained for human society, then environmentalist arguments against scientific and industrial development fail, particularly if that development brings other benefits such as employment opportunities, housing and increased convenience.

Environmentalism is also used here to cover all those organisations which are rooted in an environmentalist perspective. For example, the National Trust, Royal Society for the Protection of Birds (R.S.P.B.) and the Woodland Trust argue in favour of keeping some areas of nature free from industrial and urban development and have used a number of strategies to achieve this goal, from public education and recruiting supporters to buying tracts of land which they manage and maintain themselves. In their own terms these efforts have had some successes, but for Greens these efforts do not go far enough, as they fail to address the root causes of ecological damage and hence do not call for significant social changes.

Reform environmentalist approaches are sometimes accused of adopting a managerial stance towards the natural world, and one which is ultimately self-defeating. Almost all conservation, preservation and amenity organisations fall into this category, as they tend to argue for and are involved in managing nature reserves, areas of outstanding natural beauty, public access areas and buildings of historical value and interest.[1] Environmental organisations do these things largely for human-centred reasons. For example, one aspect of the work of the R.S.P.B., is that it owns nature reserves which it manages ostensibly for the benefit of birdlife, but also for its own members who have access to these reserves for observation. In this way, environmentalism argues for nature preservation and conservation as part of the creation and maintenance of a high quality of life for humans.

Radical ecologists might argue that this strategy may indeed protect some wildlife in the short term, but the establishment of green 'oases' does nothing to prevent the large-scale destruction of nature by commercial and industrial practices all over the planet, which will make localised environmentalist efforts largely irrelevant. Further, some eco-radicals argue that the very idea of human beings being able to 'manage' naturally occurring ecosystems in their own interests is a clear indication of modern human hubris and Western 'Enlightenment' thinking, itself one of the root causes of global environmental damage revealed by the recent evidence on global ecological damage. In this sense, the destructive modern attitudes towards the natural world are reproduced within reformist organisations, whose very existence then tends to militate against the development of a more 'ecocentric' perspective. As Evernden (1985: 10) notes, enlightened self-interest is not an adequate basis for nature politics because '... environmentalists have ensured their own failure whenever self-interest can be perceived as lying elsewhere'. An example of this would be a more short-term materialistic adherence to the benefits of economic growth as being more conducive to 'self-interest'. In this way, radical ecology has come to define itself not only in opposition to further industrial modernisation, but also in opposition to more established forms of managerial environmentalism.

Further than this though, the analysis of modern societies offered by radical ecology is claimed to go much 'deeper' than that of environmentalism, to penetrate to the causes of ecological damage, and thus it is said to contain, 'all the truths of the shallower view, plus some additional ones as well' (Goodin 1992: 43), and hence to go beyond 'mere' environmentalism. It is argued that the emergence of a radical ecological perspective could lead to the radicalisation of reformist environmental organisations and the creation of a mass movement pursuing the transformation of the destructive society/nature relationship currently embodied in modern culture. It is worth remembering though, that the real reforms achieved by the early environmental groups have come to be largely taken for granted by those which followed, and in this sense the descriptive chronological contrast between 'reformists' and 'radicals', though useful in some respects, tends also to act as a barrier to seeing this contrast against the backdrop of the longer-term development of British environmentalism. This long-term development is a major theme running throughout this study.

Radical Ecology

Trying adequately to characterise the radical ecological perspective is notoriously difficult, due to the variety of approaches which fall within this general 'worldview'. In attempting to differentiate radical ecology from environmentalism I do not want to be drawn into a protracted discussion about this internal variety.[2] Here I am attempting to provide a guide to the fundamental differences of approach of the two perspectives and their respective solutions to environmental problems in order to show why some researchers have come to see the contemporary ecological movement as 'new.'

As a working definition I use the term 'radical ecology' to refer to those approaches which attempt to move away from a human-centred concern for nature protection towards an ecocentric perspective which emphasises the interrelatedness of living things (including humans) in ecosystems. By ecocentric I mean 'a mode of thought which regards humans as subject to ecological and systems laws' (Pepper 1996: 329). More than this though, ecocentrics argue that non-human nature is worthy of protection and defence in its own right, without recourse to arguments about the necessity for this protection to be related to human survival and well-being. As Goodin (1992:

8) has observed, '... it is clear that nature is now taken to have an independent role in the creation of value. The value of nature is no longer regarded as wholly reducible to its value to God or to humanity. And it is this insight that drives, most powerfully, the current wave of environmental concern'. In this sense, radical ecology wants to shift the burden of proof on to those who would interfere with natural systems and intervene in areas of 'wild' nature in the name of development, to demonstrate why it is justifiable to destroy valuable ecosystems and disrupt natural processes. In the absence of such justifications, radical ecologists argue that the natural world should be maintained intact.

In opposition to environmentalism, radical ecology approaches generally argue that ecological problems cannot be solved within the present socio-economic, political framework, which usually means more technological fixes such as recycling plants, catalytic converters and so on. Whilst these may provide short-term solutions, they also require industrial production themselves and therefore can only add to long-term global ecological problems caused by industrial development, as well as propagating the notion that no radical social change is required. In addition, radical ecology approaches, despite using the findings of scientific research to substantiate their calls for urgent action, are critical of the contribution of classical scientific thinking to an anthropocentric worldview which legitimises ecological damage in the interests of progress and development. There are many statements of faith which could be used to illustrate their point here. For example, Marx's thesis (cited in Bottomore and Rubel 1990: 68) that '... mankind always sets itself only such problems as it can solve; since, on closer examination, it will always be found that the problem itself arises only when the material conditions necessary for its solution already exist or are at least in the process of formation'. One of the more recent statements in this vein is the following from P.B. and J.S. Medawar (1972: 15):

We believe that technological remedies can be found for evils of technological origin and are prepared to marvel at people who think otherwise. One had hoped that a journey to the far side of the moon had convinced everyone that any accomplishment which is not at odds with the laws of physics is within human capability. [3]

This represents a clear 'technocentric' orientation (O'Riordan 1981) against which many radical ecologists are reacting. Instead they propose a return to simpler lifestyles, usually in decentralised communities, lower levels of consumption in the Western nation-states and the reorganisation of highly industrialised societies and cultures in favour of ecologically benign (or 'soft') technologies and anti-materialist attitudes which advocate 'treading softly on the Earth'. So, although managerial environmentalist measures may receive some support from radical ecologists, they will tend to be perceived by the latter as not going far enough in their analysis of the *causes* of ecological degradation, and therefore to understate the size of the problem hence avoiding any discussion of necessary social changes. 'If it [Green politics] stops at mere reforms in conservation and pollution control, then it will merely be operating as a leaky safety valve for the existing systems of exploitative politics' (Ecology Party 1983: 34).

Radical ecology therefore sees itself as going beyond the rather narrow confines of the environmentalist approach and moving nature politics in the direction of a thoroughgoing critique of modernity itself, particularly in so far as this is based on criticisms of the rationalistic Enlightenment 'project' and 'classical' methods of scientific inquiry. Many radical ecologists trace the origins of the contemporary 'ecological crisis' back to the advent of dualistic modes of thinking and a mechanistic worldview introduced via the sixteenth and seventeenth century scientific revolution.[4]   Fritjof Capra (1983: 38) summarises why this is so.

> The medieval outlook changed radically in the sixteenth and seventeenth centuries. The notion of an organic, living, and spiritual universe was replaced by that of the world as a machine, and the world-machine became the dominant metaphor of the modern era. This development was brought about by revolutionary changes in physics and astronomy, culminating in the achievements of Copernicus, Galileo, and Newton.

By locating one of the sources of destructive modern attitudes to nature in the scientific 'worldview', radical ecologists differ from environmentalists who will typically draw on expert scientific research to support their arguments for nature preservation. It should be noted though that radical ecologists are much more impressed by recent developments in theoretical physics, particularly the emergence of 'chaos theory' and quantum (sub-atomic) physics which appear to be more amenable to an 'ecological' reading of their implications (as in, Prigogine and Stengers 1985). Capra (1975: 71) argues for example that, 'Quantum theory thus reveals a basic oneness of the universe ...' which supports the radical ecological focus on interrelatedness.[5]

Table 1.1 Shallow versus deep ecological perspectives

Shallow Ecology	Deep Ecology
Natural diversity is a valuable resource for us.	Natural diversity has its own (intrinsic) value.
It is nonsense to talk about as value except as value for mankind.	Equating value with value for humans reveals a racial prejudice.
Plant species should be saved because of their value as genetic reserves for human agriculture and medicine.	Plant species should be saved because of their intrinsic value.
Pollution should be decreased if it threatens economic growth.	Decrease of pollution has priority over economic growth.
Developing nations' population growth threatens ecological equilibrium.	World population at the present level threatens ecosystems but the population and behaviour of industrial states more than any others. Human population is today excessive.
"Resource" means resource for humans.	"Resource" means resource for living beings.
People will not tolerate a broad decrease in their standard of living.	People should not tolerate a broad decrease in the quality of life but in the standard of living of over-developed nations.
Nature is cruel and necessarily so.	Man is cruel but not necessarily so.

(Source: Naess cited in Devall 1990: 33)

In this way the links which Toulmin (1982) finds between the 'new' physics and postmodernism can be extended to radical ecology, as part of the postmodernist undermining of the certainties and metanarratives of modernity (Lyotard 1984). Generally, I will be arguing against this kind of interpretation, which seems to ignore modernity's 'dualistic' character (Eder 1993 and Chapter 3 this volume).

By way of a summary, Arne Naess's characterisation in Table 1.1 above, gives a good indication of the key difference of emphasis between environmentalism and radical ecology, though it should be borne in mind that the terms of the divide have been set from the radical side. Nevertheless, despite the polemical intent here, Naess manages to capture the broad differences of emphasis of the two approaches and gives us a feel for the solutions they offer. However, I will argue *pace* Naess, that (shallow) environmentalism is not a restricted form of deep ecology, rather the two are different perspectives, and as Goodin (1992) has argued, which one is 'correct' is a matter of political intent and genuine debate. More than this, I will be attempting to show that the histories of the environmental movement and radical ecological ideas in Britain are significantly interrelated.

Post-Industrialism and the New Social Movements

Post-industrial society theories are now an established part of sociological discourse, having been propounded in several forms since Daniel Bell's initial statement of the thesis in the USA in 1963. The most influential interpretation in Europe has probably been Alain Touraine's work (1971, 1981, 1983) which puts a stronger emphasis on the displacement of industrial class conflict than Bell, and the subsequent struggle of new social actors to step into the place vacated by the labour movement. I will have more to say about Touraine than Bell as it is the former's attempt to locate which new movement has the potential to fill the void which brings us into contact with the self-conceptions of Green activists and writers.

However much their respective analyses differ in emphasising one aspect of post-industrial theory over others, there is a quite remarkable degree of agreement amongst post-industrial theorists on the key features of the new society (Kumar 1986: 193). An initial characterisation of these would include:

1. The long-term decline of manufacturing industry and with it the proportion of the workforce directly involved in the processes of manufacturing material goods. A corollary of this is that the service sector of the economy expands, leading to a rise in the numbers of service sector workers, in particular a shift away from blue-collar work and towards white-collar work takes place.

2. A certain kind of technological change gathers pace, based on information technologies which not only creates powerful new groups of information professionals but also results in a thorough - going 'informationalising' of manufacturing processes, resulting in a speeding up of the removal of industrial workers from the manufacturing sector.

3. The emergence of groups of information professionals begins to change the dominant sources of social power and although there is disagreement over just how powerful these information professionals are or will become, both Bell and Touraine argue that the development is significant. Bell reads a major importance into the emergence of these groups from his perception of a shift in modern society's 'axial principle' towards the production of theoretical knowledge rather than manufactured goods (though he later repudiated the idea of a 'knowledge elite' in Bell 1980).

Touraine (1971) sees the emergence of a new 'class' conflict between a growing 'technocracy' and a variety of social groups opposed to different aspects of the post-industrialising process, or in his own terms, in opposition to the 'programming' of more and more aspects of social life. In order to be an effective opposition though, Touraine argues that these diverse groups must coalesce into one genuine social movement. The task for sociologists is to explore which of the fledgling movements has the potential to develop in this way. In recent times, the environmental and Green movements have been seen as the most likely to be able to unite the various strands of opposition (Eder 1993).

These aspects of contemporary social change provide the necessary structural context for the development of new social concerns and protest which feed into the emergence of new social movements such as environmentalism, animal rights, women's movements, disability rights, anti-nuclear and peace movements and various urban movements. It is here that post-industrial theories meet those which define new social movements as a special category of social movements more generally. New social movements are said to be different from previously existing 'old' social movements in a number of ways including: organisational form, issues of concern, participants involved and value orientation. The generalising of these common features to all new social movements I find difficult to accept on empirical and historical grounds and will be concerned not only to argue against the grain of new social movement theories, but also to produce a more discriminating and historically realistic description and explanation of the development of environmental and Green movements. At this stage it may help to outline a few of the key questions and problems which are raised in relation to the linking of post-industrialism, new social movement theory and the history of the environmental movement, to set the scene, as it were, for what follows.

Ecological writers and many sociologists have identified contemporary nature politics as 'anti-industrial' in tenor, often explicitly so. In the USA, Theodore Roszak (1981: 33) identifies the 'convergence of all urban-industrial economies' as the main problem, because all such societies are 'devoted to maximum productivity and the unbridled assertion of human dominance'. Whilst one of the classic statements of the British Greens' anti-industrial position comes from Jonathon Porritt (1984: 43-4):

> The politics of the Industrial Age, left, right, and centre, is like a three lane-motorway, with different vehicles in different lanes, but *all* heading in the same direction. Greens feel it is the very direction that is wrong, rather than the choice of any one lane in preference to the others. It is our perception that the motorway of industrialism inevitably leads to the abyss - hence our decision to get off it, and seek an entirely different direction.

The use (and waste) of the Earth's resources in the production of consumer goods; the degradation of natural environments, rapidly increasing extinction of species, creation of global problems such as ozone depletion and global warming, pollution, technological disasters such as oil 'spills' at sea and the Chernobyl nuclear explosion, and many other 'dysfunctions' are all seen by Greens as products of industrialisation and its destructive mind-set. The latter leads to an unrealistic technological optimism and faith in modern industrial societies to solve the problems it sets itself. Greens have no such faith and are, in Cotgrove and Duff's (1982) terms, 'catastrophists' not 'cornucopians' seeing natural limits to human development.

One question we can ask at this point is why, if Green movements are opposed to industrialisation, have they only emerged in the final quarter of the twentieth century? Why did Green politics not find a fundamental place within the oppositional forces in industrial capitalist societies much earlier? In Britain, the origins of the modern Industrial Revolution can be traced back to 1750-1830, the period of 'industrial take-off', and industrialisation has continued apace ever since. With hindsight, perhaps we should be surprised at the lack of resistance to industrial development during the nineteenth and early twentieth centuries. The apparent dismissal, or lack of interest in this problem is evident from several contemporary Green texts which seemed all too willing to accept the idea that they were contributing to the development of a radically new social movement. For example, the 1983 U.K. Ecology Party (1983: 4) Manifesto claimed that 'Green politics is the single most significant international movement since the birth of socialism at the end of the 19th century'. The Ecology Party had adopted the 'Blueprint for Survival' (1972), a document drawn up by the editors of the British environmental journal The Ecologist, as its manifesto. The latter claimed that '... our Blueprint for survival heralds the formation of the movement for survival and, it is hoped, the dawn of a new age in which Man will learn to live with the rest of nature rather than against it' (Goldsmith et al 1972: 10).

To compound the problem, it appears that at the precise moment when sociology begins to produce and embrace post-industrial and postmodern theories which describe a historical transition *beyond* industrialism and modernity, a radical social movement emerges which professes an implacable opposition to continuing industrialisation. How do these two 'fit' together and how can we make sense of the apparent incongruity?

One further problem needs to be mentioned. Organisations whose aims have included the conservation of nature, protection of wild animals, defence of natural beauty and access rights for the public to the countryside have been in existence in Britain long before the 1970s. This fact is often acknowledged but often dismissed on the basis that a few middle class 'societies' constitute a social movement. Others ignore early conservationist groups as irrelevant to the understanding of contemporary nature politics which seems to have radical political aspirations in contrast to the localised and reformist nature of earlier conservationist efforts. At the heart of this study is the contention that we cannot understand the character and prospects of contemporary environmental and Green movements without locating them in their proper historical context. This means taking seriously the earlier forms of nature conservation as well as the longer-term development of the environmental movement *and* its constituent organisations which are often neglected in contemporary discussions.[6]

Notes

1   Conwentz's (1909) term, 'natural monuments', gives some sense of the connections that early environmentalists found between preserving both 'natural' and 'human-made' objects.

2   See Eckersley 1992 for a reliable engagement with these varied positions.

3   It is somewhat ironic that space travel, rather than lending support to a technocentric orientation to ecological problems, helped to drive home the radical ecological message of how beautiful and fragile life on Earth is. As one former astronaut of the former German Democratic Republic put it, 'Before I flew I was already aware of how small and vulnerable our planet is; but only when I saw it from space, in all its ineffable beauty and fragility, did I realize that humankind's most urgent task is to cherish and preserve it for future generations' (Jahn quoted in Kelley 1988; plate 141).

4   See for example Fritjof Capra's *The Turning Point* (1983), Carolyn Merchant's *The Death of Nature* (1982) and Vandana Shiva's *Staying Alive* (1988) for good examples of this argument. All three find links between the rise of Western science and the oppression of women, thus leading the way into an ecofeminism based on inverting modernity's negative symbolic evaluations of both nature and women.

5   Such a reading seems inexorably to lead in the direction of new age idealism with all the problems this brings. Zukav (1980: 117) argues that 'Since particle - like behaviour and wave-like behaviour are the only properties that we ascribe to light and since these properties now are recognised to belong not to light itself but to our interaction with light, then it appears that light has no properties independent of us'. This is clearly not consistent with ecological realism which stresses the intrinsic properties and value of natural objects, rather, it is strikingly reminiscent of some forms of extreme social constructionism (as in Tester 1991).

6   The reading of contemporary Green ideas as 'new' leads to some curious positions. For instance, in a largely excellent account, O'Riordan (1981 : 239) notes that in advocating a return to the land as a solution to the evils of civilization, 'Kropotkin was a hundred years ahead of his time'. However, the recourse to nature as a healing salve expressed by Kropotkin (and others) in the late nineteenth century, has been a recurring feature in oppositional politics since at least the early nineteenth century. In this sense, Kropotkin was very much 'of his time'.

2 Theories of Old and New Social Movements

Introduction

A sociological perspective on contemporary social movement activity, which emphasises the novel or historically 'new' aspects of these movements, has been widespread amongst researchers in this field since the 1970s. Since a wave of contemporary environmental and Green organisations and protest actions appears to have emerged around this time, 'new social movement' (NSM) theory would seem to have been, at least partly, developed to try to account for this wave of nature politics. 'Ecological' movements have been described as typical 'new' social movements, and as I am extremely sceptical of many of the claims of NSM theories, a reconstruction of the historical development of nature politics, taking in 'Green' ideas, actions and organisation building provides a good test case for the utility or otherwise of this perspective. Chapter Four begins this reconstruction.

In this chapter I outline the main themes of NSM theories, but I particularly want to highlight two underlying issues. Firstly, differences notwithstanding, NSM theories seem to be drawn inexorably towards a reliance on large-scale theories of social-structural change, primarily though not exclusively, some version of the post-industrial society thesis, as a way of structurally anchoring, and hence providing a framework within which the rise of NSMs can be explained. In British sociology the ideas of 'New Times' (Hall and Jacques 1989) associated with the (now defunct) journal *Marxism Today*, theories of post-fordism (Murray 1989), and Lash and Urry's thesis of the disorganisation of British capitalism (1988, 1985), make some similar claims to post-industrial theories (Bagguley 1992: 26-7), though there are differences of emphasis among the various analyses. I shall discuss post-industrial theories here, and will only refer to the more recent British research when it adds something extra to the main claims of the older theories. I consider the apparent connection between NSM theory and post-industrialism to be problematic in several respects, and will explain why.

Secondly, I return to an issue already raised, namely the continuity of social movements across time. I consider that the relative neglect of this dimension in NSM theory has detrimental consequences for this theory's ability to cope with the historical evidence on environmentalism. The critique of NSM theory leads into a re-evaluation of structural post-industrial theories, and Part Three makes some progress towards a more realistic and long-term approach to understanding the development of environmental movements in Britain.

Definitions of 'Social Movement'

Though definitions of the concept 'social movement' abound in the literature, and each gives special emphasis to some aspect or other, there is fairly broad agreement on what it is that differentiates social movements from other forms of collective action such as political interest groups and political parties. A representative attempt at a definition is the following from Alan Scott (1990: 6):

> A social movement is a collective actor constituted by individuals who understand themselves to have common interests and, for at least some significant part of their social existence, a common identity. Social movements are distinguished from other collective actors, such as political parties and pressure groups, in that they have mass mobilization, or the threat of mobilization, as their prime source of social sanction, and hence of power. They are further distinguished from other collectivities, such as voluntary associations or clubs, in being chiefly concerned to defend or change society, or the relative position of the group in society.

There are I think, four important points in this definition:

1. Social movements are 'collective actors'. That is, there is a unity to their activity.
2. They have, or aim to create, a 'common identity'. This alerts us to the ways in which people can come to take their involvement in a social movement as a fundamental part of their own self - identity which they share with others in the movement.

3. Social Movements must be able to at least threaten 'mass mobilization'. It is unclear exactly what 'mass' means here. It could mean that movement activists must themselves constitute a mass, or that movement activists are able to mobilise their concerns amongst the non-committed public. I am happier with the latter, as most mass mobilisations are broad - based alliances of activists and supporters drawn from different 'movements' rather than being exclusively drawn from a single movement.

4. Movements aim to 'defend or change society'. In short, they have some collective goals and values which are part of a wider vision of what society should be like. In this way, there is often a moral or ethical dimension to movement activity.

Pakulski's (1991: 32) more concise definition below, remains broadly consistent with that of Scott, despite the differences of emphasis in their work:

> The term 'social movement' refers to a recurrent pattern of partially institutionalised collective activity which is anti-systemic in its value orientation, form and symbolism. When it attracts a relatively large number of supporters and sympathisers, it is called a 'mass social movement'.

Although this more action-oriented approach makes a distinction between 'social movements' and 'mass' social movements, and does not recognise movements aimed at defending the existing social order, Pakulski nevertheless notes similar characteristics to Scott as the defining features of social movements, namely:

1. collective activities which are,
2. value-oriented,
3. attract supporters and sympathisers, and which are,
4. 'anti-systemic'.

What is perhaps not brought out explicitly in these definitions is that unlike more spontaneous political protest actions against specific state policies, social movements tend to endure over time, often despite the marginalisation or even demise of the organisations which originally gave form to them. This is because movements are not simply organisations, nor are they the sum total of organisations pursuing similar changes within society. Rather, social movements can be seen as involving more or less coherent belief systems or 'ideological packages' which may exceed the scope of the movement's organisational forms at any time. The utility of this idea is pushed further in the work of the 'resource mobilization' theorists, McCarthy and Zald.

Within the resource mobilization paradigm, McCarthy and Zald's conceptual scheme has been one of the most widely discussed and used. Their alternative definition argues that,

> A social movement is a set of opinions and beliefs in a population representing preferences for changing some elements of the social structure or reward distribution, or both, of a society. A countermovement is a set of opinions and beliefs in a population opposed to a social movement. As is clear, we view social movements as nothing more than preference structures directed toward social change, very similar to what political scientists would term issue cleavages (1987: 20).

In addition they note the existence of 'social movement organizations' (SMOs) together with 'social movement industries' (SMIs). A SMO is, '... a complex, or formal organization that identifies its goals with the preferences of a social movement or a counter-movement and attempts to implement those goals ...', whilst SMIs are, '... the organizational analogue of a social movement ...', that is to say 'All SMOs that have as their goal the attainment of the broadest preferences of a social movement ...' (ibid: 20-1).

As McCarthy and Zald themselves note, there is a clear parallel between the concepts of SMI and SMO, and that of commercial 'industries' in economics. Movement organisations are treated as analogous to business corporations competing against each other within an economic sector. In this perspective, there is competition between SMOs which constantly strive for control of access to scarce financial and cultural resources. Chief among these resources is of course people themselves as supporters, members and activists. The highlighting of this competitive dimension of social movement activity (which clearly does exist) is often a useful corrective to discussions which over-emphasise the unity and collective purpose of movements, or what Melucci (1985: 793) calls the mistaken notion of 'a sort of deep mind of the movement'. Nonetheless, if pushed too far, this sort of perspective makes it difficult to visualise the sense in which social movements can attain and sustain any kind of unity at all, and we should be careful not to overstate the antagonisms within broad social movements. The competitive dimension is only one part of the reality of social movements, and in relation to the formation of early environmentalism, it is also clear that there was also co-operation between organisations, as well as overlapping memberships.

McCarthy and Zald separate 'opinions and beliefs' or 'issue cleavages' (what they take to *be* social movements) from the organisations through which the social movement is given concrete form(s) (SMOs), and the totality of these organisations which make up SMIs, or what can be termed 'social movement sectors'. If applied to the contemporary environmental movement in Britain, we could say that the primary concern or fundamental issue cleavage, is to change the form of the relationship between society and the natural world. One of the more successful organisations within the social movement is Friends of the Earth which campaigns on a number of related problems which require changes in the way society thinks about, values and treats the natural world. The environmental movement sector (or SMI) would also include the National Trust, Greenpeace, R.S.P.B., World Wide Fund for Nature (W.W.F.) and others.

Whilst this approach would seem to 'fit' the movement and its organisations quite well, and therefore give us a useful research strategy, a main problem is that the separation of 'issues' from 'organisations' does not hold analytically. In many cases the two are combined and interrelated in complex ways. For example, the issues pursued by movement organisations often develop within those organisations as a result of the successes and failures of their campaigns, or the political opportunities which arise somewhat unpredictably, for pursuing and publicising particular causes. Movement organisations often campaign on issues they think they can win, not necessarily those which are fundamental to fulfilling their ideological principles and which express their core values. This means that any definition of social movements must include the organisations through which the movement operates as these are not separable from the key issues. In short, movements cannot be reduced simply to 'issue cleavages'.

I now want to turn to contemporary theories of new social movements which have been developed in Western Europe since the 1970s. These theories attempt to modify previous ideas of social movements in a number of ways, in the light of the emergence of 'new' movements which, it is argued, are different from previous forms of social movement.

Approaches to New Social Movements

Since the outbreak of a number of mass and collective protests and demonstrations throughout the Western world during the 1960s, there has been a re-awakening of interest in the study of social movements within the social sciences.[1] However, despite the generation of a number of analytical frameworks, no single approach to social movement research has been able to take on a paradigmatic status, and to dominate the field. In particular, as several analysts have noted, there has been a visible divide between the resource mobilisation approaches popular in North America, and the new social movement theories in Western Europe (Klandermans et al 1988, Klandermans 1991; Melucci 1985, 1989; Eyerman and Jamison 1991: Ch.1). These differing perspectives reflect the historical development of social science on the two continents, but they also see social movements from different angles. In short, they ask different questions about what social movements are, how they are formed and what we should expect from them.

As Melucci (1989) has pointed out, the resource mobilisation approach (though by no means a unified one) focuses on the 'how' of movements. That is, it looks at the ways in which individual choices are made, for example whether to participate or not, and organisations built, asking what resources are required and available. The roots of resource mobilisation approaches lie in the development of rational choice theories of collective behaviour as a reaction against the dominance of functionalist interpretations (Olson 1965; Oberschall 1973; Gamson 1975). On the other hand, new social movement theories concentrate on the 'why' of movement activity, and are typically concerned with macro-social changes which generate new issues and stimulate new groups of people to mobilise. In particular, as I have already argued, NSM theories are inextricably tied to some version of the now widespread thesis of a shift towards post-industrialism (Brzezinski 1970; Touraine 1971, 1981; Bell 1974; Gorz 1985). [2]

Clearly these European approaches are influenced by problems in marxist theory, namely a disillusionment with 'actually existing socialism' as it developed in the former Soviet Union, and the apparent failure of the West European working class to fulfil its 'historical mission' to bring about social revolution. When casting around for explanations for the emergence of 'new' movements, social-structural change is invariably invoked. While resource mobilisation approaches neglect social - structural change, new social movement theories largely ignore the practical matters of resource availability, organisation building and the individual's capacity for making 'rational' decisions (Melucci 1989).

With this in mind, it may appear that a judicious combination of these two approaches would lead to a better informed explanation of contemporary social movement activities. New movement theories could be used to provide answers as to why movements are 'new' in terms of shifts and long-term changes in the structure of society (post-industrialism), and resource mobilization to investigate how new social conflicts and grievances are turned into visible, and more or less organised forms. A problem here though is that,

> ... the answers to the "why" and "how" questions may be interdependent ... A better understanding of social movements and of the power of social movement theories is furthered by systematic comparative research on movements and movement sectors across time, societal contexts, and types of movements (Kitschelt 1991: 343).

I think that this is an important point, and this study can be read as an attempt to follow Sydney Tarrow's (1991: 401) injunction that '... comparison across time can provide a healthy dose of realism - or add empirical backing - to claims that 'new social movements' are fundamentally different than what has come before'. I am arguing of course that new movements are not fundamentally different from earlier ones, and as well as a comparison across time, I am concentrating on one 'new' movement, environmentalism/Green politics as far as possible, in order to redress what I see as the over-generalised conception of what is really a quite diverse range of movements, together with the mistaken identification of a post-industrial transformation as generating the 'conditions of possibility' for their emergence as a bloc.

Distinctiveness of the New Social Movements

In this section I will draw on the work of several theorists of NSMs including Touraine (1971, 1981), Melucci (1980, 1985, 1989), Offe (1985), Frankel (1987), and Rucht (1990), together with others who have attempted to bring together the common themes contained in the various accounts (D'Anieri et al 1990; Bagguley 1992; Boggs 1986b; Eder 1985, 1990; Scott

1990). In doing so, I aim to produce something of an 'ideal-typical' new social movement as an heuristic device with which to approach environmental and Green movements. I am conscious that this runs the risk of setting up a model which corresponds to no 'real' movement and which could therefore be construed as a misguided endeavour. However, this strategy is justified because the features attributed to new movements are scattered across a number of works, and the production of an ideal-type will help to draw these strands together. As Weber (1949: 89-92) notes, 'In its conceptual purity, this mental construct cannot be found anywhere in reality. It is a utopia. Historical research faces the task of determining in each individual case, the extent to which this ideal-construct approximates to, or diverges from reality ...'. So the construction of an ideal type does not constitute a claim to represent definitively an aspect of social reality, but works to sensitise us to social phenomena.

The ideal-typical new social movement does alert us to some features of contemporary movement activity such as attempts to confront authorities and the public with symbolic protests. However, there is in this case a need to bring NSM characteristics into contact with empirical and historical evidence in order to test their efficacy, as I have argued that an over-concentration on contemporary actions has led to something of a distortion of the picture of environmentalism and Green activity. If the synthesised new social movement is unable to demonstrate that its key features *are* novel when confronted with the test of historical comparison, then we have to question whether the NSM concept really is a useful one.

The word 'new' is often equated with the word 'contemporary' to identify a phenomenon which is with us *now*. This usage carries only a temporal meaning and has no evaluative implications. When applied to the concept of social movements, I have no problem with the notion that some social movements notably those concerned with ecology, feminism, civil rights, anti-nuclear, animal rights etc., are features of many industrialised societies today. Of course there is a related meaning of the term 'new' in this context, namely that these movements have emerged recently. Even this need not intimate any absolute break with previous forms, it merely makes the point that some movement activity (or 'wave' of activity) has recently taken place. If this was the intended meaning of the word 'new' in theories of NSMs, then the gap between the theory and historical reality would be minimal, provided that we could reach agreement on the concept of social movement.

For NSM theorists though, 'new' has wider and more controversial meanings. Its usage cannot be properly understood without reference to perceived 'old' social movements, the contrast with which gives NSM theories their descriptive and seemingly explanatory force. New movements are not simply contemporary manifestations, they also display apparently unique features which old movements did not, and in many cases they consciously react against the forms, values and institutionalisation of old movements.

To speak of new movements in this sense is to dwell within discourses of post-industrialism, postmaterial values and postmodern cultural forms, and it becomes difficult to disentangle what is useful in the NSM theory from what can be dismissed. The attempt critically to assess new social movement theory seems to lead inexorably into arguments about the nature of contemporary society. For example, by challenging the contention that new social movements favour specific organisational forms, we also seem to be calling into question post-industrial society theories, which give NSM theories a structural base, and postmodernism as a new dominant culture which breaks down hierarchical forms of authority. Perhaps this is the inevitable result of theorising social change in static terms which lends itself to the creation of dualisms: material/postmaterial values, modernism/postmodernism, industrial/post-industrial societies, old/new movements.

Like the word 'new', the use of 'social' has a wider and more far-reaching meaning than at first it may appear. The study of social movements has become popular in sociology only over the past twenty-five years or so, although most commentators accept that social movements are and have been a feature of all industrialised societies. Indeed if one of the defining characteristics of social movements is that they are self-conscious, more or less organised projects of social change, then they must surely be 'modern' phenomena.

All movements are social in the unproblematic sense that collectivities of people are involved. Social movements can however, be classified as 'political', 'religious' or 'moral', and although they remain 'social' movements in the sense above, these movements are thought to be somehow different from genuinely social movements. For NSM theorists, to describe social movements as political movements amounts to reductionism. Clearly the word 'social' has taken on a new significance here. This is because, for NSM theorists, 'social' refers not only to group or collective actions but to the location in which this action occurs, namely civil society or the realm of 'everyday life'. That is to say, outside the formal, institutionalised political channels and the state. This characterisation has implications for the evaluation of a movement's success or failure.

A politically reductionist evaluation of social movements would stress the extent to which the key issues identified by the movement were taken up within the realm of formal politics and policy-making. Success here is equivalent to inclusion into the system. So the election of Green Party M.P.s and the adoption of policy suggestions by government and political parties would qualify as successes in these terms. However, this evaluation fails to acknowledge the effects of movement membership and active participation and support on the individual, consciousness and social relations, and on the whole realm of cultural life more generally. In this way, the political reduction performs an ideological function in analysis by closing off possibilities and only acknowledging social movement effects within the sphere of existing formal politics, when its effects really go much wider.

In NSM theories then, the social location of new movements is emphasised (Melucci 1985, 1988, 1989; Habermas 1981; Offe 1985; Boggs 1986b). This is partly due to the post-industrial theories they rely on for explanation, which argue that cultural changes occur before these feed into changes in political life, but also because this social location contrasts sharply with the institutionalisation and establishment of old movements within the existing formal political system. 'Social' used in this way, acts as a device for demarcation between old and new movements, and tends to take the political elements of old movements as constitutive of those movements *in toto*, thus ignoring or bypassing the social forms of old movements which were part of their historical development and which may continue to exist. Ironically then, NSM theories perform their own form of political reduction on old social movements in order to generate a distinctive, descriptive contrast. The laudatory aim of avoiding reductionism is therefore somewhat marred by their refusal to take seriously the continuing social nature of old social movements and movement networks (Klandermans 1990).[3]

In most Western nations, the 1950s and '60s economic 'boom' brought more economic security and rising living standards, but this was only achieved via the expansion of the welfare state and increasing state intervention into previously untouched areas of social life such as consumption, services and social relations more generally. New social movements are thought to arise at least in part, as attempts to take back control of the individual's everyday life. As Habermas puts it, to resist the 'colonisation of the life-world' (*Lebenswelt*), hence their antagonism to the state, and the slogan 'the personal is political', first used by feminists (D'Anieri et al 1990: 446).

The idea of a post-industrial transformation goes further than Habermas's (1975) discussion of the legitimation crisis faced by the modern state however. Post-industrialism includes the following features:

1. The shift away from manufacturing to service, tertiary, quaternary and quinary sector employment.
2. A consequent 'power shift' away from capitalist entrepreneurs towards a newly emerging 'technocracy' (Touraine 1971) or 'technostructure' (Galbraith 1972), which exercises control over informational resources.
3. The installation of 'theoretical knowledge' as the key or 'axial principle' of the new society and the widespread application of information technologies (Bell 1974).
4. The long - term displacement of the working class as a potentially revolutionary collective actor due to changes in the significance of workplace politics and the undermining of class-based politics, leading to new forms of social conflict (Touraine 1971; Bauman 1982;Gorz 1985).

As a result of these significant changes,

> ... new social movement scholars explain the emergence and nature of the recent movements by examining grievances which they argue arise from the structural condition of postindustrial society. New social movement theorists argue that recent social movements represent an entirely new form of social protest and reflect specific properties of advanced industrial societies (D'Anieri et al 1990: 446).[4]

We can identify four main areas where post-industrial new social movements are said to differ from previous social movements: in their goals and values, organisational forms, participants and campaigning styles. I shall deal with these in turn.

Rather than articulating the interests of a particular social class or social group, NSMs tend to promote issues which are non- or cross-class in nature, such as the concern for 'clean environments', and which consequently attract a much wider constituency. This is consistent with Inglehart's (1977) thesis of the 'glacier-like' shift towards postmaterial values from the 1950s, when post-scarcity socialisation begins to lead to a new level of concerns such as the state of the natural environment, personal autonomy and self-actualisation through activities such as 'consciousness-raising', a renewed interest in spirituality and a Foucauldian 'care of the self'. Somewhat ironically then, the emergence of 'anti-systemic' movements appears to follow on the back of the very successes of the industrial system in meeting people's most urgent needs.[5] Inglehart's (1990) more recent research suggests that the shift to postmaterialism has continued.

The postmaterial goals which new movements seek, stand to bring potential benefits for society as a whole, and typically these goals are pursued from outside the formal political system and the state. Green movements for example, advocate changes in individual lifestyles rather than attempting to capture state power. It is possible to argue therefore that new movements have universalist goals in contrast to the class specific goals of the labour movement, and that this is a key point of difference between old and new movements. However, I show in Chapter Four that some elements of late-nineteenth century socialism and anarchism also couched their arguments in universalist terms rather than being narrowly class-specific, thus there is much less of a contrast than at first glance.

It is argued that the forms which NSMs take are a reflection of their disillusionment with, and thus distanciation from, the forms of old social movements such as trades unions and organised labour. NSMs reject representative internal democracy in favour of direct participation wherever possible. They deliberately avoid building hierarchical, career-oriented structures into their organisations to try to prevent the accumulation of power at the top. The British Green Party's recurring struggles around the issue of whether or not to elect a party leader, and their experiments with new internal structures is a good example of the tensions within a party which seeks to work in a participatory way, whilst simultaneously pursuing electoral support in an unsympathetic pre-existing political framework.

Other loose networks of activists such as anti-roads protests under the umbrella of 'Reclaim the Streets' or 'Critical Mass' would also be examples of the kind of new organisational forms attributed to NSMs, but the idea that these loose networks are typical of the wider environmental movement is not proven. Nor is it clear that the numbers of activists involved in these protests really amount to a new social movement. I do not think that social movements, new or old can really be defined by one organisational form. This is because a variety of forms can be shown to exist, but also because organisations change over time, very often in the direction of more centralisation, developing hierarchical and bureaucratic structures in order to deal with increasing membership, attempts to recruit more supporters, and to facilitate effective fund-raising.

Whereas old social movements had their base in class divisions, particularly within the workplace, NSMs are said to attract members from across the traditional class cleavage of capital/labour. This would seem understandable for environmental/Green movements as the issues they raise potentially affect all people in society not simply one sectional interest. However, environmental and Green movements are not as amorphous as this characterisation suggests. The majority of surveys conducted into environmental and Green organisations lead us to the conclusion that an overwhelming proportion of their activists come from a new middle class employed in services, education and the public sector generally. Cotgrove and Duff's (Cotgrove 1982; Cotgrove and Duff 1980, 1981) work on British environmental organisations during the early 1980s is a good empirical example of the extent of new middle class involvement in movement activity. Nevertheless, NSM theorists argue that 'New middle class politics is, in contrast to most working class politics, typically a politics of a class, but not on behalf of a class' (Offe 1985: 77). In relation to Green politics, Eckersley describes this as an orientation towards 'virtue', not 'selfishness' (Eckersley 1989).

These arguments draw on the idea that the new middle class is not directly involved in industrial production and therefore supports the Green critique of expanding economic growth. There is also the suggestion that this class is frustrated at being excluded from the decision-making structures of neo-corporatism, hence their advocacy of Green politics reflects their status as outsiders. It is possible though, that the new middle class may perform a leadership role in many social movements because they possess the skills which movement organisations actively seek out. Bagguley (1992: 40) points out that the specific class interests of the new middle class are expressed through workplace unions and associations, but do not 'spill out' into society. We need more research into the 'ordinary' supporters of organisations such as Greenpeace before we can reach firmer conclusions on this matter.

One further important feature which is recognised by NSM theorists is what we could call action repertoires. It is argued that new movements use a much wider range of protest and lobbying actions than old movements did, and that NSMs typically adopt unconventional tactics (Rucht 1990). Most noticeably there is a stress on direct action rather than using the existing channels of interest mediation and negotiation. This seems to describe accurately some of the actions of anti-roads campaigns, many symbolic demonstrations staged by Greenpeace and Friends of the Earth, and the more recent 'ecotage' of Earth First!.[6] It should be noted however that some researchers have noted that Greenpeace and Friends of the Earth have become increasingly professionalised and are now just as involved in lobbying the state for legislative reform and the inclusion of environmental policy into the existing party platforms as with direct actions (McCormick 1991; Yearley 1994; Allen 1992).

Also, as we will see in Chapter Four, even in the earliest phase of environmental organisation-building in the late nineteenth century, a range of strategies and campaigning methods were used, including direct actions, and therefore there is no simple descriptive distinction to be found between the methods of old and new environmentalism. Of course, some of the newly formed organisations make use of new technologies such as video, television and the internet, but so do many of the older, more established ones. It is just not the case that we can clearly identify significant old and new campaigning styles and repertoires of action.

This characterisation of NSMs has drawn on a variety of sources including theorists of new movements and others who have attempted to synthesise the main themes from NSM theories.[7] I have deliberately avoided a discussion of any one author as the NSM perspective is spread across a number of works. However, I now want to turn to the work of Alain Touraine and Alberto Melucci in more detail to show how, despite their macro and micro approaches respectively, both remain tied to some version of the post-industrial thesis for their explanation of the emergence of NSMs. Melucci was one of the first researchers to specifically use the term new social movement, although Touraine had clearly identified new movements as significant phenomena much earlier, and despite some changes in emphasis, both have continued to use the term, both descriptively and theoretically. Melucci's work is interesting because it demonstrates how dependent the NSM thesis is on the central assumptions of post-industrialism theory, even when the latter is not explicitly formulated.

Social Movements in Programmed Societies: Alain Touraine

In the work of Touraine, the connection between new movements and post-industrialism is explicit and since the 1970s has attracted much interest as much for his controversial methodological advocacy of 'sociological intervention' as for the content of his theory of the changing nature of industrial societies and the role of social movements within them (Freiberg 1975: 370-3; Rucht 1991). Touraine's work attracted many others to social movement research and remains probably the most controversial both in substance and methodology within the field. In my view, it is a hybrid of both old and new methodologies and theories of social movements. For instance, he develops a theory of post-industrialism, but draws on Marx and Engels's framework of antagonistic class conflicts. He talks of new social movements in the plural, but his research effort is directed towards identifying which single movement will emerge from the present phase of activity to become the dominant oppositional force. However, Touraine's work does attest to a historical reality of the domination of oppositional politics by the organised labour movement which has often made other movements 'invisible' or seemingly less important. It has also contributed to a misleading image of the labour movement in NSM theories, which see the latter as typified by the Labour Party and highly organised trades unionism. I turn first to Touraine then because it is he who makes explicit the case for developing a theory, not only of new social movements but of post-industrial or 'programmed' society.

Touraine does not treat social movements as marginal phenomena, rather he locates social movements at the heart of society and therefore of sociology. For Touraine, sociology is or should be the study of social movements. His explicit aim is '... to reorganize the entire body of sociological analysis around this new idea, that of the social movement' (1981: 78). In a sense what he wants to do is displace what he sees as the static concept of 'society' with the more dynamic notion of 'social movements', as he argues that the latter are engaged in the continual process of creating society. To this end, he argues that sociology should adopt

> ... an image of society as an ensemble of systems of action, as a drama in which the social movements play the main roles ... this sociology of action ceases to believe that conduct must be a response to a situation

and claims rather that the situation is merely the changing and unstable result of relations between the actors, who through their conflicts and via their cultural orientations produce society (1981: 30).

This means that Touraine's is an 'action sociology' which stands opposed to most social-structural accounts of social reality, such as functionalism and marxism. Society is the conflictual production of itself and consists of two main components. Firstly, its 'historicity' - 'The great cultural orientations by which a society's environmental relationships are normatively organised', and secondly, the social movements - 'through which these orientations become social practices' (ibid: 26).

Social movements lie at the heart of society as the major actors on the stage where social reality is continually (re)created. It should not be thought though that social movements aim simply at modernization, nor are they carriers of Marxian social contradictions. Rather, a social movement '.. is defending another society ... The idea of superseding must be replaced by the search for an alternative' (ibid: 80). In this conception, sociological analysis focuses on the creativity of social movements in the production of innovation whilst institutions and formal organisations are largely bypassed.

Touraine seems to work in the spirit of Marx and Engels whilst rejecting their stress on productive class conflict and societal contradictions. What he takes from the marxist tradition is its insistence that 'class' antagonisms are truly social conflicts involving both social relations and cultural orientations. Although these may crystallise into political organisations which become involved in negotiation and interaction with the state, the social movement cannot be reduced to this level of conflict. Where he breaks with marxist concepts is with the insistence that social movements are not reducible in any simple way to objective class interests, and in his dismissal of the notion of social 'contradictions' which demand resolution through social revolution.

Touraine's concept of social movement relates to what he calls a 'triangle of forces'. These are: Identity, Opposition and Totality. 'Identity' refers to the conflictually created self-consciousness of a social actor (Rucht 1991: 364). This self-consciousness can only be formed through the experience of a conflict ('Opposition') with the actor's 'class' adversary, a social force whose object is the control of 'historicity'. Totality is therefore the 'historical action system' in which class opponents strive for dominance. Touraine's methodological proposition of 'sociological intervention' is devised to facilitate a potential social movement in realising the stakes involved in their local struggles, and in this way, to raise these struggles to the level of historicity. I will not dwell on this methodological aspect of Touraine's work which has received much attention and criticism over recent years (see Freiberg 1973, 273; Melucci 1989; Rucht 1991), as I am more interested in the substance of his thesis.

The main consequence of Touraine's conception of a 'triangle of forces' is that only two truly social movements can exist in any 'society', for example bourgeois groups and workers make up capitalist society. 'Corresponding to a system of historical action there is a main class relation and consequently a pair of antagonistic social movements' (1981: 94). I think that Touraine's use of the term 'class' is often confusing and sometimes contradictory. At times he seems almost to equate 'class' with 'social movement'. For example,

> Social movement and class struggle are synonymous expressions; only the former will be used here, because to speak of class struggle would seem to indicate that classes, objectively defined, enter the struggle to defend contradictory interests. To speak of social movements is to state, on the contrary, that there exist no class relations separable from class action, from its cultural orientations and from the social conflict in which the movement occurs (ibid: 91).

Later however, he argues that '... the term class has to be replaced by that of social movement' (1986: 26). This terminological and possibly conceptual confusion results from Touraine's attempts to dynamise what he takes to be static concepts. His objections to the concept of class are similar to those he makes concerning the concept of society, namely that these concepts imply a static object when in fact the reality they attempt to express cannot be separated from the actions of the groups involved in their production. In effect, he tries to dispense with Marx's objective class-in-itself whilst holding on to the class-for-itself. Unlike some post-modern theorists, Touraine continues to see social movements as 'personages', and maintains, as Melucci (1989: 25) rightly says, an image of 'Social movements ... as figures in an epic tragedy, as heroes or villains who are moving toward some grand ideal or dramatic destiny'.

With the de-centring of the struggle between Capital and Labour, the problem for Touraine becomes that of discovering the progressive social movement which will replace organised labour as part of post-industrial or as he puts it, 'programmed' societies in direct opposition to the power of a growing technocracy. Touraine's thesis that the variety of contemporary movements constitutes a 'transitional phase' of social change is dependent on an acceptance of his theory of the shift to a new form of social organisation beyond industrial capitalism. His most general thesis is that 'A new society is being born. If we want to define it by its technology ... let's call it the programmed society. If ... from the nature of its ruling class, we'll call it technocratic society' (1971: 27). In keeping with his action sociology, Touraine argues that a new ruling class is forming, a technocracy whose monopoly is not now one of capital or material resources, but over information. Control over informational production, access and distribution replaces that of control over capital and physical resources. Old class conflicts between organised labour and capitalists are no longer the chief source of the social conflict over historicity. 'In the programmed society, the working class is no longer a privileged historic agent ... simply because the exercise of power within a capitalist firm no longer places one at the centre of the economic system and its social conflicts' (1971: 17). This does not imply the disappearance of the working class or trades unionism, these struggles still go on. What it does mean though is that the power of the working class to transform society due to its strategically crucial social location is lost.

In the transitional period to a programmed society, a range of new social movements emerge as resistances to technocratic power at several levels and locations. For Touraine, this period of diversity and pluralism of movements cannot be permanent or long-lived if a successful challenge to the emerging technocracy is to be mounted. A single oppositional movement must be formed which will become the principal actor in the struggle over historicity. In his own terms, during the conflictual process of construction of its own identity, a social movement must identify its opponent. Signs of this are evident he argues, in his studies of anti-nuclear mobilisations in France which recognised the 'techno-economic apparatus' as its adversary (Touraine 1983). Though this is an important first step, it is not enough. The emerging social movement must become aware of the stakes involved, namely the production of society's form itself, and it is in this aspect of movement activity that Touraine believes sociology can perform a useful function. He argues that sociologists should adopt his method of 'intervention' in order to create a dialogue with movement activists so that they can reach an understanding of the highest level to which their struggles aspire or can be made to aspire. For Touraine, there is no question of an uninvolved or detached sociology.

Essentially, Touraine's conception of the emerging programmed society differs little from many other such accounts of a shift to some form of post-industrial society. Central to these accounts is the idea that post-industrial societies' production and use of informational resources brings about or demonstrates the rise to prominence of a dominant technocracy or technostructure which is not co-terminous with the capitalist class, and which begins to usurp the latter's power. As we will see, this theoretical reliance on post-industrialism causes problems for NSM theorists from which it becomes difficult for them to extricate themselves.

Touraine's work has certainly stimulated interest in the subject of social movements, and his thoughts on NSMs have become a starting point for many other studies which diverge from his own theories and concepts. However, his work shows clearly the problems that are generated by theories of new movements. In his attempts to demonstrate the emergence of a new type of society, Touraine uses as evidence anti-nuclear, ecological and women's protests and mobilisations. In doing so he claims to show that these are separate from and different to earlier conflicts in the workplace over control of the production process and distribution of material rewards, in fact that new movements are signs of a fundamental transition.

There is a circular logic at work here. Post-industrial society brings forth new movements, and new movements demonstrate the emergence of post-industrial society. In his own terms of course this is inevitable as 'society' is simply the name we give to express a dynamic social reality which consists not of institutions but rather, of action and social relations. A new set of fundamental social relations *is* a new society. Therefore if it can be demonstrated that genuinely new social movements exist, we would have to admit the existence of social-structural change. Unfortunately Touraine fails to show that this has indeed happened. Even if we accept that social conflicts around ecology, women's struggles, peace movements etc. are new, and I do not, this is not synonymous with identifying new *social movements* in Touraine's sense of the term. If we are in a transitional phase to a programmed society, then how can we justify giving the control of informational resources priority in the definition of the new social conflict over historicity? At best, all we could say would be that new social conflicts have emerged alongside that of Capital/Labour. We have no real basis for concluding that any of these conflicts (and there are significant differences between them) will become the dominant one.

Touraine comes close to endorsing the ecology or Green movement as being the most likely to develop into a genuine social movement in opposition to technocratic power, but others working outside Touraine's scheme, argue in favour of feminism (Habermas 1981), and Touraine himself believed at one time that the student movement could fulfil this role. In 1969 he wrote that 'The student movement is a truly social movement' (1969: 97). With hindsight we would have to disagree with this claim. It seems that by placing social movements at the centre of society and sociology, Touraine inevitably becomes drawn to premature conclusions regarding the destiny of emergent social conflicts, whilst his reliance on a theory of post-industrialism only serves to reinforce this conclusion. There are also few convincing reasons to believe that only two social movements can co-exist within a society. As Rucht (1991: 372) argues, 'Even if we would assume that in past history there was only one pair of social movements in a given society, this may change in future societies'. I would go even further than this and argue that there have been more than two social movements throughout the history of modernity, but the ability of some forcibly to press their claims, blinds us to the existence and activities of others. Rather than trying to seek out elements in contemporary protests which might coalesce to form a genuine social movement in the future, we should revise our ideas about what social movements are. In short, I think that Touraine takes an historical episode - the dominance of a central class conflict (Capital and Labour) - and develops it into a general theory of social movements and societies which cannot be supported empirically.

Despite the speculative and problematic generalisations in Touraine's account of the nature and significance of social movements, there is something persuasive about his account of old social movements. The Capital/Labour conflict has indeed been both practically and theoretically, the primary one in the industrialised societies during the nineteenth and twentieth centuries. So much so, that many other movements and movement organisations have received little or no attention from sociologists despite their successes in the production of social and cultural change. What we need to hold on to is the fact of this historical dominance in order to understand why other movements either failed to develop and survive, or have been treated as secondary and derivative. The question of whether one or another of these conflicts stands to become dominant in the future must remain open, it is not a matter which can be resolved by recourse to post-industrial theory.

Social Movements as Signs: Alberto Melucci

Melucci (1989: 42) was one of the first to use the concept of new social movements, and although he expresses concern that the perspective may now be developing into something like a paradigm, he continues to speak of new forms and characteristics when discussing recent developments, as well as presenting in a somewhat patchy way, a theory of post-industrialism or, 'complex society'.[8] It is appropriate then to turn to Melucci as he rejects Touraine's dynamic macro-sociological explanation and tries to approach NSMs from a micro-sociological perspective. Despite this though, he continues to rely on some version of the post-industrial thesis which demonstrates how closely the two theories are related and how difficult it is to extricate one from the other.

Melucci aims to develop a new framework for the analysis of collective behaviour, one which dispenses with the theatrical analogy with its heroes and villains, and which he sees in Touraine's work. As he says:

> ... sociological analysis must abandon the traditional view of movements as characters moving on an historical stage. In the tradition of both progressive and conservative thought, conflict is often represented through the image of theatre. Social movements are cast as figures in an epic tragedy, as heroes or villains who are moving toward some grand ideal of dramatic destiny. There is a stage on which the characters act; the players follow a script that foreshadows a happy or tragic ending, usually defined from the point of view of the author (1989: 25).

This starting point is clearly at odds with the ideas of Touraine and others, whose sociology is premised on the idea that social movements can be discussed as 'personages'.[9] Melucci insists that collective action should not be seen as an entity or a unitary empirical phenomenon. To do so would be to accept a reified view of what remains essentially a social process. 'Whatever unity exists should be considered the result and not the starting point, a fact to be explained rather than assumed' (Melucci 1989: 26). Not to do this is '... to assume that there is a sort of deep 'mind' of the movement, instead of considering it as a system of social relationships' (1985: 793). This shift of emphasis then leads to a concern with the social construction of collective action, which must be built by '... aims, beliefs, decisions and exchanges operating in a systemic field. A collective identity is nothing else than a shared definition of the field of opportunities and constraints offered to collective action' (ibid: 793).

Visible protest actions and mobilisations are not thrown up in any simplistic fashion by state policies, planning decisions etc., rather these manifest forms rely on a pre-existing latent level of local groups, networks and alternative cultures which exist submerged in everyday life. To focus only on public demonstrations is to miss these 'social laboratories' in which people can experiment with alternative lifestyles and cultural codes and quite often leads to a form of political reductionism (1989: 43; 1995: 112). This is a worthwhile point which alerts us to the creation of identities and solidarity. For example, Hetherington (1993: 768) has noted that movements are also 'emotional communities': 'Social movements ... provide a form of affectual solidarity that allows, through the creation of distinct lifestyles, shared symbols and solidarity, a revalorization of self-identity'. It is evident though that the kind of analysis Melucci proposes can be applied to all social movements, not just new ones, and there is no reason to suppose that new movements are the only ones to operate at the submerged levels of society identified by him.

Though his work diverges quite sharply from that of Touraine, Melucci's definition of social movement carries more than an echo of the latter's conception of a triangle of forces. He argues that a social movement is a 'specific class of collective phenomena which contains three dimensions' (1989: 29). Presumably other forms of collective behaviour do not exhibit all three dimensions together. The defining dimensions are; solidarity, conflict and the breaking of the limits of the system in which the action takes place. There is a clear parallel here with Touraine's concepts of identity, opposition and totality. Solidarity is the actor's '... mutual recognition that they are part of a single social unit' (Melucci 1989: 29), or what Scott (1990: 6) we noted earlier, terms a 'common identity'. A social movement must also be engaged in conflict, that is it must be '...in opposition to an adversary who lays claim to the same goods or values.' Finally, the activities of a social movement '...violate the boundaries or tolerance limits of a system, thereby pushing the system beyond the range of variations that it can tolerate without altering its structure' (Melucci 1989: 29). Though this definition does draw heavily on

Touraine, it is clear that Melucci sees social movements as localised and fragmented. He holds out no prospect of any kind of 'total' revolution or planned social transformation. In this sense, and in contrast to Touraine's modernist theory, Melucci's work can be seen as a postmodern reading of the field of social movements, concentrating on diversity and fragmentation. He envisages Western societies today as complex societies, not amenable to the grand narratives of emancipatory struggle which characterised social movements during capitalist industrialism.

Melucci argues that contemporary movements challenge the administrative logic of complex systems on symbolic grounds. Movement forms are not simply instrumental means to ends. Rather, they act as signs for the rest of society, making visible previously unseen problems concerned with the 'grammar of life'. Individuals practise in the present the changes they wish to see in the future, and this gives them a 'prophetic function'. Whilst this postmodern interpretation of contemporary movements is consonant with the ideal-typical new social movement as I described it earlier, there is no reason to suppose that these aspects of social movement activity are restricted to the contemporary situation. Many of the activities of utopian socialists in the early nineteenth century could easily be interpreted in a similar way, that is, many other social movement activists try to 'practise in the present the changes they wish to see in the future'. This is after all what makes them visible. Animal rights activists who practise vegetarianism or become vegans, socialists who practise equality, environmentalists who work to protect natural areas, all fit this description. There is no substantial difference between old and new here which could support NSM or postindustrial theories.

Although at times he reverts to the term 'post-industrial' or 'informational society', I will stick to the term 'complex' because it differentiates Melucci from others such as Bell and Galbraith, and also because I think it is more descriptive of the general re-orientation he wishes to bring about in the study of social movements. The concept of a complex society is clearly meant to grasp the same social reality as other concepts such as post-industrial society, late-capitalism, advanced industrial society and so on. When asked what kind of society we are living in, Melucci (1989: 184) replies:

> This question is important and unavoidable in research on social movements. But the fact is that nowadays nobody has a convincing answer ... Most people feel that our systems have changed, but very few admit that we lack a language

to describe the way in which they have changed. I prefer to acknowledge this impasse, to declare it openly in order to make possible its resolution through different questions and answers.

With this uncertainty in mind, the use of the term complex rather than post-industrial does not close off possibilities, but rather, leaves open the nature of contemporary societies. This could be helpful because post-industrial theorists too often draw their demarcation lines too sharply, giving the impression that historical links with industrial societies have been radically severed, leading to an unnecessary dualism of industrial/post-industrial which we even find in the more circumspect work of Beck (1992) with his distinction between 'simple' and 'reflexive' modernity.

Unfortunately Melucci's work also demonstrates how difficult it is to hold open this question of the nature or fundamental basis of contemporary societies. He frequently reverts to the idea of 'informationalism': 'complex systems are informational systems' (1985: 796), or post-industrialism: 'Postindustrial societies no longer have an economic basis ...' (ibid: 795). He also implicitly (and sometimes explicitly) takes industrial capitalism to be a now defunct form of social organisation, for example, 'I'm convinced that we are entering an era qualitatively different from both the capitalist model of modernity and socialism as we've known it historically' (1989: 185). Or again, 'During the phase of industrial capitalism ...' (ibid: 89). And again: '...are there dimensions of the 'new' forms of collective action in complex societies which are qualitatively different from those in the phase of industrial capitalism?' (ibid: 43). I do not think that the slippage into the language of post-industrialism and informationalism is simply the problem of an inadequate language. NSM theories tend to assume theories of large-scale social-structural change as the backdrop which helps to explain what they perceive as historically unique forms of social movements. For example, Melucci (1989: 41) argues that,

[The] need for theoretical speculation is stimulated by the emergence, during the last twenty-five years, of new forms of collective action in areas untouched by social conflicts. New actors have emerged whose organizational models and repertoires of action differ from those of earlier social movements.

In spite of his protests to the contrary then, this passage contains all the elements which have led to the NSM theory taking on an almost paradigmatic form. 'New forms'; 'areas previously untouched by social conflicts'; 'new actors'; 'organizational models and repertoires of action different from those of earlier movements'. It is easy to see why, given this perception of the radically new nature of NSMs, reference to post-industrialism is necessary as the structural base on which NSM theory is grounded. There is however no need to do this. I am attempting in this analysis to hold on to the notion of industrialisation as a long term social process whilst re-thinking the place of environmental movements in modern society. In short, there are other explanations for the emergence of new movements which do not rely on post-industrialism. By taking a more historical, developmental approach which sees contemporary activity as both a continuation of, but also a development from previous environmentalism, rather than as a distinct break with it, we can better understand the current movement and its forms. However, this necessitates some re-thinking of what modern social movements are.

Revising New Social Movement Theory

In an attempt to sharpen up our view of the concept of social movement, Diani (1992: 3) has attempted to draw out some aspects of social movements which are common to four theoretical perspectives. These are the collective behaviour perspective (Turner and Killian), resource mobilization theory (Zald and McCarthy), political process theory (Tilly), and new social movement theory (Touraine, Melucci). Diani argues that in spite of their obvious differences, a 'substantial convergence' can be found on three defining features of social movements. 'A social movement is a network of informal interactions between a plurality of individuals, groups and/or organizations, engaged in a political or cultural conflict, on the basis of a shared collective identity' (1992: 13).

He notes that '... any organization which fulfils the requirements I have pointed out (interactions with other actors, conflict and collective identity) may be considered part of a given movement' (ibid: 14), and does not rule out that political parties may on occasion be included as part of a social movement. This redefinition is useful as it does not take specific organisational forms to be defining characteristics of social movements, something which I have argued is difficult to substantiate in NSM theories. The NSM focus on 'loose organisational structures' or 'networks of interactions' as defining features of new movements is problematic because it effectively rules out the possibility that:

1. the form of movement organisations may be related to the stage of development of the movement as a whole, and therefore,
2. that the form of movement organisations may change over time. Also that,
3. social movements (new and old) can involve a variety of organisations with quite different internal structures.

As organisations grow, it is quite likely that they will adopt a more formalised, rigid structure in order to increase their effectiveness in recruiting members and raising funds. This has clearly happened with Greenpeace for example. Similarly, some organisations which consider themselves to be part of a social movement, may see a tight internal structure as necessary for the maintenance of its members' collective identity in the face of a hostile political environment, for instance in the case of early trades unions. In short, the question of organisational form is an empirical one which cannot be answered at the theoretical level of analysis.

Although Diani's essay is a useful move towards the inclusion of movement organisations in social movement study, there are still some problems. Firstly, he describes the focus on 'conflictual issues' as a basic component of social movement activity (1992: 17). I prefer to see social movements as resistances to dominant social processes, as in the case of environmentalism, to continuing industrialisation and urban development. The main advantage of this is that what I contend is a key feature of social movements, namely their continuing existence over time, transformed to be sure, is more easily explained. To focus on issues as opposed to resistance to processes creates the problem of accounting for an organisation or group's switch from one specific issue to another, without that issue's resolution. It also leaves unanswered the question of how different issues are related to each other in the view of movement members, and thus of what constitutes the unity of the movement.

Secondly, whilst Diani sees the interactions between individuals, groups and organisations as constitutive of movements, I see the actions, protest campaigns and organisational activities of (and within) movement organisations as just as much a part of what constitutes social movements. This is because I am arguing that movement organisations themselves are the key factor in maintaining the continuity of the social movement over time. So, despite diminishing interactions between organisations, it is possible for those organisations to become more, not less active. Indeed, the levels of interaction may be inversely related to a movement's success. In the early stages, movement organisations may interact more with each other, partly to foster a sense of collective identity, partly as a result of negotiations between them as to how they should proceed. As organisations become established, a division of functions may emerge and interactions between them diminish, but this does not necessarily mean that the movement loses its sense of purpose, the reverse may in fact be true. We can see something of this in the early environmentalism, where interrelationships and co-operation were prominent features as the movement fought to become established. Once established the necessity for continually reinforcing collective identities is reduced and movement organisations can concentrate on their own area of interest. Social movements are not defined simply by the interactions between movement organisations, but also by the activities of and within those organisations.

The validity of the theory of new social movements relies on a contrast with the features and types of old movements, and even when it is not explicitly stated (as in Melucci), assumes post-industrial social change. It is my contention that taken together, these assumptions present contentious areas of debate and theories of social-structural change as consensually resolved when this is simply not the case. The theory of post-industrialism for example, not only remains unclear in its own terms, but has been strongly challenged (Gershuny 1978; Kumar 1986; Callinicos 1989; Pollert 1990). The characteristics which supposedly demonstrate this social transformation: decline of manufacturing industries, growth of the service sector and a flexible workforce, emergence of information technology and its application to increasing numbers of production plants and into social life more generally, necessarily implies a view of what industrial society was. There is some confusion concerning the main features, significance and chronology of British industrialisation which leads us to reject any direct comparison between the process of industrialisation and the changes attributed to post-industrialism. Post-industrial theorists tend to misrepresent or under-emphasise the significance of the industrialisation process in human development, and to assume that, having existed for two and a half centuries, industrial societies are now themselves 'traditional' social structures. I do not think that this is a realistic assessment of the significance of industrialisation. [10]

Disjunctive NSM interpretations work within a framework of static social states; 'old' and 'new', 'industrial' and 'post-industrial', and whilst some relevant changes can be identified in this way, such as the international focus of some environmental organisations, the framework tells us very little about the transition from old to new. There is also little sense of social process or development, and no real awareness of significant continuities over time. My reconstructive approach, whilst recognising sometimes quite distinct 'waves' or 'phases' of counter-cultural activity which make recourse to arguments about the benefits of 'natural' living, contributes to redressing the balance in the social movement literature by focusing on long-term continuities and the development of social movements in relation to the dominant social processes in which they are enveloped. Only in this way can we arrive at an evaluation of the potential of contemporary movements.

Notes

1 Though this interest does appear to be waning at the time of writing.
2 Margaret Rose (1991) demonstrates that discussions of post - industrialism can be traced back as early as 1914 to Coomaraswamy and Penty's *Essays in Post-Industrialism: A Symposium of Prophecy Concerning the Future of Society*. However, the meanings attached to the term here differ significantly from those of Bell, Touraine, Gorz et al. For Penty, post-industrialism means '... the state of society that will follow the break-up of Industrialism, and might therefore be used to cover the speculations of all who recognize Industrialism is doomed (cited in Rose 1991: 23). This meaning is in fact closer to that of present day Greens or deep ecologists, but also to Green socialists such as William Morris and Edward Carpenter than to theorists such as Bell, for whom post-industrialism refers to a further stage of technological development, going beyond simple industrialism.
3 Klandermans work discusses some recent connections and interrelationships between old and new movements and movement networks.
4 Note the terminological confusion here. 'Post - industrial society' and 'advanced industrial society' are used synonymously even by critics of the former concept. My own view is that the characterisation of modern societies as 'advanced industrial' is probably more reality congruent than the alternative post-industrial tag, and that these two concepts should be seen as alternative and conflicting characterisations, not as synonymous expressions.
5 Differences between 'Northern' environmentalists in the relatively rich countries and those in the relatively poor countries of the 'South' which are aired in international conferences such as the 1992 Rio Earth Summit, often demonstrate that the regimes of 'plenitude' and 'scarcity' identified by Shils (1972) produce very different attitudes to

science and technological development. This can be illustrated by a comment from Marcel Roche (In Medawar, P.B and J.S. 1972: 18), former Director of the Venezuelan Institute for Scientific Research that '... in fact, 90 per cent of the world's people still passionately desire science and a share in it as a source of human happiness; we even wish for pollution, as a sure sign of prosperity!'.

6 'Ecotage' is Earth First!'s shorthand for ecological sabotage. That is, the disabling of machinery to stop ecological damage, and, for example, the American EF! tactic of driving nails into trees to delay or prevent logging.

7 In the first group are Habermas 1981; Melucci 1980, 1985, 1989; Touraine 1971, 1981; Offe 1985; Rucht 1990; Kitschelt 1990 and Boggs 1986. In the second group are Pakulski 1991; Scott 1990; D'Anieri et al 1990 and Eyerman and Jamison 1991.

8 Melucci (1989: 41-2) writes, 'As one of those who introduced the term 'new social movements' to sociological literature, I have noticed the increasing ontologization of this expression, and its subsequent characterization as a 'paradigm".

9 Touraine (1981: 78) in fact argues against Melucci, that the originally nineteenth century industrial image of social conflict 'never introduced the image of a historical actor, i.e., one who is guided by normative orientations, by a plan, in fact, by a call to historicity'. This industrial (and plainly marxist) image of conflict presented movements as 'conveyors of contradictions', not as creative self-conscious actors in their own right.

10 This misrepresentation leads Callinicos (1989: 125) despairingly to comment that 'The idea of a post - industrial society is of course nonsense'. A more subtle perspective is that being developed by Giddens, Beck and Lash, who all (though in different ways) theorise contemporary industrialised societies as characterised by 'reflexive modernization'. Beck talks of a 'risk society', Giddens of a 'post-traditional society'.

3 The Rise of Environmentalism and Radical Ecology

Contemporary Environmentalism and Radical Ecology

There are currently a number of competing explanations for the rise of environmental or radical ecology movements, most of which attempt to account for their emergence from the 1960s. In the previous chapter I explored the explanation most widely referred to, that which sees the Greens as part of a bloc of new social movements in post-industrial societies. As the NSM thesis has been so influential it was important to consider it separately. In this chapter I want briefly to cover other possible explanations for rising environmental and Green movements before considering explanations which take a more historical view of the present situation.

In the first section I make use of recent discussions of the major explanations for the rise of environmentalism and radical ecology movements. Most of these are rooted in the assumption, misleading in my view, that significant environmental activity is really only a product of the last thirty years or so. Because this study brings out important continuities in the development of the environmental movement, in the second section I look in more detail at three other approaches, those of Brand, Eder, and Beck, which in their various ways and to varying degrees, show a keener awareness of the history of environmental activism and organisation building, rather than simply concentrating on the contemporary period.

Contemporaneous Explanations

Explanations for the rise of post-1960s environmentalism and radical ecology can usefully be separated according to the central focus of the explanation (Martell 1994: 108-9). In broad terms the main explanations currently concentrate on:

1. Socio - economic structure: post - industrial theories see significant

43

structural change leading to the marginalisation of the labour movement and the rise to prominence of a series of new social movements based in the growth of a new middle class, including environmentalism and radical ecology.

2. Culture: notably Inglehart's (1977, 1990) 'postmaterialist values thesis' (or a version of it) which looks to post-second world war affluence and its effects on socialisation processes as a key explanatory factor accounting for the rise of quality of life issues.

3. Politics: the closure of 'corporatist' forms of interest mediation to new demands (such as ecology) and the subsequent channelling of these into non-established forms of social movement activity.

4. Agency: the concentration on the activities of influential social groups, notably scientists, media professionals and movement activists themselves in bringing new issues before the public.

I have already dealt with new social movement and social - structural explanations (1) so there is no need to cover these here. I will briefly outline the others in turn, showing why they can constitute only partial explanations for environmentalism and Green activism.

Postmaterialist arguments emphasise the capacity of the post-war industrialised societies to fulfil basic needs and hence to stimulate concerns of a non distributional, non-materialist kind. To be more precise, these new concerns are, as the thesis suggests, genuinely *post*-material. That is, it is important to bear in mind that for 'quality of life' issues such as environmentalism to come to the fore, basic material needs (however these are defined) must continue to be met. Therefore postmaterial values are not really non- or anti-materialistic *per se*, but are related to levels of material satisfaction in society, so that postmaterial trends could be reversed if material satisfaction levels are reduced, say in times of severe economic depression. Inglehart's thesis (1977, 1990) concentrates on the 1950s economic boom in most Western nations and the creation of welfare state provisions within a peaceful climate, as the main reasons for 'post-scarcity' socialisation to gain a hold on new generations, who then begin to adopt postmaterial values.

One important element of these new values is a concern for the environment or nature in the face of continuing industrial development, in so far as this impacts on the quality of life for humans. The spread of sympathies towards animals and support for animal welfare and animal rights groups could also be partly explained by this thesis, as could more widespread concerns over issues such as air and water pollution. However, Martell (1994: 125) questions the idea of a hierarchy of concerns which underlies the postmaterialist argument, (and which owes something to Maslow's theory of a 'hierarchy of needs' (1954)) suggesting that 'In societies with rising standards of living increasing material satisfactions may lead to a widening range of things regarded as basic material needs rather than a transfer to non-material needs'.[1]   It could be argued that modern consumer behaviour with its constant quest for novelty provides ample evidence for the validity of this criticism. Things once considered luxuries, such as television sets, video recorders, refrigerators and so on, have gradually come to be seen as necessities for modern living, hence 'basic' material needs are continually redefined. However, perhaps this criticism misses the mark. It is perfectly possible to envisage that the constantly shifting standard of 'basic' needs can exist alongside the spread of postmaterial values. This is because *post*material values are not synonymous with *non*-material ones, so that, *pace* Martell, the transfer from material to postmaterial values is not necessary. Non-material values would be those which reject the personal accumulation of wealth and material goods in favour of simple lifestyles, emphasising instead the alternative values of sharing and community. Small-scale 'back-to-the-land' communes or contemporary new age travellers would more closely resemble the forms of expression of these types of values. This is why there is no apparent contradiction between relatively affluent lifestyles and support for environmentalism. Indeed, this is precisely what I take Inglehart's postmaterial values thesis suggests should be occurring.

Martell (1994: 125) also cites evidence from a survey by Jehlicka (1992) which suggests that concern for the environment may be an independent explanatory factor unrelated to the spread of postmaterial values and notes that 'Post-materialism could for example, be the result rather than the cause of the rise of new social movements giving high priority to post-material issues'. In short, environmentalism could help to promote postmaterial values rather than vice versa. This is a possibility, but it is more likely that the two are mutually reinforcing. Broad shifts in social values could help to create a climate conducive to the spread of broadly environmentalist concerns, whilst environmental groups can take advantage of this climate to persuade and recruit more successfully for specific causes thus promoting postmaterial values.

Where the postmaterialist thesis really runs into difficulty is when it is used as a causal explanation for the rise of environmentalism in a specific historical period. This ignores the history of environmental concerns and more importantly, provides no account of the reasons for the formation of environmental organisations before the spread of postmaterial values. As an illustration, current concerns around the loss of animal species may seem to be a recent postmaterial-led issue, but international legislation to protect seals for example, can be traced back to the Convention for the Protection and Preservation of Fur Seals in 1911, and a similar measure to protect migratory birds was enacted by the USA and Canada in 1917 (Hannigan 1995: 147). In Britain, legislative attempts to protect birds go back even earlier, at least to the Sea Birds Preservation Act of 1869. So, although the postmaterial values thesis may be one factor in the explanation of the spread of support for environmentalism, it cannot be readily used as an explanation for the emergence of specifically environmental concerns and certainly not for the rise of environmental and Green movements as such.

Political explanations of environmentalism focus on the character of political systems of interest mediation and political opportunity structures within nation-states (Kitschelt 1986). The main argument based on political closure is that (neo) corporatist political arrangements which include government, trades unions and business, effectively exclude other lobbying interests which find it hard to make their views heard and to get their demands taken seriously within the system. With established channels apparently blocked, non-established interests and issues find expression through the looser networks of social movement activity. With regard to Green issues, political closure explanations see these concerns as lying outside those of the corporate partners. Neither business, trades unions or government have any real interest in conservation and preservation, or more realistically, these concerns are considered secondary to the generation of wealth, jobs and the pursuit of economic growth. Many Greens also make this connection when they compare their own politics of 'life' with that of the existing 'grey' (i.e., lifeless) political parties.[2] Political closure explanations also draw on the idea of the lack of influence of a growing new middle class, those white collar professionals who work in the 'non-productive' public sector, and hence the build-up of frustration within the system. Following Scott (1990), Martell notes that it is the high levels of education and articulacy coupled with this political exclusion which breeds the dissatisfaction with established politics forcing this class fraction to turn to social movement activity to press its claims.

However, critics point out that firstly '... there is no clear relationship between the strength or weakness of neo-corporatism and NSMs' (Bagguley 1992: 31, drawing conclusions from a cross-national survey by Wilson 1990). Secondly political *openness*, such as electoral systems based on proportional representation rather than the British first-past-the-post principle, rather than closure, helps to explain the successes of Green parties in Europe. And finally, that these approaches fail to explain the initial rise of environmental and Green concerns, concentrating only on why these concerns get channelled into social movement activity (Martell 1994: 118-19).

In relation to this study, political approaches, as with postmaterial theories, fail to explain the origins of environmental concern and do not pay enough attention to the creation and maintenance of environmental organisations historically. In addition there is a concentration on the publicly visible periods of intense movement activity, and the actions of Green political parties as typical of the wider environmental movement. This is understandable given their focus on the relationship between the existing political system and interest mediation, but the problem here is that it is easy to miss those cultural aspects of movement activity which are latent or 'submerged in everyday life' (Melucci 1989) and which are vital to an understanding of the periods of manifest activity. It may also be the case that Green parties are not representative of the wider environmental movement, so that to concentrate on the former gives a misleading impression of the main concerns of the movement. I think that this is a particularly pertinent point which I will return to in Chapter Five, where the British Green Party and its relationship to the environmental movement is explored more fully.

Agency explanations focus attention on the actions of specific groups in society who instigate and maintain public interest in environmental and Green issues and aims. These include scientists, media professionals and of course, environmental groups themselves. It certainly is the case that during the 1970s for example, environmental 'catastrophist' writers extrapolating current trends into the future and forecasting ecological disaster tended to be natural scientists. Biologists such as Rachel Carson, Sir Frank Fraser-

Darling, Paul Ehrlich and Garrett Hardin (amongst others) were all influential in helping to define some of the key problems, of pollution, population growth, species loss and so on.[3] However, it is unlikely that their ideas would have reached a wider audience without positive coverage in the mass media together with significant social movement involvement, so all three social groups interacted to generate public awareness of the ecological problematic.

In sociological approaches, the shift of focus from structure to agency represents a determination on the part of some writers to avoid structural determinism in the explanation of ecological protest. The action theories of Touraine (1971) and Eyerman & Jamison (1991), are examples of this. Looking at the activities of specific social groups also avoids reducing the social processes through which problems claims are constructed, to a simple awareness of the existence of an objective problem itself (Yearley 1991: 52).

Martell (1994: 124) accepts that social actors have helped to popularise ecological ideas and problems, but argues that the tendency towards a social constructionist perspective in this type of explanation can be pushed too far. That is, the '...objective existence of environmental problems...', is largely ignored in favour of an analysis of the ways in which certain environmental issues are problematised at certain times and in specific ways by influential social groups. The study of environmental problems within the framework of a social problems analysis, implies that the existence of the objective problems can never be enough in themselves to produce public concern. To become a social problem, an issue has to be defined and constructed as such. Nevertheless, in addition to the explanations outlined above, Martell sees another, namely the objective existence of environmental problems generated by human activity.

Martell's arguments against social constructionist perspectives on environmental issues seem to stem from a dissatisfaction with the way objective environmental problems are all but eliminated in the desire to show that social factors play an important part in their formulation. He says that,

> Explanations of environmentalism can be *too* socio-logical. They explain environmentalism in terms of external social factors, but they too often exclude problems identified in the content of its discourse from having a bearing on the explanation of its rise. In reducing environmentalism to social causes they deny the validity of the content of environmentalist discourse. It is reasonable to suggest that there might have been an escalation of objective

problems in industrial societies of the sort identified by greens ... (Martell 1994: 131).

If objective environmental problems are themselves an explanatory factor in the rise of the Greens, then we would expect those areas with the most pressing problems to show the most concern through, say, votes for Green parties or support for environmental organisations. Jehlicka's (1992) study suggests that this is the case in the Czech Republic, southern Germany, Belgium, Luxembourg and the Netherlands, where '... air pollution, acidification, deforestation, soil erosion and river pollution are most serious' (Martell, 1994: 134), whereas in Britain these effects are not felt as acutely, hence electoral support for the Green Party is not widespread. As one factor among others, this is an interesting area for further study, though much more comparative work is required in order to demonstrate these links. I think that one benefit of introducing objective environmental factors into our explanations is that it brings society-nature relations into sociological analysis. This is important if we are to avoid an extreme social constructionism which effectively eliminates this whole problematic.[4]

Realists like Martell see two parts to environmental problems. Firstly the objective problem itself, for example the London smog of 1952 or global warming today. Secondly, the way this problem is mediated through social processes. To focus attention only on the second aspect, though useful in some respects, can lead to the objective problem itself being ignored or omitted from sociological inquiry. In short, the content of ecological discourse with its concentration on the very real problems generated by the activities of industrial processes is excluded from the analysis.

In the context of some contemporary discussions of ecological problems, Martell provides a useful corrective to some of the wilder claims of social constructionists. I would argue though that not all ecological and environmental problems are the same, with some being more obviously amenable to expert intervention and construction than others, which then appear to affect large numbers of the public without the interventions of influential groups of (usually scientific) experts. It is easy to see the utility of a social constructionist perspective in relation to those environmental issues which are largely defined as problems by scientists, and which are not visible or knowable without specialist measuring equipment: global warming, thinning of the ozone layer and so on. However, some environmental issues such as development pressures on green belt land, which affect localities much more immediately, seem to come closer to

Martell's notion of an objective problem forcing its way into public consciousness. I am not suggesting that global warming does not really exist whereas there really are inroads being made into green belt land, only that the extent to which environmental problems are seen to be socially constructed can appear to be different according to the type of problem being considered. In this way, it is possible to see that there is a kind of sliding scale between the two extremes of a totally social constructionist approach and on one which insists on the absolute reality of objective environmental problems.

In terms of our interests in this book, which is concerned with the sociological understanding of environmentalism and radical ecology, Martell's introduction of the argument that there has been an escalation of objective problems in industrial societies has to be qualified. If this means that there are simply more objective problems than in the past, then we have to be cautious. Some environmental problems are considered less pernicious now than in the past. Water quality in the Thames has improved, restrictive regulations now cover many previously polluting industrial processes, and the problem of London smog has eased since the 1950s. On the other hand, some problems have been identified in the present which did not trouble earlier generations: fears over the potential for nuclear war, leaks from nuclear power plants, thinning of the ozone layer, climate change and so on. Whether there really are just more objective problems than previously is a contentious matter of debate. However, if escalation means that some ecological problems have now been identified which are global in scale, and affect more and more people, across larger areas of the planet, and which cannot be solved by any single nation-state acting alone, then this global awareness is clearly part of the motivation for radical ecology groups today and is a major point of difference with earlier local and national conservationism. [5]

In this first section I have outlined the main ways in which environmental and Green movements are currently explained in sociology. What should be evident from this is that these explanations are primarily concerned with post-1960s developments. There is little attempt to link contemporary environmental and Green actions with previous periods of concern and activism, and in my view this is a serious drawback. We need to be able to trace the connections between environmental initiatives over longer periods of time than these theories allow for if our understanding is to be deepened. Towards this end, in the next section I look at three explanatory frameworks which do claim to take in some of the historical aspects of environmentalism and Green politics, though they do this in different ways. This will enable us to see some of the benefits of taking a longer-term approach, and by the end of the chapter, to have a better idea of what an adequate socio-historical account of nature politics would have to cover, and what it might look like.

Historical Explanatory Frameworks

In the discussion of explanatory frameworks in this section, I cannot hope adequately to summarise the complexity and subtlety of the various authors' respective positions, and make no attempt to do so. I am interested in them only in so far as they provide examples of different kinds of frameworks for understanding the emergence and development of environmentalism and Green politics in modern societies. This strategy is justified, because part of my general critique of many current theories is that they attempt to collapse quite different movements into the same analytical space. By the end of this chapter it will be a little clearer why the authors considered here are right to take a more historical approach but also why there is a need to move from their rather abstract understanding of the development of environmentalism and radical ecology to a more empirically adequate one. This entails digging deeper into the history of the organised movement than the authors discussed in this section do in order to paint a more comprehensive picture of it.

Cyclical Approaches and Political Opportunities

One of the most influential perspectives on movement 'cycles' is that of Tarrow (1994; 1998), who has tried to show that there has been a neglect of political opportunity structures in explanations of rising protest movements. His main concern is with the way that movements do not so much carve out opportunities for themselves (agency) but rather, take advantage or not of political opportunities as they arise (structure). So although it is possible to see why movement activity erupts at particular times, it is much less easy to predict the consequences of their activities.

Tarrow makes much of the concept of 'protest cycles', explaining that,

> When I use the phrase, cycle of protest, I am referring to a phase of heightened conflict and contention across the social system that includes: a rapid diffusion of collective action from more mobilized to less mobilized sectors; a quickened pace of innovation in the forms of contention; new or transformed collective action frames; a combination of organized and unorganized participation; and sequences of intensified interaction between challengers and authorities which can end in reform, repression and sometimes revolution (1994: 153).

He identifies three groups of explanation in terms of cycles. Firstly, cultural theorists who locate cultural changes as primary and the source of political and social change (Brand 1990; Swidler 1986); second, political historians and historical economists looking for cycles of political or economic change (Schlesinger 1986; Hirschman 1982); and finally, social theorists who concentrate on the transformation of states and forms of capitalism (Tilly 1984: ch.1). In blunt terms, the first school emphasises the global nature of cycles, the second their regularity, and the third their derivation from social-structural change. However, Tarrow argues that none of these groups focus on the structure of cycles themselves. In rectifying this omission he says that the most important aspects are the broadening of political opportunities by 'early risers' or innovators in the cycle, the resultant lower 'cost' of contention for relatively weak actors and the high degree of interdependence among all actors in the cycle. In addition, at the end of the cycle it is important to look at the way political opportunities are closed off (Tarrow 1994: 154).

For Tarrow, a typical cycle develops as follows:

1. The opening up of political opportunities for 'early risers' (Ibid. 155) which then makes visible the vulnerability of established authorities to further protest action.

2. A resultant heightening of conflict and the diffusion of protest to groups not usually involved, at least during the course of the cycle.

3. The 'action repertoires' of movements leave traces in the culture for future risings and 'frames of meaning' whilst ideologies (such as that of human rights) help to justify collective action, but also motivate new supporters.

4. At their peak, cycles produce new organizations or rejuvenate old ones. Tarrow (1994: 157) suggests that 'organizations born in collective action continue to use it. Once formed, movement organizations compete for support through collective action. The common spiral of radicalisation observed in many protest cycles is the outcome of such competition for support'.

5. Increased interaction between groups of challengers and the authorities tend to increase in frequency and intensity and become multipolar rather than bipolar.

This cyclical structure is similar for all protest cycles, but Tarrow is at pains to remind us that the *outcomes* of cycles of protest are diverse. In particular, he says that 'the involvement of foreign powers turned the ends of these cycles into different directions' (1994: 168) though generally the outcome is determined via a process of political struggle. That is, '... the structure of politics through which movement demands are processed forces them into a common crucible from which modest reforms are the most likely outcome' (ibid.: 170). But why do movement cycles seem to end in incremental reform? Tarrow's answer is that 'Since movements are born, diffused and processed through the logic of political opportunities, it is the changing structure of opportunity emerging from a protest cycle that determines who wins and who loses, and when struggle will lead to reform' (ibid.: 177). In short, the end result is not strictly in the hands of the protesters themselves, rather, the structure of the protest cycle will tend to determine outcomes, often leading to unintended consequences, but more often leading to incremental reforms rather than revolutionary changes.

In order to show this empirically, Tarrow compares the student movement of 1968 and the American women's movement in the same period. The former was 'an instant marvel yet a long term failure; whereas the second, although seeming to go from disappointment to disappointment, has brought about profound change in American politics and society'" (1994: 177) The question is why? In terms of his 'four powers in movement', although women had a slow start in the 1960s, the opportunity structure actually favoured them in the following ways:

1. In their repertoires of contention, women used 'conventional and symbolic' actions which placed their arguments in the mainstream of

American collective action, whereas the student movement 'alarmed public opinion' with its strategies and repertoires (sit-ins, violence, barricades etc.) (1994: 181; see also Swidler 1986).

2. In their respective 'framing' of collective action and discourse, the framing of students had little resonance outside of their peer group. Ideas of 'power to the imagination' and so on held no appeal for working people. In the case of the women's movement though, incremental changes to language were introduced which drew on already existing repertoires of meaning, subverting them in the process. For example, they promoted subtle shifts in language use, 'women' not 'girls', 'gender' not 'sex', 'partner' not 'girlfriend' (1994: 182).

3. In terms of the way these movements organised, their 'mobilising structures', the student movement depended on students whose university life is necessarily short-lived, and this almost inevitably led to organizational instability. The women's movement used a variety of organisational forms such as loose networks of activists, formal organisations such as the National Organisation of Women (NOW) and women's studies educational programmes. It was also important that a network of contacts already existed before the 1960s outburst and the relatively small group character of these facilitated stronger solidarity.

4. Finally - and this is Tarrow's main argument in relation to protest cycles - all of this activity depended on the opening up and closing down of political opportunities. The French government was elected with a reinforced majority after the student protests and dealt effectively with educational reform, so defusing the movement's more radical demands. Whilst in the USA, the womens movement took advantage of the Democratic Party's use of representative groups to ensure that feminists gained a foothold and a presence in the American political system. Let us hear Tarrow's own summary of this argument:

In summary, French students erupted on the scene far more dramatically than American women. But the uncontrolled repertoire of the French students, their obscure and abstract discourse, their lack of consistent mobilizing structures and permanent networks and, especially, the migration of political opportunities from the movements of May to the government converged to reduce the power of their movement. American women, who first mobilized in the shadow of the Civil Rights movement, combined a rich and varied repertoire, a meaningful discursive politics, a network structure embedded in society and institutions and an electoral advantage that have made the women's movement among the most successful in American social history, effecting - among other things - a profound shift in political culture (1994: 184).

At the end of this account, Tarrow raises the possibility that we may be moving to a situation where 'movements arise more easily than previously, a 'movement society" (ibid.: 186) which is largely due to the process of globalisation and increasing transnational connections which appear to be freeing social movements from the influence of the national state and internal political processes. In short, movements may now be spreading more rapidly when they arise and are less easily defused by national political actions.

Critical Remarks

Clearly Tarrow's analysis is important and fruitful in terms of asking questions which lead to empirical and comparative research, and the introduction of political opportunity structures into the study of social movements brings a new dimension to the large scale theorising of scholars such as Touraine. However, the focus on opportunity structures does not of itself explain why particular social movements emerge or why they persist over time, even after the end of a highly visible protest cycle. In relation to the development of the environmental movement in Britain for example, the most striking feature is the continuous expansion of the movement over the last 100 years, not disjunctive changes in cycles of action. In addition to a theory of the 'structure of protest cycles' we need to explore changes at the level of culture in order to show why it is that the environment has become a focus for campaigns for social change, and a particularly clear example of this is Brand's (1990) work on movement cycles and their relationship to the wider society and I turn to this next.

Karl Werner Brand: A Cyclical Phenomenon?

One way of understanding and explaining the emergence of a wave of new social movements in Western democracies is to place them within the broader context of a changing general cultural mood or '*Zeitgeist*.' Shifts in the 'cultural climate' can provide fertile ground for the concerns of social movements to gain credibility, and to spread these concerns to a wider public, thus opening up new possibilities for political action and the institutionalisation of social movement problematics into 'normal' politics. I want to discuss an interesting example of this kind of approach which is provided by Brand (1990),[6] focusing particularly on the way his study relates to our understanding of the environmental and radical ecology movements in Britain, though I will also refer to other cyclical ideas where necessary.

Brand (1990: 33-4) identifies three periods of broadly based 'cultural criticism' in Britain, America and Germany which fall roughly 70 years apart with each lasting around two decades. These are: 1830-1850, 1890-1910 and 1960-1980.   His thesis is that these periods coincide with the mobilization phases of social movements including women's movements, peace and environmental movements and alternative movements, during which new members are recruited, activism increases, organisations are formed and alternative (counter-) cultures develop. By using the term *Zeitgeist*, Brand (ibid: 28) means '... the specific configuration of world-views, thoughts and emotions, fears and hopes, beliefs and utopias, feelings of crisis or security, of pessimism or optimism, which prevail in this period'. He is particularly concerned with the specific social mood he calls 'modernisation critique' which includes criticism of the central institutional dimensions of modern societies such as 'commercialisation, industrialisation, political centralisation, bureaucratisation and democratisation, cultural rationalisation and pluralisation' (ibid.). Modernisation critiques can take the form of pre-modernist recourse to tradition, anti-modernist appeals to nature as a source of authority, or artistic/aesthetic reaction evidenced for example by the European Romanticism of the early nineteenth century, though Brand suggests that all three forms generally appear together.

The shape and specific nature of modernisation critiques depends to some extent on the particular features of national political life and political culture, and more research would perhaps bring out these cross-national differences, but this should not detract from the general picture which emerges across increasingly interdependent nations and economies. Brand argues that the *Zeitgeist* of the 1830s and 40s was characterised by the tensions and problems associated with the shift from agrarian society towards industrialisation and the spread of capitalism. Later, at the turn of the century, social movements were able to feed on more widespread sentiments and feelings of Victorian 'over-civilisation' and repression, when people began to question accepted notions of progress as the darker side of industrialisation became clearer. In the 1960s and 70s the earlier promises of the post-war affluent society were questioned and found wanting, with the technocratic solutions proposed by socially defined experts to society's problems no longer appearing believable. Critique took a subjective turn towards a new interest in self-identity and personal politics, culminating in the 1980s postmodern mood of 'anything goes' (Brand 1990: 30-3).

It must be re-iterated that Brand is talking about broad changes in the cultural climate which potentially feed into the operations and organisation of many social movements, not just environmentalism, and in this way he tends to bypass the distinct experiences and reactions of different social groups to these broad cultural shifts. In relation to the cultural aspects of environmentalism and a growing interest in nature, Brand notes the emergence of animal welfare and protection sentiments (for example, the formation of the Society for the Prevention of Cruelty to Animals in Britain in 1824) and the increasing numbers of natural history societies in the early nineteenth century, but he argues that the first real phase of environmental social movement mobilisation occurred in the late-nineteenth century when,

> ... the increasing anti-urbanism and the nostalgic idealization of wilderness and rural life gave these efforts the impetus of a true mass movement, speeding up legislation of nature and monument preservation, animal and plant protection, and the establishment of national parks. Outside activities, such as cycling, hiking and camping came into fashion (Brand 1990: 36).

There are some problems here caused by the attempt to reach general conclusions across three nation-states. Specific initiatives did not simply cross national borders. For example, Britain's ten National Parks were not designated until after 1950 (Evans 1992: 82), much later than in the USA. However Brand is right to point to the late nineteenth century as a particularly active period of mobilization and organisation building, what I call the first 'phase' of organised environmental activity in Britain.

Despite an increase in popularity and political significance during the inter-war years, Brand argues that it is only during the 1960s and 70s that a second-wave of environmental mobilisation occurs and a real mass movement emerges.[7] In trying to explain these two waves, he attempts to test their fit with the long waves of economic up-swings and down-swings of capitalist economies, the so-called Kondratieff cycles, which last '40 to 60 years', concluding that although there is no direct causal relationship between these cycles and periods of general modernisation critique, his findings do suggest that,

> ... optimistic versions of cultural criticism appear rather in times of economic prosperity (as between the turn of the century and World War I or in the 1960s); pessimistic versions appear in phases of economic down-swing and depression (as in the 1830s and 1840s, in the last two decades of the nineteenth century, in part in the 1920s, and again in the 1970s) (1990: 39).[8]

Economic conditions seem to influence the particular character and direction of modernisation critiques once these have been set in train, and these critiques then feed into the activities and arguments of social movements.[9]

In relation to environmentalism and Green ideas, Brand's argument suggests that pessimistic versions should have occurred in the late nineteenth century, and again in the 1970s, but as I will show in the next chapter, both an optimistic environmentalism and a more pessimistic Green politics have existed at one and the same time. In my view, this is because attempts to reform and regulate industrialism and more radical Green ideas of transcending this society altogether are interrelated, with reformists trying to translate radical ideals into practical measures, whilst radicals accept these but continue to push for more.[10] In short, although the balance of reformism and radicalism does shift in different periods, the long-term development of environmentalism and Green politics has been more processual than the thesis of recurring modernisation critiques allows.

Brand also argues that one general conclusion can be drawn from his analysis. This is that cultural criticism and middle class radicalism 'spread in the wake of a period of rapid industrial growth and social transformation, favoured by the establishment of a new model of political integration and development promising progress and the solution of long-standing problems and social conflicts' (1990: 41). Here it is clear that Brand wants to stress (rightly) that the 1960s and '70s modernisation critique was not unique, but rather that such periods have not been uncommon since they are linked to

'...the dynamic of capitalist and industrial development which does not come about gradually, but in discontinuous processes of crisis, disorganisation and restructuring' (ibid.). This need not necessarily mean that social movements appear and disappear like waves rushing on to the shoreline however. Though Brand does not say so, it is implicit in his thesis that social movements may lie dormant or remain at the level of social networks, only rising to public prominence when the cultural climate changes in their favour, and a reasonable argument could be developed in this vein to describe the (re)emergence of a discourse and more public manifestation of radical ecology in the late twentieth century. However, cyclical approaches generally tend to focus on the contexts in which social movements find themselves at the expense of studying the movement's organisations themselves. The concept of *Zeitgeist* or 'spirit of the age' can be invoked to describe the complex of ideas and sentiments which feed environmentalist sympathies and arguments, but this is not sufficient in itself to explain the continuance of movement organisations even after the ending of a period of cultural criticism. It is difficult to see why environmental organisations would become institutionally established and continue to expand their memberships unless some of the same concerns which provoked their formation also exercised following generations.

Another example of a cyclical explanation is Lowe and Goyder's (1983) important study of the British environmental movement which Brand is aware of.[11] Like Brand, they characterise the movement's development as 'episodic', with one 'episode' in the late nineteenth century, one in the 1970s and '80s, though they also identify a further one between the Two World Wars,[12] suggesting that an expansive process of suburbanisation gathered pace during the latter period which led to increasing concerns about development in the countryside. Evans (1992: 61) notes for example that,

> Between 1920 and 1940, no fewer than 4 million houses were built. The yearly net loss to concrete more than doubled in the late 1920s and the annual loss of over 25,000 ha in each and every year of the 1930s has never been approached since. The word 'suburbia' has an ugly ring to it these days; in the 1930s, suburbia was the place to be. But the sprawl was seen as a terrible menace to the landscape and probably did more than anything else to trigger the alarm of conservationists about the countryside.

Unlike Brand however, Lowe and Goyder use the dates of formation of environmental *organisations* as the key indicator of increased public awareness and concern for the natural world. Though this is a much narrower measure of environmental concern than the myriad cultural manifestations identified by Brand, I think that the focus on organisations is justified in relation to environmentalism *as a social movement*. As I will argue later, it is precisely through its organisational forms that the movement is able to endure over time, rather than fading completely from view. The focus on organisations forces us, in spite of pointing up more or less distinct episodes of environmental concern, to take seriously the continuity of the environmental movement in Britain since the 1860s, a key argument I will make throughout this study.

The formation of organisations within the environmental movement is a very important factor which helps to bring an environmentalist perspective to the wider population (and hence expand the movement), by providing a focus for policy-making, the development of ideas, creation of self-identities and so on. Organisations by their active lobbying also enhance the possibility of established political parties being forced to take account of environmental issues. More than this though, environmental organisations can form the crucial bridge which is capable of bringing ideas previously perceived as marginal into the mainstream. In short, organisations smooth the transition for outsider groups to become established and in so doing, potentially change the existing institutional order. I argue that it is in this way that dominant social processes and institutions can be regulated and even transformed.

What is missing from Brand's cyclical approach to periods of environmental concern is attention to the campaigning activities and organisation building of movement activists themselves. Environmental organisations can continue to provide a focus for maintaining public interest in environmental concerns, even after the demise of a wave of cultural critique. A cyclical approach is useful in so far as it can highlight specific periods when broad cultural changes facilitate the growth of social movements by providing a more sympathetic climate within which they operate, and it may be during such periods that, for example, legislative change may be pursued with greater success than previously. The prevailing cultural climate may also influence the shaping of a movement's range of arguments and to some extent its organisational forms. But by concentrating on periods when social movement activities become more publicly acceptable and visible, we should not lose sight of the continuities between periods or phases, or the endurance of movement organisations over quite long periods of time despite the demise of vigorous modernisation critiques.

The main problem with Brand's perspective is that there is not enough sense of direction or development of the environmental movement. I think that this is a major drawback in relation to organised environmentalism which has a fairly continuous history and a clear line of expansive development over time. However, the idea of recurring periods of cultural critique does fit the anti-industrial tenor of contemporary radical ecology much better. Radical ecology has not given rise to specific social movement organisations which could carry its key ideas forward. Indeed, radical ecologists try hard to resist the drive towards formal organisation as they are suspicious of bureaucratic forms, career hierarchies and establishment. Because of this, radical ideals are much less likely to survive the ending of a period of vigorous modernisation critique. Hence Brand's approach does alert us to the influence of counter-cultural periods on the rise of Green ideas, but we need a different kind of perspective if we are adequately to explain continuities within the environmental movement.

A deeper understanding of the periodic eruption of widespread cultural critiques in modern societies could be achieved by examining the relationship between these and the dominant culture which they seek to criticise. For instance, it may well be that '... the critique of modernity has been part of the modern spirit since its very inception' (Wellmer 1991: vii). Klaus Eder has developed just such an approach which tries to show how a deep-seated alternative cultural tradition, normally suppressed, in different historical periods punctures the fabric of the dominant culture, resulting in a flowering of counter-cultural movements and ideas of the kind identified by Brand, and it is to this perspective on the rise of cultural movements that I now turn.

Klaus Eder: The Emergence of a Submerged Counter-Culture

A different kind of specifically cultural explanation of contemporary ecological movements is provided by Klaus Eder (1985; 1990; 1993). Rather than focusing on historically specific episodes of cultural criticism and social movement mobilisation, Eder attempts a re-visioning of modern culture in order to bring out the longevity of what he describes as an alternative, 'submerged' cultural tradition in Western societies. This has now become not only visible, but quite fundamental to the creation of what Eder somewhat confusingly calls a developing new 'class' conflict over society's relationship to nature.

Eder argues that modern culture is not a homogenous whole but is characterised by a 'double cultural tradition' (one dominant, one subordinate) whose origins can be traced back to early modern Europe. He says that '... the dominant tradition is the one tied to industrialism; the other one is a dominated tradition that has manifested itself in the Romantic model (which was reacting to Enlightenment as its better alternative) and that has been feeding counterculture movements throughout the last two centuries ' (1993: 140). If we call these two traditions modernism and romanticism respectively, then they carry different images of society's relationship to nature. It is not that modernism was a new dominant culture and critics turned to an older romantic tradition in order to oppose it. Rather, '... the Romantics were as modern and as new as the rationalists' (Calhoun 1993: 79). Both modernism and romanticism came into being as constitutive parts of modern culture, but romanticism took a subordinate form.

Modernism distances itself from all previous cultural traditions and 'attempts to constitute society beyond nature' (Eder 1993: 124). In this sense, modernism attaches negative symbolic value both to other cultural traditions and to nature, and although Eder uses Marx and marxism as an exemplar of the modernist tradition, it is clear that the classical physical sciences and the social sciences are modernist in Eder's sense. These basic features of the dominant cultural tradition find some sympathy in the critique of modernity offered by the contemporary radical ecology movement which often points to the way industrialisation and a rational, scientific outlook have de-throned nature as *the* source of value thus enabling and legitimising environmental damage (Merchant 1982; Capra 1983).[13] Although radical ecological ideas cannot be reduced to the description of anti-scientific, some radical ecologists are extremely critical of 'mechanistic' science, so there are some parallels with the anti-science movements which also seem to have been recurring phenomena in the experience of modernity. For example, Toulmin (1972: 24) wonders whether anti-science movements

> ... [are] not a generational or secular phenomenon, as predictable as the tides. Throughout the last half-millennium, at least, anti-scientific attitudes seem to have peaked at intervals of 130 years or so, if not every 65 or 30-35 years. ... can we not see today's anti-science, similarly, as a recurrent expression of the same preoccupations that underlay the hostility of Goethe, Schiller and William Blake to the Newtonian science of their time? Or the scorn of

Jonathon Swift for the activities of the early Royal Society? Or the insistence of Michel de Montaigne that intellectual life should be focused on matters of humane concern, rather than on hubristic attempts to theorize about aspects of nature quite foreign to human needs?

The timing of these cyclical peaks of anti-science sentiments is somewhat vague in Toulmin's account but the thrust of the thesis is quite close to that of Eder. Like Eder, Toulmin (1972: 23) argues that the underlying generative cause of these waves of anti-science is a vein of (counter) cultural attitudes '... which are normally there below the surface, and have occasionally blown up to serious proportions'. Opposition to scientific rationalism and to the institutional organisation of scientific research today are just the '... contemporary expression of deeper-seated and longer-standing attitudes and interests ...' (ibid.). One possible explanation for the wave-like recurrence of anti-science attitudes, particularly amongst intellectuals, is provided by Varcoe (1995: 79) who argues that the 'swing effect' of enthusiasm for and revulsion against science, is linked to the position of modern intellectuals who 'find themselves caught between an increasingly dominant world culture (of science) and the disjunctions it induces everywhere ... On the one hand, science has done so much to improve the lot of humankind. On the other, it seems to be the source of new divisions and injustices'. This may go some way towards explaining the ambivalence to science amongst radical ecological intellectuals.

A critical attitude to science can be seen in the way that some radical ecologists portray 'non-scientific' societies as in some ways less ecologically damaging, and look to Eastern philosophies and religions such as Buddhism, Taoism and Hinduism for traditions which contain a greater respect for nature (Pepper 1996: 19). For example, it is often asserted that the social organisation of 'primitive' cultures such as the Native American Indians or Australian Aboriginal groups led to a more harmonious relationship between society and nature than in the modern West (Manes 1990; Young 1990).[14]

In contrast to modernism, early romanticism gave a positive symbolic valuation to nature which it saw as '... representing life and therefore required the application of moral principles. Nature was enshrined as the real world beyond the artificial world of society and politics' (Eder 1993: 128).[15] Although the most visible aspects of this counter-cultural tradition were intellectual and artistic works, Eder notes that glimpses of it can be seen throughout the nineteenth and twentieth centuries in, for example, communal and vegetarian movements, late - nineteenth century agrarian communes in Germany and other communal experiments. For Eder (ibid: 129) what these examples show is that '... nature has since the beginning of modernity been the latent field of social and cultural struggles'.[16] Modernity, or rather modern culture, must then be seen as 'Janus-faced', with a dominant cultural tradition repressing but frequently being punctured by, a subordinate one which poses a challenge to the way the society/nature relationship is constructed and valued. Eder's thesis finds support among spiritual 'deep' ecologists like Capra (1982: 459), who argues that,

> The Deep Ecology movement, then, is not proposing an entirely new philosophy but is reviving an awareness which is part of our cultural heritage. What is new, perhaps, is the extension of the ecological vision to the planetary level, supported by the powerful experience of the astronauts and expressed in images like 'spaceship Earth' and the 'whole Earth' as well as the new maxim 'think globally, act locally'.

In contrast to truly cyclical theories as in Toulmin and Brand, Eder suggests that the contemporary situation marks the end of recurring cycles of romantic and anti-science protests. This is because modern societies have undergone significant changes which have led to the romantic model of society/nature relations moving out of its subordinated, latent situation and becoming manifest, leading to the increasing centrality of conflicts over 'nature' in modern societies. He identifies two main reasons for this.

Firstly, 'The ecological crisis has made nature the arena of public disputes', and second, '... an increasing reflexivity in dealing with cultural traditions has led us to thematize competing notions of relating to nature' (Eder 1993: 129). It is not clear from Eder's work how this increasing reflexivity has come about, nor is it apparent that an ecological crisis actually exists, or whether any consensus even exists on what this phrase might mean. However, for our purposes here it is important to emphasise again that Eder does not see the contemporary interest in ecology and nature as *wholly* new, but rather as part of an increasing conflict over the future direction of modernity, or what Touraine (1981: 26) calls the 'struggle over historicity', that is, over 'The great cultural orientations by which a society's environmental relationships are normatively organised'. What has changed though, is that concerns over society/nature relations have become more visible and now increasingly play a central role in oppositional politics.

Eder also notes implicitly that there is a third factor which has promoted the emergence of counter-cultural concerns, this is the development of a new middle class concentrated in service sector occupations. This group 'are also potentially a new social class', who are '... the potential carriers of a new relationship with nature', because the 'ecological crisis' has come to pose threats to their lifestyles which tend to place a high value on 'quality of life' issues' (Eder 1993: 134-5). Unlike older middle class groups, the new middle class has a crucial strategic role because the service sector in which they are employed '... is apparently becoming the key sector of the emerging postindustrial society' (ibid: 134), and it is this new importance which brings Eder to the conclusion that it is the new middle class which is 'shaping an emerging new class structure'. He notes that middle class leisure pursuits such as '... wandering, climbing, excursions into the countryside [and] all forms of tourism', (ibid.) make it clear that nature has had a special significance for the middle classes, who are '... emotionally tied not only to a just world but to a good world to live in, and they react much more intensely to the effects of exploiting the natural environment' (ibid: 135).

As in other theories of the role of the new middle class in new movements and counter-cultures, Eder mistakes the participation of this group in leadership roles and amongst activists, for an exclusive 'interest' of the middle classes in the substantive concerns of environmentalism. It is certainly clear that many founders of early (late-nineteenth century) environmental organisations enjoyed outdoor pursuits, nature study and so on, partly as a way of getting close to 'God's works'. A love of nature almost becoming a post-Darwinian religion (see for example, Aveling 1883).[17] And yet, this kind of interpretation fails to appreciate the interest in nature of many other groups, including manual workers. Indeed, there is no reason to believe that working class lifestyles proved wholly impenetrable to the same broad cultural shifts towards the adoption of non-utilitarian attitudes towards nature (Thomas 1984) that Eder sees in the middle classes.

As early as the 1770s, botanical field clubs began to spring up around the country, many in manufacturing districts where '... all their members, without exception, were manual workers, most of them factory operatives or jobbing gardeners' (Allen 1978: 159). A similar kind of society devised by weavers and workers in the tailoring trade had been noted in Norwich during the mid-eighteenth century, and the silk weavers of Spitalfields enjoyed collecting colourful insects. *The Encyclopaedia of Gardening* of 1822 noted that 'Wherever the silk, linen or cotton manufactures are carried on ... the operatives are found to possess a taste for, and occupy part of their leisure time in, the culture of flowers' (cited in Allen ibid.). An interest in nature study and collecting was not confined to the more exclusive clubs which charged membership fees and conducted their hobby in a spirit of academic seriousness. Also since the late-nineteenth century, the tradition of allotment holding has been common amongst manual workers and has passed down through generations. By the turn of the century there were around half a million allotment holders. The Committee of Enquiry into Allotments (1969) found that eighty per cent of holders lived in towns, and forty-five per cent were manual workers. Similarly, gardening has long been a working class activity.

Perhaps the difference is partly one of visibility. Manual workers tended not to be the ones who wrote articles for newspapers or books on natural history, nor did they hire debating chambers, pay for the establishment of museums or publish their transactions (Allen 1978). Nevertheless, this should not disguise the fact that, although workers played almost no part in the founding of environmental organisations, this probably owes more to their lack of material resources and free time to do so, rather than to any fundamental resistance to their objectives.[18]

Because he is concerned with broadly based cultural traditions and counter-cultural groups, Eder is less interested in social movements and their constituent organisations. In his case this is because part of his argument is that *social* movements are reactions to and protests against modernisation and modernity, whilst *cultural* movements are potentially the carriers of a new type of society. In the context of an emerging ecological crisis, cultural movements come to conflict openly with social movements which they perceive to be pursuing a more 'rational' modernity in its present form. He argues that cultural movements have, for the first time, become established as 'a new historical actor' (Eder 1993: 137).

It is possible to make this analysis more concrete. Eder seems to have in mind the differences between the established environmental movement (as a social movement) and the counter-cultural radical ecology movement which defines itself (in part) in opposition to the established groups. There is some validity in this characterisation of the differences between environmentalists and radical ecologists, which can be seen in the latter's criticism of the former. However, it is often the case that cultural movements can feed into social movement activity, and help to provide a more favourable cultural climate for the expression of social movement interests, as well as providing an attentive public and new opportunities for recruitment and organisation-building. In short, cultural movements and social movements within a movement sector may be mutually supportive *in spite of* their apparent and often highly visible conflicts. In particular, counter-cultural attitudes can spill over into increased support for existing social movement organisations. Indeed, later I will argue that this is what seems to have happened during both the first organisational phase of environmentalism (1860-1900) and its expansionist phase (1960-90), when the tensions between reformists and radicals were highly visible. In both periods, environmental reformers sought to translate radical ideas into more immediate practical proposals for the control of industrial development. I spend much of the rest of the book looking in more detail at the history of the British environmental movement in order to discover whether the quite radical conclusions that Eder (and others) draw from the activities of contemporary radical ecology can be supported.

Because Eder reads the contemporary period of nature politics as in some way different from all earlier such periods (i.e., a shift from a latent phase to a manifest one) it is clear that he thinks that the context in which social and cultural movements operate has fundamentally changed. As I noted earlier, his own arguments which suggest that a new 'ecological crisis', an increasing 'reflexivity in relation to other cultural traditions', together with the growing new middle class constitute this new context I find somewhat unconvincing. In the absence of any compelling evidence to the contrary, I think that the distinction Eder draws between modernist and romantic aspects of modernity must be seen as continuing into the present period, finding its way into the discourses of environmentalism and radical ecology, for example, in the latter's ambivalent stance towards scientific research and attempts to criticise modern rationalistic modes of thought for their limited concept of rationality (Porritt 1984: 15-21). What this suggests is that, along with other oppositional movements, environmentalism and radical ecology contain both rational *and* non-rational, modern *and* romantic elements, a conclusion Karl Mannheim (1953: 124) reached some time ago, in relation to romanticism and conservative thought,

> ... the romantic movement is not just a purely retrogressive reaction. The romantic mind has already absorbed and neutralized the contribution of modern rationalism. It is not adequate to think of romanticism simply as a diametrically opposed and entirely heterogeneous counter - movement to rationalism. It should rather be compared to the swing of a pendulum - a

sudden reversal from an extreme point reached in one direction. The change-over from rationalism into irrationalism - both in the emotional life and in the intellectual activities of the individual - occurs even among the chief representatives of the Enlightenment itself. Thus in Rousseau and Montesquieu an extreme rationalism and its opposite exist peacefully side by side.

Eder's thesis takes the shifting balance or 'pendulum swing' in the present period as evidence for a radical social transformation, but I do not think that this conclusion can be justified. It places much too heavy an emphasis on the transformation of reform environmentalism into a more radical ecology, an interpretation which is not supported by the evidence from the longer-term development of the environmental movement. Therefore we must affirm that contemporary radical ecology does not take us beyond modernity. As Calhoun (1995: 102) remarks on this issue,

> The complexity of interplay across rationalist and romantic lines is important to grasp. ... There may be an important battle between rationalist universalism and attention to the irrational, between the value of the particular and the repressive, disempowering, and deceptive side of individualism. But to equate that with a battle between modernity and its putative successor is to fail to recognize how deeply a part of modernity that whole battle, that whole frame of reference is. And this is only to speak of Western modernity.

What Eder sees in the present period as a conflict between established social movements pursuing a more rational modernity, and (counter-) cultural movements which are carriers of a different society, I argue is better interpreted as a constant tension between a reformist environmentalism and a radical Green analysis of society/nature relations. These two have co-existed since at least the late nineteenth century when the first environmental organisations were formed and radical 'back-to-nature' ideas, communal experiments and so on were prominent. One aspect of my alternative approach is that this interplay between reformism and radicalism has been a major factor in shaping the current situation, and in this respect it is not so surprising that contemporary radical ecology has tried to distance itself from existing environmental organisations and arguments.

Nevertheless, by introducing the idea of an 'ecological crisis' as a key factor in changing the context in which social and cultural movements operate, Eder raises the question of what the nature of this crisis really is, and this is an issue we can usefully pursue in Ulrich Beck's (1992) influential theory of the emergence of a 'risk society', an examination of which will help to flesh out the social context of contemporary nature politics.

Ulrich Beck: Reflexive Modernization and the Risk Society

Apart from interest in environmentalism and radical ecology within social movement research, discussions of nature politics within sociology have tended to be within the broader context of the social production of risks (Giddens 1990; 1991; 1994), and further, in the emergence of a 'risk society' following the influential analysis of Beck (1992; 1994). Discussions of the risks produced by the *normal* operation (functioning) of (post)modern (post)industrialised societies would seem to interlock well with the concerns of contemporary radical ecologists, especially in so far as these risks refer to the destruction of valued environments, industrial pollution of rivers and waterways, fears around modern food production methods, production of climate change and so on. Certainly many of the dire warnings of radical ecologists now seem to be accepted as at least real possibilities and as such are taken seriously within academic discourse.

Beck and Giddens' work on reflexivity, 'reflexive modernisation' and the development of a risk society also presents an alternative analysis to that offered by the concept of post-modernity. Whereas the latter is often taken as marking a break with modernity, the thesis of reflexive modernisation argues that risk societies are produced by the continuing processes of industrial modernisation. So although Beck, for example, argues that risk societies are in some sense new, he also says they are products of the previous industrial societies. I will outline Beck's view of the nature of modern societies, drawing on Giddens where necessary, as it is Beck who has more to say on the 'problem of nature' in relation to the production and construction of risks.

Beck envisages a three-stage periodisation of the history of modernity (Lash and Wynne 1992: 3), namely:

1. Pre-Modernity   2. Simple Modernity   3.Reflexive Modernity,
    (feudal/agrarian)   (modern/industrial)   (modern/risk society)

It must be said though, that no specific dates are attached to this typology, and in truth Beck is only concerned with the change from a 'simple' to a 'reflexive' form of modernity. Lash and Wynne (ibid.) provide an accessible introduction to Beck's understanding of this change, which they describe in the following passage:

> ... modernity is very much coextensive with industrial society and the new reflexive modernity with the risk society. Industrial society and risk society are for Beck distinct social formations. The axial principle of industrial society is the distribution of goods, while that of the risk society is the distribution of 'bads' or dangers. Further, industrial society is structured through social classes while the risk society is individualised.

Industrial societies produce material goods, but as these social formations develop over time, their normal production processes and institutionalised modes of development produce side effects (industrial waste, pollution, the transformation of nature) which gradually come to dominate at the expense of goods production itself. More time and energy is spent dealing with the effects of industrial production than with that production itself, hence it is justified to speak of the emergence of a 'risk society'.[19] As Beck (1992: 20-1) says:

> ... the knowledge is spreading that the sources of wealth are 'polluted' by growing 'hazardous side effects'. This is not at all new, but it has remained unnoticed for a long time in the efforts to overcome poverty ... To put it differently, in the risk society the unknown and unintended consequences come to be a dominant force in history and society.

What Beck (1994: 2) is theorising here is the 'creative (self-)destruction for an entire epoch: that of industrial society'. This occurs not through some revolutionary political movement or directed social project, but largely as an unplanned and unpredicted development behind the backs of everyone. Although initially the unplanned nature of this development was not explicit in his work, later Beck makes it clear that 'reflexivity' is not the same as 'reflection.' He suggests that we should '... call the autonomous, undesired and unseen, transition from industrial to risk society *reflexivity*' (1994: 6), whilst 'reflection' is a secondary activity in which 'public, political and scientific' reflection on this change takes place.[20] This means that reflexive modernity is a shift in the form and character of the modernisation process, producing a new condition of society, which first comes into existence, and only later becomes the subject of public and academic debate.

Beck seems to be arguing that the emergence of the risk society replaces the industrial society, and yet he also insists that risk societies are still in some sense industrialised societies. This is because it is industrial processes which continue to create the bulk of modern risks. It is difficult to see how these two claims could be compatible. Perhaps the problem is that, like post-industrial theories, Beck is being drawn into a form of theorising where societies are seen as static 'things' rather than focusing on industrialisation as a continuing social process. Elias's advocacy of process theories could be helpful here (Elias 1970; Goudsblom 1989). If we see that the industrialisation process leads to more risks, and gradually to 'higher consequence' risks (global warming etc.) which become major social and politically contested problems, then it is possible to avoid positing static social states (industrial versus risk societies).

For example, even if a majority of workers in some national societies are now employed in service occupations rather than manufacturing industry (as Eder argues), this does not mean that they can avoid or opt out of the consequences of industrialisation at the global level. A concern with global environmental problems is one aspect of a heightened sensitivity to transnational connections in the current period (Sklair 1994), and a source of support for contemporary environmental and radical ecology movements. As Kilminster (1997: 258) notes, 'The more extensive and intensive people's dependence on each other becomes globally, the more it is in their mutual interests to mitigate the unintended harmful environmental effects as well as to reduce the risk of a nuclear war'.

A further problem with the theory of reflexive modernisation occurs with Beck's concept of 'risk' itself. He defines risk as 'a systematic way of dealing with hazards and insecurities induced and introduced by modernization itself' (1992: 21). But if risk is a way of dealing with hazards, then risk does not refer to the hazards themselves. However, at times he seems to be saying that risks *are* real social hazards such as industrial pollution and radioactivity which people really face, whilst also and at the same time, noting that risks are 'particularly open to social definition and construction' (ibid: 23). This is somewhat confusing. As we saw in the first section of this chapter, Beck is not alone in trying to wrestle with the problems of realism versus social constructionism. The debate between these two seemingly intractably opposed positions has become more openly contested in recent years, and some major contributions have occurred in relation to discussions of nature politics in modern societies. For example Dickens (1992), Benton (1991, 1994), and Martell (1994) have argued from realist positions, whilst Yearley (1991), Tester (1991), Hannigan (1995) and Macnaghten and Urry (1995) promote the utility of social constructionism.[21] However, Beck seems to take an ambiguous position in this debate in relation to the reality or otherwise of modern risks.

Nevertheless, and moving against his own position somewhat, what we can usefully derive from Beck's work is that industrialisation is still one of the dominant forces or processes in and amongst national societies. I think that this is a clear advance over those post-industrial approaches which posit a radical break with industrial society and culture in a postmodern age, and unless we adopt a more developmental view of the industrialisation process, we can easily be led to see industrial societies as historical aberrations. The next question is how does the reflexive modernization thesis deal with the politics of nature?

Back to Society: The End of Nature

Beck suggests that late-twentieth century ecological protests have increased in significance because nature, previously considered to be outside of society and politics, has now become a social and political issue. Nature has been drawn into the (reflexive) modernisation process itself, meaning that what we previously thought of as nature is at an end. Similarly, Giddens (1994: 77) argues that 'Nature has become socialised. Today, among all the other endings, we may speak in a real sense of the end of nature - a way of referring to its thoroughgoing socialization'. For both Beck and Giddens, nature has apparently lost its capacity for 'otherness' in relation to Western societies. 'If human beings once knew what 'nature' was, they do so no longer. What is 'natural' is now so thoroughly entangled with what is 'social' that there can be nothing taken for granted about it any more' (Beck/Giddens/Lash 1994: vii). This assessment really restates the argument advanced by McKibben (1990: 59), that the effects of industrial activity have reached a point where they partly shape natural cycles themselves, so that 'A child born now will never know a natural summer, a natural autumn, winter or spring. Summer is going extinct, replaced by something else that will be called 'summer''.

If this is the case, then we could legitimately ask environmentalists and radical ecologists who claim to be acting in defence of nature, what exactly is this thing called 'nature' that they are supposed to be defending? Certainly not, according to Beck and Giddens, something outside of or beyond human society, something wild, autopoietic or beyond human interference. Advances in genetic engineering techniques, in vitro fertilisation, human-generated changes in global weather systems, all point in the direction of acknowledging at least the blurring of the boundary between society and nature. As Beck (1994: 27) puts it,

> It is already becoming recognizable that nature, the great constant of the industrial epoch, is losing its pre-ordained character, it is becoming a product, the integral, shapeable 'inner nature' of (in this sense) post-industrial society. The abstraction of nature leads into industrial society. The integration of nature into society leads beyond industrial society. 'Nature' becomes a social project, a utopia that is to be reconstructed, shaped and transformed. Renaturalization means denaturalization. Here the claim of modernity to shape things has been perfected under the banner of nature. Nature becomes politics.

This does not mean that humans are in control of natural forces, but that nature has now been drawn into the field of politics, and what Beck hints at here is not the end but the paradoxical triumph of modernity. Paradoxical because despite integrating nature into society, modern development now produces risks which cannot be scientifically calculated with any certainty. Scientific experts in specialised fields can be legitimately challenged by lay actors with local knowledge, (as shown for example in Wynne's (1996) study of Cumbrian sheep farmers' interactions and conflicts with 'experts' after the Chernobyl nuclear accident in 1986).[22] Risks which seem to emanate from the natural world can actually be shown to stem from human, industrial activities, and it is these which now become political concerns for oppositional movements, with some Greens advocating a policy of de-industrialisation. Workers' movements tied into industrial processes, and whose livelihoods depend on these are in no position to provide an effective, critical opposition, hence new social (and cultural) movements have become more visible as well as more significant for the future development of society.

Beck is clearly aware that many conservationist and preservationist organisations trace their origins back to the period he describes as one of 'simple modernity' (i.e., industrial societies) rather than 'reflexive modernity', but he argues that there are significant differences between the 'old' and 'new' nature politics, or between what I am calling environmentalism and radical ecology. He notes that,

> Conservation movements have existed since the beginning of industrialization. Yet the selective critique expressed by conservation organizations (which in addition involved neither large costs for nor a fundamental critique of industrialization) was never able to shake off the nimbus of hostility to progress and backwardness that surrounded it. This only changed when the social evidence of threats to nature through industrialization grew and at the same time scientific interpretations completely detached from the old ideas of conservation were offered and accepted. These explained the growing public discontent with the obviously destructive consequences of industrialization, supported it, freed it from concrete individual cases and occasions, generalized it and joined in a broad protest against industrialization and technification (Beck 1992: 162).

Beck's argument here is that the old environmentalist critique was selective, localised, and unrelated to scientific research whereas the new radical ecology produces a general critique of the industrialisation process as such, but he also attaches much importance to the development of the link between radical ecology and scientific research. What he has in mind here are disciplines or sub-disciplines such as conservation biology, ecology and marine biology etc., which have provided evidence of the harmful effects of industrial processes on the natural world. This has helped to legitimise the protest movements and taken their concerns into established political systems. In this sense, contemporary radical ecology movements can be seen as signs of the emergence of what Beck describes as the reflexive phase of modernity. This is because they are concerned with the 'dark side' of industrialisation, rather than its formal, public, institutionalised expressions. Radical ecology movements signal the end of industrial societies. Beck (1992: 11) puts this in his own way:

> ... in its mere continuity industrial society *exits the stage of world history on the tip-toes of normality, via the back stairs of side effects,* and not in the manner predicted in the picture books of social theory: with a political (revolution, democratic elections) explosion. Furthermore, this perspective implies that the countermodernistic scenario currently upsetting the world - new social movements and criticism of science, technology and progress - does

not stand in contradiction of modernity, but is rather an expression of reflexive modernization beyond the outlines of industrial society.

In one sense, this type of account is persuasive as it describes significant social change as part of a process of 'normal' industrial development which does not require recourse to radical social and political movements or rapid, disjunctive social-structural shifts. This does not mean that the latter should be ruled out as explanations of course, only that they are genuinely revolutionary periods, and hence unusual events. In relation to the (re)emergence of a highly visible politics of nature since the 1970s, Beck makes some salient points. Unfortunately his dismissal of earlier periods of environmental concern prevents the risk society thesis from addressing the movement as a whole, and therefore of the place of contemporary radical ecology movements within the history of nature politics. The early environmentalism is dismissed much too readily. It is just not the case that early environmentalism was unconnected to science for example. The growth of nineteenth century natural history societies which categorised and classified plant species, brought home the consequences of population growth and industrial and urban development. There is also little awareness in Beck's thesis of the cyclical recurrence of modernisation critiques or anti-science movements, as in Brand and Toulmin respectively. I do not think that we can arrive at an adequate understanding of the environmental and radical ecology movements unless these kinds of historical precursors are taken seriously.

It is also unclear why Beck feels the need to oppose the concept of a risk society to that of industrial society. As he himself at times implies, industrial societies can also be seen, and in a real sense I would argue always have been, risk societies. This is so to the extent that forms of modernisation based on the production of technological fixes to deal with the side effects (consequences?) of industrialisation have always gone hand in hand with a simple industrialisation process, though of course, we may be more aware of this linkage today than in the past. To argue that modernisation has now become dominated by an ecological orientation is just not proven. Hajer (1996: 246) is in my view correct to state that '...it is better to refrain from speaking of today's predicament in terms of 'our ecological crisis' (which suggests it is time and space specific) and to speak of the ecological dilemma of industrial society instead'. This is a much more realistic assessment which also leads us to the conclusion that this dilemma has been evident since at least the creation of late-nineteenth century environmental organisations.

Finally, in relation to contemporary nature politics, both reformist and radical, Lash (in Beck et al 1994: 211) argues that 'one can surely agree with Beck and Giddens (and David Harvey) that environmental politics is in the end about damage limitation'. But if this is the case then there would appear to be little or no difference between late-twentieth century radical ecology and late-nineteenth century attempts at conservation, both of which seek to prevent damage to nature, whether this is perceived as valued local environments or a planetary bio-sphere. This assessment also does not sit well with Beck's thesis that reflexive modernisation marks a clear break with the past, taking us beyond industrial society and simple modernity.

I think that environmental politics *is* about damage limitation, and it is difficult to see how it could be anything else given that human societies exist in constant interchange with non-human nature. But this appraisal in itself tells us little about the character of environmentalism in different periods, nor does it help us to understand how the environmental movement has developed over time or its range of concerns broadened. Despite its attempt to link simple and reflexive forms of modernity, the conclusions Beck draws from the risk society thesis as it stands, lack empirical support and must therefore be seen as somewhat speculative.

Conclusion

Explanations which aim to account for the (re)emergence of a wave of activity and protest from the late 1960s which take the problem of nature as a central concern, fall short of an adequate understanding of environmentalism and radical ecology. None of them provides a comprehensive framework within which to locate contemporary manifestations of nature politics, which include a wide range of elements such as changes in personal lifestyles, networks of protest activity, environmental ethics, the formation of specific organisations and so on. Part of the reason for this is that there has not been enough empirical research into the movements themselves, but just as seriously the concentration on contemporary movements diverts attention from some very real continuities and development over time and helps to create a misleading picture of old and new. Because of this neglect, the historical explanatory frameworks discussed in part two of this chapter represent a clear advance over those which restrict the analysis to contemporary manifestations of environmental and Green concern.

They show us that modern concerns with society-nature relations go back a long way, and seem to intensify and erupt into public visibility in particular periods. These concerns can and have taken the form of opposition to scientific modes of thought, dissatisfaction with civilisation and the idealisation of mediaeval or simpler societies, notions and experiments of returning to the land and a hatred of industrial development, to name just a few. Brand is right to point out that at times, fairly distinct counter-cultures develop which flower for a time before fading from view, and I will argue later that the efflorescence of radical ecology movements in many Western societies from the late 1960s can be seen as one aspect of just such a counter-cultural movement, which is rooted in the tilting of the balance from modernism towards romanticism (Eder 1993). Perhaps it is only now, as this counter-cultural period has drawn to an end that we are able to achieve enough critical distance to place it into a proper historical context, and in this sense both Brand and Eder provide some useful insights into the counter-cultural aspects of radical ecology. However we must bear in mind that radical ecology is only a part of what constitutes contemporary nature politics.

Beck, Brand and Eder pay little attention to the history of specific environmental movement organisations and their development, and even where a greater awareness of this history is shown earlier periods of activity and organisational forms are quite quickly dismissed and separated from contemporary ones. Given the centrality of nature politics for the validity of their broader theories this is somewhat surprising. Later I discuss the continuous development of British environmentalism in order to show the relevance of the history of environmental movements for an adequate understanding of the current situation.

A main theme of this study is that environmentalism and radical ecology are not only moderate and radical approaches to society/nature relations respectively, but are and have been related and in continuous tension. In the present period the more rapid shift towards an international environmentalism has gone hand in hand with the development of a radical global ecological perspective, but I will show that as a social movement tied in to the processes of industrial development, environmentalism has developed over a much longer period of time into its present form. The radical ecological perspective lacks organisational continuity, and can be said to have an intermittent history, rising to prominence during periods of widespread counter-cultural activity. This means that any explanation of contemporary environmentalism and radical ecology must be sensitive to these differing histories, and must also trace the origins of environmental concern and the ways in which this has been expressed and channelled into organisational forms. This is the task taken up in Chapter Four.

Notes

1   This is an argument reminiscent of Durkheim's point in relation to the incidence of suicide. Giddens (1971: 71) summarises Durkheim's argument as follows: 'If the effect of satisfying wants is simply to stimulate further wants, then the disparity between desires and their satisfaction may become actually broadened'. In short, there is a question over the connection between levels of material wealth and the spread of new social values. It would appear just as likely that the satisfaction of material needs and wants would lead to new material needs and wants rather than a shift to non-material ones. Nonetheless, although this is a theoretical possibility, the survey evidence produced in favour of the postmaterialist argument suggests that this has in fact not happened.

2   A typical expression of this is the following from the British Green Party's 1992 General Election Campaign Manifesto: 'At some point in the future, people - who are not as stupid as grey politicians seem to think - will choose to make the change from the politics of extinction to the politics of sustainability' (1992: 1).

3   See Chisholm, A (1972) for a representative selection of the natural scientists arguing for social and political change at this time.

4   See the debate on this issue in the journal *Sociology,* stemming from Murphy, R. 1994: 'The Sociological Construction of Science Without Nature', in *Sociology* 28, 4.

5   The extent to which global ecological problems are socially constructed will not be my central concern in this study. Useful discussions of the merits of social constructionism in this area can be found in Hannigan 1995 and Burningham and Cooper 1999.

6   A cyclical approach is also developed in Bürklin (1987).

7   Interestingly, Brand (1990: 36) notes that 'Whereas these movements [environmental movements] showed a gradual (even though discontinuous) growth in the nineteenth and twentieth centuries, *alternative movements* manifested much less organizational continuity'. So, although his focus is ostensibly on waves of cultural criticism, he is clearly aware that the environmental movement does display organisational continuity since the formation of early conservation and preservationist organisations. In this respect, cyclical approaches are not necessarily opposed to my own in this work which is concerned to show the developmental nature of the environmental movement in Britain compared with the intermittent periods of counter - cultural movements. However, Brand does not provide any explanation for the continuities and development

of the environmental movement, concentrating instead on the highly visible counter-cultural waves, and this is a serious drawback if we are to understand the present situation.

8   Brand is aware that the theory of Kondratieff cycles is controversial, but argues that it is useful as an heuristic device rather than as a causal explanation. Dicken (1992: 99-100) identifies four cycles, with the upswing within each being rooted in the appearance of a connected series of technological developments. These are:

1) 1780-1830: steam, cotton, textiles, iron.
2) 1830-1880: railways, iron and steel.
3) 1880-1940: electricity, chemicals, autos.
4) 1940-2000: electronics, synthetics, petrochemicals.

This seems to show that these cycles provide no simple causal explanation for the emergence of intense periods of modernization critique, and in that sense supports Brand's contention that economic cycles may influence their character but not emergence.

9   Cotgrove's (1982) work on environmentalism's pessimistic catastrophist leanings in the 1970s would seem to provide some evidence to support this thesis of pessimistic cultural critique within the new environmentalism or what I am calling radical ecology. However, in Chapter Five I show that the more 'optimistic' reform environmentalism also gained members at this time. Unlike Cotgrove, I argue that the new organisations such as Greenpeace and Friends of the Earth are best seen as part of the development of environmentalism, not marking a clean break with it.

10 This is evident in the present period in the identification of 'shades of Green' within environmental and radical ecology, as well as in the distinction between a shallow and deep ecology (Naess 1972) or 'light' and 'dark' Green forms of nature politics (Porritt 1984).

11 Brand (1990: 42) notes that as well as Lowe and Goyder, O'Riordan (1971) also refers to three, not two, discrete episodes of environmentalist activity. Again though, this gives the impression of discontinuity, whereas my argument is that continuous development at the organisational level is much more striking.

12 Brand (1990: 42) points out that in the inter-war years, the environmental movement in the USA was not a 'mass-based movement', while in Britain environmental interest was restricted to 'groups organising outdoor activities', the implication being that this period did not constitute a distinct phase of movement activity. However, it is difficult to defend this position. It is quite clear that the origins of the organised environmental movement in Britain in the late-nineteenth century cannot be described as a mass movement either, but Brand's chronology implies that it should have been. Environmental activity in the inter - war years also involved more than simply 'organising outdoor activities'. A number of nature protection organisations were also formed in this period and the attempt to squeeze the evidence into a theoretical framework of 'cycles' seems to have led here to a misreading of the evidence.

13 Some see much earlier roots to ecological destruction than this however. As early as 1967, Lynn White Jr (cited in Barr 1971: 11) pointed to Christianity as a key source of legitimacy for human exemptionalism and the domination of nature, arguing that 'Especially in its Western form, Christianity is the most anthropocentric religion the

world has seen ... Christianity, in absolute contrast to ancient paganism and Asia's religions (except perhaps Zoroastrianism), not only established a dualism of man and nature but also insisted that it is God's will that man exploit nature for his proper ends'.

14 Lewis (1994: 242) recounts the story of how 'Chief Seattle's' 'ecocentric' speech on the American Indians' respect for nature, often referred to by radical ecologists as pointing up the exploitative nature of Western societies, was uncovered as a hoax, and had actually been written by a 'white American screen writer, working for the Southern Baptist Convention'. (See also Church (1988)). It must be noted though, that the recourse to 'primitivism' as a source of ecological wisdom has never been wholly accepted and a more realistic understanding of 'traditional' societies is evident amongst many radical ecologists today.

15 This recognition of a 'real' and an 'artificial' world is reproduced in a lot of radical ecological writing, particularly where an attempt is made to argue that nature has intrinsic value rather than relying on human valuations of it. Edward Goldsmith describes this contrast as that between a 'real world' (the biosphere as a whole) and a 'surrogate world' (human creations such as cities, machines, commodities etc.) (1988).

16 There are some parallels here with Campbell's work on the 'romantic ethic' (1987), which he claims helped to produce and legitimise the practices of modern consumerism. This would seem to go against the grain of Eder's position which sees romanticism as an oppositional counter-culture working *against* the dominant trends of modernity. Campbell's study sees the romantic ethic as one *part of* these dominant trends. Richards (1990) argues that the consumerist 'commodity culture' really began to take shape around the time of the Great Exhibition (1851), but was restricted to the middle classes.

17 For example, James Bryce who was influential in the creation of several conservationist organisations, was an '.. avid outdoorsman, rambler and botanist. He assaulted the White Mountains of New Hampshire and made a solo ascent of Mount Ararat' (Ranlett 1983: 200). Many others were amateur naturalists.

18 The popular socialist 'Clarion' cycling clubs in the late nineteenth century also demonstrated a love of the outdoor life amongst politically active workers.

19 This shift has been theorised as a different kind of specifically 'ecological' modernisation.

20 Beck's own work could then be said to be a form of reflection rather than reflexivity.

21 There are of course differences in the extent to which social constructionism is pushed within these broad positions between authors. For example, Yearley and Hannigan are more circumspect than Tester in relation to the social construction of natural phenomena. Hannigan (1995: 188) says that 'the assertion that global warming should not necessarily be taken at face value as an established scientific fact but rather be seen as something which is open to the social construction of scientific and popular knowledge does not constitute a denial that greenhouse gas emissions exist or that they might possibly have global impacts'. At the extreme end, Tester (1991: 46) argues that 'A fish is only a fish if it is socially classified as one, and that classification is only concerned with fish to the extent that scaly things living in the sea help society define itself', thus effectively removing the objective reality and properties of fish.

22 It should be noted here that Wynne is highly critical of Beck's distinction between a non-reflexive period of simple modernity contrasted with a new reflexive modernity. He argues that theorists of new reflexivity seem to take a lack of overt protest amongst lay actors as evidence of positive trust and approval of expert knowledge, when, even in the period of simple modernity this was not the case. 'In other words, the reality of social dependency on expert systems should not be equated with positive trust, when it could be better characterised as 'virtual' trust, or 'as if' trust' (1996: 50). This would cast some doubt on Beck's periodisation.

4 The Origins of Organised Environmentalism

Introduction

In contrast to the self-understanding of many radical ecology activists and new social movement theorists, the latter decades of the nineteenth century in Britain have been described as 'the most fecund and important period of green politics before 1980' (Gould 1988: viii).[1] Gould details a variety of ideas, initiatives and activities in late nineteenth century Britain which he argues, could easily fall within an ecological or Green perspective today. Yet despite this, one historian of cultural responses to industrialisation and urbanisation in this period has noted that:

> When I first became intrigued by the subject I searched the general histories dealing with the period for accounts and references to the movement, which was everywhere visible in the literature of the time. I found virtually none, no doubt because history records only the dominant events and ideas, those that influence and determine what happens next (Marsh 1982: 245).

It would seem that nineteenth century 'Green' ideas and actions have not been considered significant enough to be included in general histories until recently. Evidently 'what happened next' was not influenced by Green ideas and arguments and did not involve a large scale return to living on the land in close contact with nature. Nor was there a significant move towards the simplification of lifestyles and the establishment of networks of small 'human-scale' communes, both of which were advocated by political radicals at the time. Instead, the state became increasingly active in many areas of social life, industrialisation and urbanisation continued apace and the disparate elements of the labour movement began to crystallise into an effective, organised force capable of bringing 'the social question' to the attention of all classes in society, working through as well as outside existing political institutions (Przeworski 1985). Gould (1988: 22) notes that, 'simple life' thinking has been neglected in favour of the proposals of the 'ideological victors'. Perhaps this goes some way towards explaining the lack of interest in the problem of nature amongst historians and sociologists too, and can help us to see why an increasing interest in this problem today has lent support to the idea that the Green and environmental movements must be in some sense, new. It may be that when characterising the most significant events and movements of a particular period, just as in a painting, some elements are open to view in the foreground, whilst others are partially hidden in the background behind them. Environmental initiatives have been in the background, out of direct view and attention, whilst other movements have been more successful and hence visible in the foreground.[2]

The relationship between society and nature which had pre-occupied some anarchist and socialist groups (and others) was thus removed from the concerns of 'progressive' politics as it was thought irrelevant to the more immediate material needs of working people. But although I agree with Gould (and Marsh), that 'Green' ideas almost disappeared from view towards the end of the nineteenth century,[3] this does not mean that concern for the natural world simply collapsed, to be re-awakened in the 1960s, 70s and 80s in the form of a new social movement displaying the radically different characteristics attributed to these post-industrial forms of collective action.

An increasingly organised environmentalism also developed in Britain (and elsewhere) in the late nineteenth century producing a series of interlinked conservationist and preservationist societies and organisations, which had some success in promoting the regulation and control of human (industrial) activities which impact on the natural world. If, as I argued earlier, a social movement emerges at the point when groups of people join together to intervene collectively in the shaping of a dominant social process, in this case industrialisation, then environmentalism as a social movement began in the late nineteenth century and has continued to develop throughout the twentieth. This means that the movement has a longer history than post-industrial theories allow for, and it is my intention in this chapter to examine the characteristics of these early forms and to explore some of the similarities between these and the features attributed to new social movements today.

Maintaining the working distinction established in Chapter One, between environmentalism and radical ecology, the bulk of this chapter will concentrate on environmentalism, but some late-nineteenth century 'Green' ideas will be included for the purpose of comparison, both with later Green thinking and forms of environmentalism. This will enable us to deepen our understanding of environmentalism by exploring the way that the 'reformism versus radicalism' axis of movement politics contributed to the shaping of the arguments and forms of nature politics in the period. But first we need to dig a little deeper into what is meant by 'nature' in this context.

A Background of Changing Sensibilities

'Nature' says Raymond Williams (1987: 219-21), 'is perhaps the most complex word in the language', noting that '... any full history of the uses of nature would be a history of a large part of human thought'.[4] He identifies three main areas of meaning of the word which have developed over time and which co-exist today. Chronologically these meanings are:

1. Nature as the essential quality and character of something (this meaning can be traced back to the thirteenth century).
2. Nature as the inherent force which directs either the world or human beings or both (from the fourteenth century).
3. Nature as the material world itself, taken as either including or not including human beings (from the seventeenth century).[5]

In the 1850s John Stuart Mill (in Clayre 1979: 306) argued that the two principal meanings of nature were the second and third of these, and although all three meanings can be found today within environmental and radical ecology discourses, meaning '3' is most relevant to environmentalism, which defines itself as a movement aiming to defend the non-human natural world against encroachments from unregulated human activity, in particular from industrial and urban development.[6] Williams notes that from the seventeenth century, a change in the use of the word 'nature' is discernible, from the description of a process to that of a thing. This shift in meaning is important because environmentalism was in part, based on the defence of thing-like natural (and historical) objects which could be clearly identified and protected, and in this sense the idea is rooted in one of modern culture's most basic dualisms, that of culture/nature, which radical ecologists today argue, needs to be overturned.[7] Since the eighteenth century the countryside, 'unspoiled places', and 'plants and creatures other than man' have come to be seen as natural (Williams 1987: 223).

The gradual emergence of a new dominant meaning of the word 'nature' can be seen as one outcome of a gradual, long term change in modern sensibilities. However, it should be noted that early environmentalist arguments in defence of nature usually related this to the continuing well-being of humans, and in this sense the orientation of the movement could be characterised as 'human-centred' (humanist or anthropocentric) rather than 'nature-centred' (or 'ecocentric'). The attempt to construct a coherent ecocentric orientation in the present period (Eckersley 1989,1992; Fox 1984; Naess 1973, 1984; Goodin 1992) constitutes a subtle change of emphasis, both from earlier 'Green' ideas and environmentalism, and has been criticised on a number of counts (Neuhaus 1971; Mellos 1990; Harvey 1993; O'Neill 1994). Ecocentric philosophies often try to argue that Nature has 'intrinsic value' and its value therefore exceeds the scope of human beneficence and is not reduced to being valued by humans simply because this is in their own interests. This kind of argument is not wholly new as there are similarities in some of the ideas of William Morris, for example. However, as a socialist, Morris's primary concern was with the quality of life for people, and to attribute an ecocentric orientation to his motivation would be wrong. Nevertheless, Morris is closer to today's radical ecologists than to his contemporary J.S. Mill. In his criticism of the idea that people's actions should conform to nature, Mill ((1851) cited in Clayre 1979: 307) asks, 'If the artificial is not better than the natural, to what end are all the arts of life?', noting that,

Everybody professes to approve and admire many great triumphs of Art over Nature: the junction by bridges of shores which Nature had made separate, the draining of Nature's marshes, the excavation of her wells, the dragging to light of what she has buried at immense depths in the earth; the turning away of her thunderbolts by lightning rods, of her ocean by breakwaters. But to commend these and similar feats, is to acknowledge that the ways of Nature are to be conquered not obeyed: that her powers are often towards man in the position of enemies, from whom he must wrest, by force or ingenuity, what little he can for his own use, and deserves to be applauded when that little is rather more than might be expected from his physical weakness in comparison to those gigantic powers.

Early 'Green' thinkers like Morris could not have agreed with this 'technocentric' statement, and nor would today's radical ecologists, who call into question the ability and right of humans to interfere in natural processes.

They certainly did not 'admire the many great triumphs of Art over Nature', and to see why this is so it is necessary to go back to the reasons for the emergence of different sensibilities in relation to the natural world.

A growing interest in and concern for the non-human natural world amongst some social groups predates the formation of the first environmental organisations by at least two centuries, and forms part of the necessary cultural background to the formation of specialised organisations whose aims were to intervene in the management of society's relationship with the non-human nature. The gradual changes in cultural values and emotional sensibilities provided a base of support for the aims of early environmentalists. Thomas (1984) demonstrates that attitudes in England underwent a gradual change, over a very long time-scale, between 1500 and 1800. The overall direction of this change could be described as being towards a non-utilitarian attitude towards non-human nature. Rather than seeing nature as God's creation *for* humans which they could therefore legitimately utilise at will, a concern for the well-being of non-human animals gradually came to be expressed, along with growing interest in the effects of human actions on the integrity of Nature 'writ large.' Thomas (1984: 301) provides some insights into this process, and explains the changes thus:

> The growth of towns had led to a new longing for the countryside. The progress of cultivation had fostered a taste for weeds, mountains and un-subdued nature. The new-found security from wild animals has generated an increasing concern to protect birds and preserve wild creatures in their natural state. Economic independence of animal power and urban isolation from animal farming had nourished emotional attitudes which were hard, if not impossible, to reconcile with the exploitation of animals by which most people lived.

A non-utilitarian attitude towards the natural world can therefore be seen to stem from the distanciation of everyday life and social production from nature, together with a gradual reduction in the level of fears in relation to natural events and forces. In sociological terms, Thomas seems to be describing the psychological and emotional effects of a very gradual alteration in orientation to the natural world promoted by changes in social organisation and the rise of a scientific worldview. In the work of Elias (1987b) the possibility of increasing control over, and hence the reduction of fears in relation to natural events is also connected to growing chains of interdependence between greater numbers of people across larger geographical areas of the world: '... as humans have gradually come to understand natural forces more, fear them less and use them more effectively for human ends, this has gone hand in hand with specific changes in human relationships. More and more people have tended to become more and more interdependent with each other in longer chains and denser webs' (Mennell 1992: 169-70). And this reduction in fear has helped to produce different moral evaluations of the natural world.

The reduction of fears in relation to the natural world does not arise wholly because of the ability of humans to protect themselves from the unpredictability of natural forces or threats from wild animals, though of course these probably played the most important part. Fears of this kind were also generated by the threats posed by the activities of humans, for example robbers and bandits for whom wild woods and forests provided opportunities for attacks. In this respect the non-utilitarian attitudes to nature which gathered pace from the sixteenth century are related to the pacification of larger areas of social life, described by Elias as part of a 'civilising process'. As Elias (1994: 496-7) points out,

> The manner in which "nature" is experienced is fundamentally affected, slowly at the end of the Middle Ages and then more quickly from the sixteenth century onwards, by the pacification of larger and larger populated areas. Only now do forests, meadows and mountains gradually cease to be danger zones of the first order, from which anxiety and fear constantly intrude into individual life. ...[P]eople - more precisely the town-people for whom forest and field are no longer their everyday background but a place of relaxation - grow more sensitive and begin to see the open country in a more differentiated way ... They take pleasure in the harmony of colour and lines, become open to what is called the beauty of nature ...

Changes in the direction of a non-utilitarian attitude to the natural world leading to an aesthetic appreciation of nature formed one part of the complex of shifts in sensibility which provided the cultural context for later nineteenth century environmental campaigns to protect natural spaces. However, the development of a scientific interest in nature study from the seventeenth century helped to give conservationist arguments credibility and make them politically respectable, and preservationist arguments emphasising the need to 'save man from himself' also played a part (Gilig 1981: 97-8).[8] It is also worth remembering that although cultural shifts of this kind provide the necessary backdrop to the formation of environmental movements and organisations, they do not in themselves account for the specific character of those organisations. Resource mobilization theorists are right to point out that the actual formation and maintenance of organisations forms an area of study in its own right.

Both Thomas and Elias take a long-term or gradualist view of the changing sensibilities with which we are familiar today. We should add though, that not only did these new sensibilities develop over a long period of time, they also spread gradually across different social groups. For many the perception and experience of living in an industrial society came relatively late, and the movement of people from rural to urban locations was a transformation whose implications did not really become widespread until after the mid-nineteenth century. This would imply that the spread of non-utilitarian attitudes towards nature to many social groups would have been drawn out well into the twentieth century and possibly beyond.

In the context of the gradual transformation of attitudes and sensibilities outlined above, the formation of organisations dedicated to the preservation of the natural world and access to are not unusual. Rather, they are one consequence of the intensifying spread of industrialisation and urbanisation. Of course, organisations have to be built and support for them garnered, and during this process the arguments and even the goals of the initial founders may change. To examine this process we need to start with the first environmental organisations which were founded in the late nineteenth century.

Origins of the Organised Environmental Movement

The origin of the organised environmental movement in England can be precisely dated. It began on 19th July 1865, the date of the formative meeting of the Commons Preservation Society (C.P.S.), possibly 'the world's first private environmental group' (McCormick 1991: 31).[9] Before this time there were no organisations dedicated to environmental conservation in Britain, but following this early example, and a further decade during which the C.P.S. demonstrated that successes in the field of nature protection were possible, came a flurry of organisational activity.

The end of the nineteenth century marks the close of a very active initial phase of organisation building in the emerging environmental movement. However, it does not coincide with Brand's identification of periods of counter-cultural modernisation critique, which he sees as flowering between 1830-1850 and 1890-1910. As we will see, new environmental organisations have continued to be established regularly throughout the twentieth century, and my reading of this history taken as a whole is one of continuous development rather than one of spurts of activity following periods of inactivity. [10]

Table 4.1   Dates of formation of selected nineteenth century environmental organisations

Organisation	Date of Formation
Commons Preservation Society	1865
The Kyrle Society	1876
Society for the Protection of Ancient Buildings	1877
The Sunday Tramps	1879
Metropolitan Public Gardens Association	1882
Lake District Defence Society	1883
National Footpaths Preservation Society	1884
The Selbourne League	1885
Society for the Protection of Birds	1889
Society for Checking the Abuses of Public Advertising	1893
The National Trust for Places of Historic Interest or Natural Beauty	1895
Coal Smoke Abatement Society	1898

Sources: McCormick, J. 1991; Young, S.C. 1993; Gould, P. 1988; Evans, D. 1992.

Despite the apparently single-issue character of many of these public amenity and conservationist groups, their leaders and memberships did not see them as such. High levels of overlapping membership and close links between the organisations, demonstrated a perceived similarity of interest and common purpose which can best be summarised as a desire to protect and preserve the natural world against the increasing encroachment of the industrial and commercial way of life. Development had to be controlled and managed to prevent damage to, and the destruction of, valued natural (and historical) environments. As one prominent campaigner put it, the aim was to preserve 'the beauties of wild nature against the inroads of industrialism, so fast encroaching on the world's green places' (Bryce (1905) cited in Ranlett, 1983: 200).

Thus the general tone of late-nineteenth century environmentalism was not revolutionary. Despite decrying the worst excesses of industrialism, environmentalists in the period sought only to contribute towards the ordering of the relationship between the solidifying industrial society and the natural world. They did not like some of the manifestations of industrialisation, but most saw it as a path on which there was no real prospect of turning back. What was deemed possible was the effective regulation of industrial activity to prevent further despoliation of nature, and a number of arguments for the defence of nature were advanced.

The spreading towns and growing cities together with the continued rapid expansion of population and Census evidence of a seemingly irreversible shift from rural to urban lifestyles prompted much concern in the period. Magazines and newspapers carried articles on the subject of the problems created by continued urbanisation. For example, one writer observed that 'The growth of large towns is admittedly one of the great evils of our time. We cannot prevent this growth, though we may deplore it' (Lewes 1887: 680), and proposed a provision for open spaces to be written in law. Cities were perceived as unhealthy places to live, *The Manchester Guardian* noting that out of 11,000 armed forces volunteers in the Manchester area, only around 1,000 were 'fully fit' and Rowntree's survey showed that between 1897 and 1901 only half of army recruits were 'medically acceptable' (Read 1979: 297). In the capital, Lord Brabazon, founder of the Metropolitan Gardens Association (M.P.G.A.) and one of the leading critics of urban life for its effects on the health of the population, worried for the future of Britain's armed forces. He noted with concern that 'Taking town and country recruits together, out of 64,000 men who enlisted in 1884, no fewer than 30,000 were rejected for physical incapacity, a proportion which cannot fail to give occasion for very serious reflection' (Brabazon 1887: 673). The problem did not lie with the rural recruits however, but with the urban: 'In this instance the remedy which naturally suggests itself, is the minimizing of the unhealthy conditions of urban life which have led to such a sad result' (ibid., 674). The contrast between the 'natural' and the 'artificial' which has resurfaced in today's radical ecology is plain to see in this statement.

Another conservation enthusiast, Octavia Hill, had been influenced (as were many) by John Ruskin, and her role in the formation of the National Trust in 1895 seems to have been an extension of her attempts to improve the conditions of the urban poor (Hill 1884).[11] The establishment of 'open spaces' in London was part of the latter endeavour which led seamlessly into a concern to preserve other areas of natural landscape and historic buildings (Hunter 1898; Hill 1899). Gould (1988: 92-3) argues that Hill's work 'indirectly strengthened private property' by promoting a perception of communal land ownership amongst the masses, when none existed in reality, and thus blurring, 'the reality of inequality in land ownership', and removing the potential threat of real conflict. However, there was much evidence of the unhealthiness of cities, including the medical evidence from Dr William Farr in 1865, that despite the greater accessibility of fruit and vegetables in towns and cities, and a generally improved diet, mortality was higher there than in the countryside. Even when Farr's study was repeated in 1900-02, '... open-air work together with the church, again offered the best hope of long life: gardener, gamekeeper, farmer, railway-engine driver or stoker, and farm labourer were the healthiest occupations after clergyman' (cited in Clapp 1994: 66). Reformers argued that fresh air, country life and access to nature were the keys to a healthier population, and this is part of the reason for the symbolic associations of the country and the city with which we are now familiar and which troubles Williams (1973: 1) when he observes that,

> On the country has gathered the idea of a natural way of life: of peace, innocence and simple virtue. On the city has gathered the idea of an achieved centre: of learning, communication, light. Powerful hostile associations have also developed: on the city as a place of noise, worldliness and ambition: on the country as a place of backwardness, ignorance, limitation.

The 'hostile associations' which gathered on the city can still be found amongst late-twentieth century political ecologists today. As spokesman for the anarchistic 'social ecology' strand of contemporary radical ecology, Murray Bookchin has been at the forefront of the critique of modern cities. He argues that,

> Civilization as we know it today is more mute than the nature for which it professes to speak, and more blind than the elemental forces it professes to control. Indeed, "civilization" lives in hatred of the world around it and in grim hatred of itself. Its gutted cities, wasted lands, poisoned air and water, and mean-spirited greed constitute a daily indictment of its odious morality. A world so demeaned may well be beyond redemption, at least within the terms of its own institutional and ethical framework (Bookchin 1982: 366).

Sentiments of this kind would not have been out of place amongst the early environmental and 'Green' campaigners, and demonstrate significant lines of continuity connecting the concerns of industrial critics across the twentieth century. In the late nineteenth century, it was the association between ill health, industrial pollution and city life which pushed people like Brabazon, despite their general adherence to *laissez-faire* principles, voluntary works and private philanthropy to argue for state intervention. Brabazon (1883) suggested possible solutions might include better housing for the poor, 'breathing spaces' in the form of parks and playgrounds in all towns, school meals and compulsory gymnastics and callisthenics.

The foremost organisation concerned with establishing 'breathing spaces' in cities was the Commons Preservation Society whose origins were in London. Its initial aim was to save from enclosure and development some 'well-known commons in and around the capital', but gradually its interests spread to the whole of England and Wales. Despite a few setbacks, in its early years the Society succeeded in preventing the destruction of Putney Heath, Wimbledon Common, Berkamsted Common, Hampstead Heath and Epping Forest, which were potentially profitable sites for their owners given the need for house-building in the London area (C.P.S. founder, Shaw-Lefevre estimated that around 95,000 acres had been 'saved' in the Society's first twenty years).

Following from the work of the C.P.S., Lewes advocated a written provision in law for the establishment of open spaces as a condition for the building of all new towns, an idea which was to be carried forward by Patrick Geddes and realised to a limited degree by Ebeneezer Howard's Garden City Association with its mission to marry together town and country. Howard argued that 'out of joyous union will spring a new hope, a new life, and a new civilisation' (1898: 9-10). One commentator explains Howard's vision thus: 'The idea is nothing less than a vision of a transformed English industrial civilisation ... England is looking sober, prosperous, thrifty - as though the bad dream of the industrial revolution had somehow no more permanence ... the dream is broken, the ugly nineteenth century has been wiped off the slate ...' (MacFadyen 1933: 31). The establishment of Letchworth Garden City in 1903 and Welwyn Garden City in the 1920s as well as a number of 1950s 'new towns' are a testament to the continuing relevance of these reformers' desire to unite the urban and rural, town and country within one living space, for following generations. Though it must be remembered that the new towns fall far short of a radical 'transformation.'

A further argument for nature preservation linked this idea to public rights of access, leading to the formation of so-called 'amenity organisations' (Hill 1980). Public rights of access was an argument which could be used in support of the work of many early organisations' activities such as footpaths preservation, defence of areas of outstanding natural beauty (such as the Lake District), and the acquisition of land and property by the National Trust. Amenity arguments could elicit support from many social groups who had been accustomed to rights over common land and saw these rights threatened by private enclosures. It was a powerful argument which also appealed to the wealthy 'urban squirearchy' who believed that maintaining access for workers to 'God's creation' would 'strengthen the morality of the working class in resistance to subversive ideas' (Gould 1988: 89).

The maintenance of public rights over the commons was not seen only as a palliative for workers' discontent but was part of the ongoing struggle finally to wrest power from the landed classes whose dominance in Parliament was only broken during the 1880s. In 1874, 209 M.P.'s were landowners and rentiers compared to 157 from commerce and industry. By 1880, the balance had shifted decisively with 259 industrialists to 125 landowners and rentiers (Read 1979: 152). A central legislative aim of the C.P.S. was the repeal of the Statute of Merton which came into existence in 1235 to give barons rights over all land, thus marking the beginning of the long-term process of enclosure (Hardy 1979: 68). The attempts to bring this process to a halt at the end of the nineteenth century can therefore be interpreted as a symbolic demonstration of the shifting balance of social power.[12] As Wiener (1981) points out, this shifting balance of power was reflected in the adoption of aristocratic values by the urban bourgeoisie in the late nineteenth century, which also contributed to increasing support for reforms. This value system 'disdained trade and industry [and] stressed the civilised enjoyment, rather than the accumulation, of wealth, and which preferred social stability to enterprise' (Lowe and Goyder 1983: 19).

C.P.S. historian and first chairman Shaw Lefevre put forward the 'amenity' argument for public access to green spaces in cities in exactly this vein. He saw the fight for public access as a step towards the restoration of the land to the people 'which had been seized in times past by kings and barons, whose modern equivalents were equally rapacious. In winning the right to return to the land at least at weekends and holidays, the people were reversing the process of dispossession' (Marsh 1982: 47). There is no hint here though of proposals for a return to the land as an alternative way of living which was advocated by some socialists and anarchists in the period. Returning to the land for most, had now come to mean brief excursions into the countryside to escape from urban life, which was made possible by the development of the same systems of transportation whose expansion environmentalists were trying to curb, and forms one aspect of the growth of tourism as a mass leisure pursuit.

Nevertheless the access argument was important for future developments within the environmental movement. Conservationist ideas of preserving wild areas and wildlife habitats, a central feature of environmentalist activity, can be said to have developed from arguments for public access. For example, the formation of local natural history field clubs expanded during the second half of the nineteenth century, with membership reaching around 100,000 in the 1880s (Enloe 1975: 25). These were producing documented evidence of the destruction of flora and fauna and strengthening the conservationists arguments. Ironically, the Selbourne Society's 'Plant Protection Section' cited (amongst other practices) 'nature-study operations' as one of the *causes* of the demise of some wild plants (Lowe and Goyder 1983: 18-19), an early awareness of the tensions between public access and conservationist arguments which continue today.[13]

The defence of 'wild nature' against 'those plagues and pests which sought to worry her out of existence' (Bryce (1905) cited in Ranlett 1983: 197) was necessary, it was argued, for the material and spiritual health of the people. Shaw-Lefevre (1894: 1-2 and 23-5) referred to the London Commons as 'oases of nature ... reservoirs of fresh air and health' and as 'lungs for the metropolis'. The founder of the M.P.G.A. believed that 'one touch of nature' made the whole world kind, whilst open spaces were described as 'almost a necessity of life. Even when shut up and neglected, hideous and desolate, they retain their primary importance to the health of the community' (Brabazon cited in Gould 1988: 94).

The championing of the beneficial effects of wild nature and the desire to preserve open spaces was indicative of the profound changes in attitudes and sensibilities we noted earlier. The trend of these shifting sensibilities can be described as idealistic preferences for country life over that of towns and cities, a love of wilderness rather than cultivation, conservation over the conquest of nature, and an increasing concern for the welfare of animals (Thomas 1984). The difference in the late nineteenth century though, was that these sensibilities and attitudes had begun to crystallise into organisations which were increasingly capable of achieving legislative change, influencing public opinion and making an impact in the regulation of industrial and urban expansion.

Undoubtedly, the early environmentalism was by and large dominated by a relatively few well-known personalities. Its leading figures and founding members were closely linked to the Liberal Party and formed an informal 'environmental establishment' in the period, through interlocking committees and informal associations (Ranlett 1983: 222) and the extent of over-lapping involvements among the leading figures can be clearly seen.

The founding committee of the Coal Smoke Abatement Society (C.S.A.S.) included Sir W.B. Richmond, the Earl of Meath (formerly Lord Brabazon), James Bryce, Sir John Lubbock and Shaw-Lefevre (Ranlett 1981). The idea for the National Trust came from a group containing Bryce, Richmond, Shaw-Lefevre, Robert Hunter, Canon Hardwicke Rawnsley and Octavia Hill (the latter had already gained a reputation as a philanthropist through her charitable work to improve the environment of the London poor, and had also organised an exhibition against smoke pollution in Kensington in 1881).[14] Six of the initial nine signatories of the National Trust were also on the original committee of Shaw-Lefevre's C.P.S. (Gould, 1988: 100), which brought together Hunter, Bryce, Hill, Lord Mount Temple, W.H. Smith M.P., Lord Arthur Russell and John Stuart Mill; whilst the Society for Checking the Abuses of Public Advertising (S.C.A.P.A.), formed by Richardson Evans, counted Bryce, Hunter, Meath, Rawnsley, Richmond, Shaw-Lefevre and William Morris amongst its prominent members.

Brabazon's Metropolitan Gardens Association (M.P.G.A.) attracted Shaw-Lefevre, Bryce, Mount Temple, Lubbock and Evans and, before his public 'conversion' to socialism, William Morris established the Society for the Protection of Ancient Buildings (S.P.A.B.), whose early members included Bryce, Lubbock and John Ruskin, whose influence can be seen in several environmentalist initiatives and 'back to nature' schemes (Gould

1988: 97 and 100; Ranlett 1983; Marsh 1982: Ch.3). Bryce was fairly typical of the founders of the early environmental organisations in that he was involved in almost all of them. He was on the original committees of the C.P.S., National Trust and C.S.A.S. and became involved in the Sunday Tramps (forerunner to the Ramblers' Association), S.C.A.P.A., M.P.G.A., and S.P.A.B.

With such a high level of overlapping membership among the leading figures, it is not surprising to find that co-operation between organisations was common. Though there was an informally established division of functions amongst the organisations, it was probably inevitable that there would be areas of common concern. The C.P.S. and S.P.A.B. joined forces to defeat plans for the destruction of London Charterhouse, Staple Inn and Barnard's Inn in the 1880s. The first Ancient Monuments Act (1882) was sponsored by Lubbock and helped through Parliament by Shaw-Lefevre, who was first Commissioner of Works in Gladstone's government. The Kyrle Society and M.P.G.A. worked together to bring about the Disused Burial Grounds Act (1884) (which authorised the transformation of derelict land, primarily burial grounds, into 'resting places for the old and playgrounds for the young') and the Selbourne Society gave its support to the M.P.G.A., C.P.S. and the Kyrle Society to save terrace gardens at Richmond and parts of Sudham and Petersham Parks. Rawnsley's Lake District Defence Society (L.D.D.S.) was also supported by the Kyrle Society and the C.P.S. in its successful campaigns against two railway extension schemes in the 1880s, whilst the C.P.S. and National Footpaths Preservation Society (N.F.P.S.) amalgamated in 1899.

Early environmentalism did not constitute a mass social movement and could not threaten mass mobilisations of supporters as a campaigning weapon. Not only was the number of activists relatively small, but the founders of the first organisations did not really intend them to become otherwise. In most cases memberships could be counted in the hundreds rather than thousands and as I noted earlier, overlapping membership generally, was in all probability relatively high. But as Bryce (Address to the Selbourne Society in 1900, cited in Ranlett 1983: 197) noted on reflection,

> [T]he existence of so many Societies with cognate aims was a great source of encouragement ... [T]hough they were largely made up of the same members ... still it looked well ... for with such a combination they could produce the impression that the attention of the whole country was directed to the question at issue.

Bryce is alluding here to the importance of creating a wider audience for environmental ideas and campaigns, something which late-twentieth century groups and organisations such as Greenpeace and anti-roads protesters understand very well in the way they make use of mass media. The Selbourne Society was something of an exception because it was the product of an amalgamation (in 1886) between the Selbourne League - whose role was partly that of a natural history society and preserver of wild flowers, forests and birds - and the Plumage League, whose campaign against the use of bird plumage as a fashion accessory had already attracted quite a large

Table 4.2   Examples of the extent of early memberships

Organisation	Membership	Year
N.F.P.S.	178	1885
C.S.A.S	300	1903
National Trust	200	1899
S.C.A.P.A.	753	1893
M.P.G.A.	680	1888
Selbourne Society	1700	1904

Sources: N.F.P.S. Annual Report 1884-85: 19, Ranlett 1983.

following amongst 'respectable' middle class women as a mark of civility and humanity (Doughty 1975).[15] As a point of comparison, total trades union membership had reached around 750,000 by 1888, with one of the largest unions, the Amalgamated Society of Engineers, having 35,000 members (Read 1979: 180-81). This is an important point in relation to the way that historians came to ignore the early forms of environmentalism in general histories of this period as it must have seemed that these were rather insignificant aspects of social reform compared with the emergence of the mass labour movement. With the formation of the Independent Labour Party in 1893, and its first electoral success in the 1906 General Election when the Party won 29 seats (Briggs 1984: 83-4), the labour movement became the central focus for radicals and oppositional politics generally.

Nonetheless, despite the relatively low numbers involved in this early phase of environmental activity, financial support was forthcoming for new ventures. This was demonstrated at the founding meeting of the C.P.S. when £1400 was made available in order to establish the Society. As well as accepting gifts of buildings and land, a judicious combination of members' subscriptions and fund-raising efforts targeted at wealthy urbanites enabled the National Trust to acquire buildings and land which would otherwise have perished or been developed. Almost from the start, the Trust took a special interest in the Lake District and a series of campaigns raised substantial funds. For example, £7000 was raised in 1901-2 to buy a stretch of land along Derwentwater, £12,000 for Gowbarrow, Ullswater and £2,400 which the Trust argued was 'a very small price to pay for securing the preservation of the famous Borrowdale Birches and public access to the 310 acres which form the heights and steep slope of Grange Fell' (National Trust Annual Report 1910). The National Trust was from the start though, not just a body for holding land but also a propagandist for conservationism and preservationism, encouraging local groups to take an interest in a diverse range of development issues.

A factor in the effectiveness of the early environmentalism was the fact that leading figures had close ties to the Liberal Party enabling the organisations to gain a sympathetic hearing as respectable bodies, both in court judgements against developers and when pursuing legislative change. Some early examples of protective legislation include the Ancient Monuments Act (1882) which obliged the state to list and survey 'sites of exceptional historical interest', the repeal of the Statute of Merton (1894), together with a number of acts aimed at protecting birds, including the 1869 Sea Birds Preservation Act (which introduced a close season from April to August on 33 species) and the 1880 Wild Birds Protection Act which extended protection to all species. The first local by-laws protecting plants were introduced in 1888 (Evans 1992: 36). This legislative route to nature conservation was the most widely used at this time and was successful in its own terms, but it is important to acknowledge that other campaigning methods were used when necessary.

Organisational Forms and Campaigning Styles

The middle class voluntary society had been established during the late eighteenth and early nineteenth century and the first environmental groups continued to adopt this organisational form. Most voluntary societies were not democratically run, unless we count the withdrawal of subscriptions over disagreements with the societies' activities as a form of democratic participation. Members subscribed but had no direct influence on how the society operated or what actions it should pursue. Committees were self-appointed and tended to be organised around one or two central, usually founding members. In short 'The dominant form of voluntary society was 'subscriber democracy" in which 'government by oligarchy was the normal practice' (Morris 1990: 184). As I will argue more fully later and in contrast to some of the more disjunctive interpretations, most contemporary environmental organisations in Britain still bear the stamp of these origins, even including the newer, apparently more radical groups such as Greenpeace and Friends of the Earth, whose organisational forms come closer to even the early environmentalism than to the loose networks of activists proposed by new social movement theories.[16]

One of the most successful organisations of the period was the National Trust, which today boasts the largest membership of any national organisation. In common with most of the nineteenth century organisations, the Trust owed its early success to its well-known and respected founding members. In particular, Robert Hunter, Canon Hardwicke Rawnsley and Octavia Hill, but as the number of properties and amounts of land the Trust acquired increased, a centralised, hierarchical, largely oligarchic organisation developed. In 1907 the Trust was granted 'inalienable rights' to its acquisitions by Parliament, giving it a specialised role and a unique status among environmental groups (Fedden 1974).[17] The Trust's policy today is decided by its council of 52, of which, half are elected at the annual general meeting, and half nominated by national institutions such as the Royal Academy, National Gallery and British Museum, together with established environmental organisations such as the S.P.A.B. and the Royal Society for Nature Conservation (R.S.N.C.). Practically, the 28 member executive committee holds most power, with the Trust's administration being carried out by its 1400 staff under the overall direction of the director general (Lowe and Goyder 1983: 140-41). The National Trust is clearly one of the most established and respected of all environmental groups, and from the start it was clear that the organisation could become a major owner of land and property. Because of this a strong administration was vital to the creation of public trust that any land and property bequeathed to the organisation was in safe hands. So, although the Trust is involved in public education campaigns and promotes environmental conservation, it does not engage in direct actions which may damage its reputation amongst supporters.

Campaigning for the environment in the early period was dominated by attempts to bring about legislative change. Sir Robert Hunter and his colleagues in the C.P.S. were keen that in matters of access and public rights of way, disputes came to court in order that legal precedents could be established. This strategy worked well on many occasions but was not the only method used by campaigners. On numerous occasions, forms of what are today described under the umbrella term of 'direct actions' can be seen in the early environmentalism. A few examples will make this clear.

Unlike the C.P.S., the N.F.P.S., in its attempts to prevent local landowners from closing off footpaths and walks 'preferred to seek redress at a lower level, using local groups, direct action and, where appropriate, the sympathies of new residents of independence and professional standing' (Marsh 1982: 50). This influx of new residents into the 'suburbs' was increasing quite substantially as the pattern of working in the city but living outside, began to be established in the late nineteenth century. In London for example, it is estimated that 800,000 people commuted to work and back by 1881, rising to 1,122,000 ten years later. Census returns show that the suburban population grew from around 940,000 in 1881 to over 2,000,000 by the turn of the century. Contrary to expectations, some found that the townsman of the middle classes who has learned to live healthily in his suburb 'was not disadvantaged compared to rural dwellers.' Rather the 'perpetual going and coming, the daily journeys by rail or tram or steamer, have not affected his health, while they have sharpened his faculties. He is more alert, more active, and more elastic than the rustic' (Low 1891: 553). Whether or not this actually was the case, the support of these new residents formed a potentially valuable cultural resource for conservation campaigners adding weight and respectability to N.F.P.S. arguments for continuing public access.[18]

Local Footpaths Associations can be traced back to the 1850s when residents campaigned to urge councils to protect areas of open land. Morris notes one such case in Leeds, where 'Resistance to encroachments upon

Woodhouse Moor began in 1838, with a meeting of freeholders at the Pack Horse Inn. By 1849, the Footpaths Association was a little more formal and part of the pressure which in 1855 persuaded the town council to purchase the (Woodhouse) Moor from the Lords of the Manor of Leeds' (1990: 184). N.F.P.S. reports also note many cases where farmers and landowners had nailed up stiles, dug up tracks or fenced off paths, only to have local people tear down the fences and continue to use the footpaths that had often been in use for generations. The setting up of local footpaths societies gave people the confidence to challenge the restrictive practices of landowners and enabled disputes to be dealt with at a relatively early stage, thus often avoiding the need for litigation. A majority of cases came to be settled in this way with the local societies eventually being consulted before any action was taken in order that a negotiated settlement could be reached.

Occasionally, the direct actions of incensed local people could lead to outbursts of frustration and anger. When One Tree Hill in South London was enclosed for the building of a golf course in 1897, residents took direct action to prevent the development. The N.F.P.S. reported that 'very riotous proceedings have taken place and fences have been broken down. Three gentlemen have called at our office to explain the case ...' (cited in Marsh 1982: 51). Unfortunately on further investigations, the Society discovered that in fact no right of way actually existed and had to explain to the demonstrators that they could not roam over any land they wished. Nevertheless, this was a sign that local people were not prepared passively to accept development proposals and were confident enough to assert their own claims to roam the land.

C.P.S. members were also not averse to organising direct action campaigns as a tactic when faced with belligerent landowners. Shaw-Lefevre's history of the early years of the Society details some of the campaigns to save London Commons. The successful campaign to save Berkamsted Common in the Chiltern Hills in 1866 involved both direct and legal actions. Grass drives across the common had been closed, copyholders were bought out individually, and a five foot high iron fence was erected preventing right of way. The landowners' solicitor claimed that the public 'has no more right to pass over the Common than a stranger has to pass through a private garden'. The C.P.S. was asked for assistance by locals and planned a symbolic demolition of the fences which would be 'not less conspicuous than their erection' (Shaw-Lefevre 1894: 62-8). Enclosure fences were removed covertly under the cover of darkness in order to buy time for the preparation of the C.P.S.'s legal case against enclosure, which was later won by the organisation on behalf of the commoners, but also as a visible demonstration of the implacable resistance of the movement.[19]

Similarly, the formation of the Lake District Defence Society (L.D.D.S.) (1883) provided a focus for opposition to private landowners' enclosure attempts. In 1885 for example, Rawnsley organised a mass action to remove all physical barriers erected by a local landowner to close off public rights of way over a footpath, and was assisted by the C.P.S. to defend this action when writs for trespass were issued against the activists (Dwyer and Hodge 1996: 72).

Demonstrations of this kind, though not definitive of the environmentalists' strategic methods, do show that symbolic direct action campaigns are not wholly novel inventions of Greenpeace and Friends of the Earth. In the context of late nineteenth century environmentalism it seems that direct action was one way of promoting the organisation and its concerns to a wider public, and demonstrating its effectiveness. This could also apply to the new, radical organisations in the 1970s, and rather than being a definitive aspect of all new social movements, is realistically one useful method by which organisations can carve out a specific niche within the wider movement.

Many C.P.S. campaigns involved supporting local people in their battles to maintain rights of access to land, the cutting of turf and lopping of firewood which stemmed from medieval times, against landowners' attempts to alter the pattern of land use in order to increase their income in an increasingly difficult period. This conflict between attempts to change land use, and resistance to those changes symbolises the 'conservatism' of early (and contemporary) environmentalism, but also its popular appeal. When Queen Victoria publicly opened Epping Forest to the public in 1882, Shaw-Lefevre (1894: 160) noted contentedly that 'Restitution was thus in a sense made by the sovereign, of land which in very ancient times had probably been taken from the folk - land for the purpose of a Royal forest, and the forest was dedicated for ever to the use and enjoyment of the people'.

Another organisation which made use of direct action campaigns was the infant Society for the Protection of Birds (formed from members of the Fur, Fin and Feather campaigners), which arose to try to stop the importation of the plumage of rare birds for the fashion trade. The Society carried on the ideas of the Plumage League, which demanded that all members sign a pledge not to wear the feathers of any bird in their hats. As early as 1868,

Professor Alfred Newton (cited in Sheail 1976: 5) was arguing that '... fair and innocent as the snowy plumes may appear on a lady's hat, I must tell the wearer the truth - she bears the murderer's brand on her forehead', another example of the changing sensibilities and extension of moral concerns outlined by Thomas (1984). The amalgamation of the League with the Selbourne Society had upset many, as the new society did not ask members to sign the pledge. The S.P.B. believed the best way to achieve its goal was to carry on taking pledges from its recruits and thus eventually destroy demand, whilst simultaneously promoting Plumage Bills in Parliament to ban international plumage trafficking. To this end, 152 branches had been formed by 1898 with the number of signatories standing at 20,000. One activist wrote that she would take note of which women wore plumed hats to church and approach them directly or send them letters pointing out their folly with information on the 'cruelty of their practice.' In 1911 a demonstration was organised in London to publicise the cause which involved the distribution of leaflets describing the 'barbaric slaughter' and the carrying of placards, whilst throughout the country, large posters were pasted onto walls and hoardings (Sheail 1976: 11-15). Again, there are some direct parallels with the activities of today's environmental and Green activism and with the protests of social movements generally. A Prohibition Act was proposed in 1908, but the Importation of Plumage Act was not finally passed until 1921, after the end of the First World War (Evans 1992: 50).

It may be objected that the R.S.P.B. is not an environmental organisation at all, but that its activities and primary concern is with animal welfare in a broad sense. However, I think this is misleading because in seeking to protect birds, the R.S.P.B. has been inevitably drawn into nature conservation. Its main policy of buying and managing land in the interests of preserving wild habitats for breeding birds, began tentatively in the late 1890s, when it provided volunteer wardens on privately owned land, but it started to acquire its own bird reserves in 1930 (Dwyer and Hodge 1996: 138). Like the National Trust therefore, the R.S.P.B. became a landowner itself, and even before this time the organisation's interests had been expanding to take in other aspects of nature conservation. For example, in the 1920s the R.S.P.B. campaigned against the effects of oil pollution on seabird numbers and raised the issue of the deleterious impact of more widespread usage of pesticides, both of which are often seen today as new areas of concern, marking the shift to a more radical ecological analysis. It is clear that this is not really a tenable proposition, as these, and many other contemporary environmental concerns are prefigured in earlier debates.[20]

Another form of campaigning was developed by the S.C.A.P.A.. The Society originated from concerns about advertising boards spoiling the natural beauty of the countryside. Between the Crystal Palace Exhibition in 1851 and the First World War, public advertising of commodities began to be adopted by companies and in the 1870s large department stores began springing up in city centres with fixed prices, standardised shop fronts and window displays 'with Whiteley and Harrods leading the way in London' (Read 1979: 257). Advertisements were, in the main, placed in newspapers but were also spreading to middle class periodicals (Richards: 1990). However one other form of advertising consisted of large metal billboards erected by the sides of roads, and as the railway system grew, alongside railway lines, to catch the vision of travellers. The S.C.A.P.A. saw these as spoiling the beautiful scenery and campaigned for restrictions on '... these hideous erections, usually of tin, with vile glazed inscriptions setting forth the names of some popular remedy, (which) are planted in the fields, so that you shall scarcely be able to glance out of a window at the country without seeing one or more of them' (in Ranlett 1983: 209-10). It was due to this that one of the first consumer boycotts came to be discussed within the Society, which arrived at 'A common understanding that the members will each at his own discretion abstain (as far as maybe) from using commodities which he personally feels are advertised in an offensive way, or patronising establishments which he regards as exceptionally unscrupulous in advertising display' (ibid.). The extent to which this proposal was adopted by members and the degree of success achieved is not known, but it was another example of the variety of imaginative direct action responses from the early environmentalists to what they perceived to be the degradation of nature and the environment.

Though some of the early organisations no longer exist, others have survived to the present. The C.P.S. has become the Open Spaces Society, The Sunday Tramps (which began in London) was the forerunner to the National Ramblers Association, and the National Trust celebrated its 100th anniversary in 1995. During the course of the twentieth century many more environmental organisations have been formed and the division of functions amongst the movement's organisations has become increasingly specialised until the advent of more inclusive international organisations such as Greenpeace and Friends of the Earth. Even these apparently more radical organisations remain close enough in aims, values, forms and actions to be seen as continuations of, or developments from the early movement rather than as a disjunctive break with it, and in this sense it is impossible to agree with Atkinson's comment that 'We can hardly speak of an 'environmental movement' as existing until about 1972' (1991: 18).

Early environmental organisations were centralised and bureaucratic, relying heavily on the enthusiasm and high social standing of their founders and leaderships. Environmentalists made use of a series of different campaigning styles including political lobbying, legal challenges, direct actions, public demonstrations and education. The arguments they produced in defence of open spaces, wildlife and nature were also diverse, including the rights of public access to land in order not to lose touch with the natural world, the benefits to be gained from maintaining natural areas and of reducing pollution in cities, and protecting natural areas from commercial development. Though industrial development was identified as a key problem and a motivation for involvement, few within the movement seriously believed that industrialisation could be reversed, nor did they argue that it should be. Industrial Britain had come to be seen as a permanent state of affairs, but continuing industrialisation needed to be controlled and regulated, rather than be allowed to spread unchecked, there were limits to its economic benefits. Many would have asked themselves the question Ruskin posed in 1859 (in Clayre (ed) 1979: 136), 'The changes in the state of this country are now so rapid ... I must necessarily ask, how much of it do you seriously intend within the next fifty years to be coal-pit, brick-field, or quarry?'.

However, some political radicals refused to accept that industrialisation should be allowed to continue. They wanted a fundamental reconstruction of society in order to bring people into closer contact with the natural world, and this meant de-industrialisation. Although produced by socialists and anarchists, many of these arguments do bear a striking resemblance to some of those propounded by today's radical ecologists. In order to facilitate a comparison between these two, we need to look in more detail at why some have described these late-nineteenth century ideas as 'Green'.

'Green' Ideas in Socialist and Anarchist Thought

In trying to explain why the late-twentieth century radical ecology movement is new, Jonathon Porritt notes that in order to address global environmental problems, Green politics has inevitably had to move beyond national boundaries. He also argues that a technocratic managerial approach to these problems will only exacerbate them by perpetuating the misplaced notion that human beings can control or manage natural systems, even at the global level. Greens today argue instead for decentralisation and the return of power to localities. This is summarised in their slogan 'think globally, act locally'. Porritt (cited in Weston 1986: 117) says that 'This dual emphasis on decentralisation and internationalism is quite unique to the green perspective'. Socialists are quick to point out though that this dual emphasis is prefigured in earlier socialist and anarchist arguments. For example, Pepper (1986: 117) argues that '...Porritt may mislead us into forgetting a whole lineage of socialist and populist thinkers who, ... emphasized both decentralisation and internationalism - Kropotkin, Proudhon and Godwin, the anarchists, and utopian socialists like William Morris and Robert Owen, not to mention the Diggers and Levellers'. In short, it is possible to find broadly 'ecological' arguments being expressed by individuals at many different times.

Some research has found that the late nineteenth century and early twentieth century in Britain was a particularly active period in the propagation of ideas concentrating on the necessity for human beings to live in close contact with the natural world (Gould 1988; Marsh 1982). However, Gould sees the period 1880-1900 as most important, whilst Brand (1990) argues for 1890-1910, as one of intense counter-cultural activity. I think that it is unrealistic to attempt to place these episodes chronologically too precisely, as their longevity depends on other factors such as the extent to which counter-cultural ideals come to be taken up by more established social movements, other political organisations such as parties and the state.

The renewed interest in the benefits of a life lived close to nature amongst socialists at this time has to be seen in the wider context of the 'socialist revival' which eventually led to the formation of the Independent Labour Party in 1893 and the gradual inclusion of working class interests into established British politics (Pelling 1965; Przeworski 1985). As Yeo (1977) points out, at this time a variety of 'socialisms' existed including ethical or

Christian socialism, socialist humanism, marxism and fabian socialism, and many followers experienced socialism as something akin to a religious conversion. It is certainly true that socialist proponents preached their 'gospel' with religious fervour with William Morris being a good example.[21] Some socialists included as part of the new gospel, the need for communion with nature. Chronicler of the early days of the Socialist League,[22] J.B. Glasier (1921: 158), wrote the following as part of his polemic on 'the meaning of socialism':

> Follow the children - freedom and wisdom are in their ways. The chains of oppression fall easily from their soft limbs, and of such is the Kingdom of Heaven. Joyously they plunge into the meadows, rolling on the grass and revelling among the wild flowers. Down to the brooks they swarm, and knee-deep, bestrew the pools with a thousand fragmentary ships. Like seagulls, they spread themselves on the beach, digging their fists and spades into the sand with Herculean might; like merlings they splash out into the waves.
> Have these things, think you, not a great meaning for us? Do they not tell us more of the secret of human happiness than all the precepts of political economy?
> Break the chains, set the people free, and the people will return to the land. The children will lead them.[23]

It is important to remember that for many in the formative period of organised labour politics, socialism meant a return to the land every bit as much as it involved matters of class, workplace issues, the rise of trades unions, and wealth distribution. At least at this stage the socialist movement was home to many interests and pursued many causes. Its goals were couched in universalist terms and were certainly wider than a simple 'selfish' class interest. Calhoun (1993: 87) has argued that,

> The nineteenth and early twentieth century working class movement (if it can be described more than tendentiously as a single movement) was multi-dimensional, only provisionally and partially unified and not univocal. It did not constitute just one collective actor in a single social drama. There was mobilization over wages, to be sure, but also over women and children working, community life, leisure activities, the status of immigrants, education, access to public services and so forth.

Interest in the relationship between humans and the natural world formed one part of the mosaic which constituted the early working class movement, and Gould (1988) identifies two broad strands of socialist and anarchist thought in relation to nature. Firstly, what he describes as 'back to nature' ideas. These were expounded by well-known socialists such as William Morris, Edward Carpenter, Robert Blatchford, and anarchists like Kropotkin.[24] Back to nature '...conveys notions of the simple life, an alternative to life in the city and work in industry, living in harmony with and as a part of Nature, the liberalisation of sexual and social relations, and a more sensitive approach to animals' (Gould 1988: ix). Second, 'back to the land' ideas included '... dissatisfaction with urban-industrial society and sympathy for things rural and natural. It demonstrates warmth towards the creation of small, self-sufficient and self-governing communities and rural regeneration' (ibid.).[25]

Back-to-nature and back-to-the-land ideas were part of a wider reaction to the increasing self-constraints and moral rigidities of late-Victorian society. Edward Carpenter was one figure who attempted to live out his ideals by setting up a market garden on which he worked, and his prolific writings advocated a return to the land in order to bring about a 'simplification of life'.[26] Carpenter's biographer wrote in 1915 that 'The modern Western world is largely divorced from nature. The centralization of population, the elaboration of machinery, the hardening of conventions, and the teaching of the Church help to account for this; the result is much unreality and infidelity. A return to a more natural life is imperative ...' (Lewis 1915: 61-2). Carpenter himself had been influenced by the Americans, Henry Thoreau and Walt Whitman who had both tried to show that a return to a simplified life in close contact with nature was not only desirable but quite possible, and Carpenter did make visits to see Whitman in America in 1877 and 1883 (Gould 1988: 22).

A group of socialists in Northern England around Robert Blatchford, also looked to contrast the virtues of a natural life to the corrupt modern society. Blatchford's *Clarion* paper, was selling around 44,000 copies by 1894, and his book *Merrie England* (1894) sold 750,000 copies in the first year (Read 1979: 329), finding support from those radicals who were arguing for the rights of workers to own land to promote self-sufficiency (Prynn 1976). The popular Clarion Cycling Clubs were formed to aid 'socialist comradeship', and in 1896 the Clarion movement could claim 700 members in over 38 clubs which compares favourably with other socialist groups of the time (Gould 1988: 43). However unlike the Fabians or the Independent Labour Party 'What was unusual in the Clarion was that man's unhappiness was so closely connected with man's despoliation of nature' (ibid: 38-9). The *Clarion* newspaper 'drew attention to the pollution of the rivers, the evils of smoke pollution, or the general trend which was converting land to 'a dull, sunless cinder-heap" (ibid.). It was in short, a type of socialism which subordinated the material betterment of the working class to the production of a more harmonious relationship between society and nature. Encouraging workers to become involved in the field clubs allowed them to perceive for themselves the contrast between 'rude' nature and polluted, commercial city life, and to be inspired by the former to attack the latter. In 1895, one leading figure amongst the Clarion socialists claimed that '... the frequent contrasts the cyclist gets of the beauties of nature and the dirty squalor of the towns makes him more anxious than ever to abolish the present system' (Groom cited in Rubenstein 1977: 69).

All of these socialist alternatives which emphasised society/nature relations were to have relatively short lives however, and a practical, reformist and inclusionary social democratic approach gradually came to the fore and became the dominant force within the wider socialist movement (Hobsbawm 1974). As early as 1872, one commentator noticed that English socialists were '... beginning to place their chief reliance upon state intervention. They seem to think that if individual efforts have been unable to achieve success, this provides the most cogent argument in favour of an appeal to the state' (Fawcett 1872, cited in Read 1979: 140), though this shift took longer to take a firm hold within the movement. Whilst back-to-nature socialism advocated a revolution in the ways of organising society, the possibility of an incremental, social democratic reformism to produce small but genuine improvements for workers came to be widely adopted. As Przeworski (1985) has argued, the formation of labour parties within an existing political context of democratic institutions, led to workers' parties adopting reformist programmes to take advantage of the potential for introducing beneficial social changes.

The shift in priorities was plainly seen in the formation of the Fabian Society, which was born in 1883 from a small group calling itself the 'Fellowship of the New Life' whose philosophy was based on an individualistic attention to self-realization and personal elevation. The social democratic Fabians however, came to the realisation that socialists had to 'accept the factory system, the city, the complexity of modern civilisation' and distance themselves from 'all those schemes and projects of bygone socialisms which have now passed out of date' (Webb 1899: 10). Presumably these included William Morris's utopia in his novel *News from Nowhere* (1890), which portrayed a reconstructed England which was 'simple instead of complex; in harmony with nature, not alienated from it; co-operative instead of competitive; and tranquil, peaceful, and stable instead of restless and ever-changing' (Wiener 1981: 59).[27] One consequence of the merging of the diverse strands of the socialist movement into a formal political party (the I.L.P) with reformist aims contesting elections, together with the strengthening and increasing power of trades unions, was that 'Green' socialist arguments and ideas were not carried forward. Rather than returning to the land, the labour movement campaigned for practical measures to include working class interests into politics, and to fight for the redistribution of wealth, thus the wave of counter-cultural activity came to an end after the turn of the century.

Galtung (1986) has argued that today's radical ecology cannot be seen as new because many aspects of the Green programme have a long history and can be seen as linked to socialist ideals. For example, he notes that practical reformism only constituted part of early socialism, and that,

> ... the socialist wave contained considerably more than that, there was also 'socialist humanism', an international peace movement, and so on. As a matter of fact, many of the tasks today taken on by the Green Movement can be seen as parts of the socialist programme, the preceding wave of social energy left unsolved (Ibid. 85-6).[28]

As I have argued, it is the case that in the period of the socialist revival (Pelling 1965) at the end of the nineteenth century, recognisably 'Green' ideas and arguments were put forward by self-proclaimed socialists and anarchists, and I can agree with Galtung that when drawing up their political programmes, radical ecologists must to some extent draw on existing theories and ideas. For instance, the fact that Green proposals for the reform of society today resemble more closely those of socialists and anarchists rather than the authoritarian tone of arguments put forward by 'catastrophists' in the 1970s, is evidence of left-wing influence, most notably perhaps in the case of Die Grünen in Germany (Fogt 1989; Hulsberg 1987). Similarly, attempts to change people's attitudes to their place in nature rather than forcibly compelling them to stop engaging in ecologically damaging practices betrays the characteristic approach of liberal individualism.

Still, just as there are varieties of socialism and conservatism, so there are varieties of 'ecologism' (Dobson 1990), and the concentration on points of overlap between ideological positions should not be allowed to obscure the essential differences between ecocentrism in the late-twentieth century and nineteenth century 'Green' socialism. The main point of difference is between a socialist anthropocentrism and a Green ecocentrism. Whilst some socialists were concerned with nature, it should be remembered that these concerns were always related to the conditions of life for people, and workers in particular. When Carpenter advocated a return to the land in small-scale communes, it was because of the benefits of this type of organisation for humans. When Morris propounded 'an epoch of rest' as an alternative to restless modern development, it was because the latter prevented human happiness. And although these arguments are repeated in discourses of radical ecology today, the latter's focus on ideas of intrinsic value in nature, and of concern with natural ecosystems does mark a shift of emphasis. In this way, late nineteenth century 'Green' socialism cannot really be seen as ecocentric in the same way that Greens today try to be.

Conclusion

The organised environmental movement emerged in the second half of the nineteenth century as a non-socialist movement with its roots in the middle classes. Environmental organisations, though often severely critical of industrial development, invariably worked within the existing social and political framework to prevent the untrammelled abuse of the natural world. In short, they were reformers not revolutionaries. The leaders and committees of these newly formed organisations consisted of men (and a few women) of property and status who saw the preservation of the countryside, maintenance of green areas in cities and the defence of nature in general, as part of the need to regulate industrial development in order to enhance the quality of life. This distinguishes them from some of the revolutionary 'Green' socialists of the time, but also from today's radical ecology which demands urgent changes in social organisation to stave off impending ecological crisis. Nonetheless, it is the case that environmental campaigners were not averse to using more radical ideas as propaganda for fund-raising and attracting support, whilst radicals like William Morris saw the benefits of trying to translate their radicalism into formal organisations and practical proposals for reform. So there was some interplay between the two forms.

In this chapter I have brought out some of the less well known and discussed aspects of early environmental campaigns such as their forms of organisation, campaigning styles and repertoires of action. In doing so I am implicitly drawing some fairly direct comparisons with the radical symbolic direct actions of post-1960s environmentalism, and in doing so reject the idea that direct actions are definitive of the latter. As I will argue later, both early and contemporary environmental groups engage(d) in a raft of strategic campaigning methods, and to characterise the new social movement by its direct actions is to focus only on the more visible forms of campaigning. For example, contemporary organisations have become increasingly concerned with legislative change, public education and information exchange. With this in mind, the early emphasis on direct actions of specific environmental organisations may be better explained by a theory of organisational development over time, which stresses the interrelationship between non-established and established organisations and the political system. This task is begun in Chapter 7.

Notes

1   Gould (1988: viii) also notes however that 'The history of green politics or social ecology can be made to stretch from pre-industrial societies', and perhaps some Green themes such as a concern for the welfare of animals and an appreciation of the natural world could be found to be expressed by individuals in any historical period. But this is not the same kind of inquiry as the attempt to trace the origins and development of environmentalism as an organised modern social movement.

2   I am indebted to Ian Varcoe for this metaphor.

3   This period was also identified by Brand (1990) as one of intensified modernization critique which ended after the first decade of the twentieth century.

4   Similarly, Harvey (1993: 1-2) has noted that '...the 'environmental issue' necessarily means such different things to different people, that in aggregate it encompasses quite literally everything there is ... words like 'nature' and 'environment' convey a commonality and universality of concern that is, precisely because of their ambiguity, open to a great diversity of interpretation'.

5   For an extended history which traces the changing idea of nature back to the Ancient Greeks, see Collingwood 1945.

6   Though Goodin argues that a 'green theory of value' is or should be at the centre of a specifically Green political theory (1992).

7   This is particularly pertinent to some ecofeminists who see the patriarchal 'hierarchical dualisms' (Eckersley 1992: 64), of modernity leading to the negative valuation of both nature and women.

8   In Britain the Royal Society was founded in 1663, partly as a result of efforts to classify species of plants (Gilig 1981: 99).

9   The Society for the Prevention of Cruelty to Animals could lay claim to this, it was formed in 1824. However, as Benton (1993: 2) says, '... it soon became clear to me that it was mistaken to lump together all movements calling for change in our relation to non - human nature. While ecological politics and radical concern about human treatment of non - human animals, for example, often shared common sentimental sources, the philosophical sources and political aims of these movements were quite distinct'. In short, the S.P.C.A was not an environmental or Green organisation. A better claim is the fact that 'The French Society for the Protection of Nature traces its origins back to 1854' (Kuechler and Dalton 1990: 278).

10   Some interpretations see the environmental movement as 'episodic' (Lowe and Goyder 1983; Young 1993), but it is part of my argument here that this could imply a lack of continuity over time which does not give enough weight to the continuation over time of environmentalist initiatives and organisations.

11   A good discussion of the range of philanthropic efforts of Victorian women is in Prochaska 1980.

12   The Statute of Merton was eventually repealed in 1894.

13   The Committee for the Study of British Vegetation, formed in 1904, sought to classify and photograph flora and became the British Ecological Society in 1913. Evans (1992: 53) notes that despite its object being '... to advance the education of the public and to advance and support research in the subject of ecology as a branch of natural science, and to disseminate the results of such research', many of its supporters would have called it 'nature study'. This echoes Worster's distinction between the 'arcadian' and 'imperialist' sides of the history of ecology, and seems to be a characteristic of the whole eco-philosophical and political ecology debate (Worster 1985).

14   See for example her article on air pollution in London (1888).

15   McCormick (1991: 30) notes that 'Popular social reform movements often borrow techniques from one another, and attract support from the same quarters. The methods of Victorian abolitionists and those opposed to cruelty to animals now began to influence naturalists. A turning point came in the 1860s when the protectionist crusade mustered its forces around the issue of the killing of birds to provide plumage for women's fashions'.

16   Though this should not be taken to imply that there are no differences either between organisations or between the old and new organisations. What is clear though is that the claims of radical novelty expressed in some new social movement theories finds little support from the development of environmentalism in Britain.

17   Fedden (1974: 85-6) notes that the inalienable rights of the Trust have only been overturned once, in 1968 by the Ministry of Transport's bypass plan on   Saltram Park in Devon. Despite its appeal, a Select Committee found in favour of the Ministry, thus overriding the Trust's rights of inalienability. As a former Deputy Director General, Fedden saw this as a 'worrying development'.

18 There are some parallels here with localised attempts to prevent the siting of polluting industries and development of waste ground - derogatively called 'N.I.M.B.Y.' (not in my backyard) - protests.

19 The C.P.S. hired 120 navvies and a special train to ensure that local people would wake the following morning to witness the symbolic laying low of the owner's fences.

20 Many radical ecologists see Rachel Carson's book *Silent Spring* (1962), which deals with the elimination of birds brought about by the accumulation of pesticides in the environment, as marking the point of transition between environmentalism and radical ecology (Atkinson 1991: 15, see also Nicholson 1970). However, Carson was only bringing to wider public attention an issue which was already being researched by the R.S.P.B.

21 A number of 'Labour Churches' were formed in the period which attracted sizeable numbers of socialists. Pelling (1965: ch.vii) gives an account of these and their brief history. Whilst William Morris's 'most devoted Socialist disciple' (MacCarthy 1996: 498), J. B. Glasier (1921: 226) argued that 'Historically, indeed, Socialism is more closely related to religious than to political propagandism. It is from the prophets, apostles, and saints, the religious mystics and heretics, rather than from statesmen, economists and political reformers, that the Socialist movement derives the example and ideals that inspire its nobler enthusiasm and hopes today'.

22 The Socialist League was formed in 1884 as a breakaway group from the Social Democratic Federation. Its founders included William Morris, Edward Aveling, Eleanor Mark and Belfort Bax. The life of the League was short, gradually winding down after Morris left in 1890 (see Pelling 1965 for a good account of the sources of disputes among early socialist organisations).

23 This passage is reminiscent of William Morris's (1908: 79) influential utopian novel *News From Nowhere* in which it is explained to the narrator how village life was restored and England de-industrialised. 'The change ... which in these matters took place very early in our epoch, was most strangely rapid. People flocked into the country villages, and, so to say, flung themselves upon the freed land like a wild beast upon his prey; and in a very little time the villages of England were more populous than they had been since the fourteenth century, and were still growing fast'.

24 The late-twentieth century anarchistic strand of radical ecology has been developed most forcefully in the prolific writings of Murray Bookchin who attempts to bring together anarchism and ecology into a perspective of 'social ecology', though his main argument really amounts to the idea that anarchism is necessarily ecological, rather than an attempt to modify the former in the light of the knowledge from ecological science.

25 The parallels between late-nineteenth century utopian socialism and aspects of contemporary radical ecological thought are evident in the following passage from Eckersley (1992: 91), who is trying to outline why an ecocentric perspective leads to the favouring of certain types of energy usage and a reduction in consumerism: 'Ecocentric theorists argue that whereas the flourishing of human life and culture is quite compatible with a human lifestyle based on low material and energy throughput, the flourishing of nonhuman life *requires* such a human lifestyle. In order to meet this requirement we need to live and experience ourselves as but one component of, and more or less keep pace with, the basic cycles and processes of nature rather than seek

to totally transcend the nonhuman world by removing all of its inconveniences and thereby obliterating its "otherness"'. Note though, that Eckersley argues in favour of a specific type of human society because 'the flourishing of non-human life demands such a human lifestyle'. In short, ecocentrics read ideal forms of social organisation of humans from the demands of nature. This kind of motivation would have been quite alien to socialists like William Morris, and demonstrates why it is overstating the case to label him (and other socialists) as Green or ecocentric in the modern sense.

26 Carpenter's own homosexuality also formed a part of his opposition to rigid Victorian morality, which he saw as effectively preventing people from expressing their natural desires (Rowbotham and Weeks 1977).

27 Morris was a key figure in the founding of the Socialist League in 1884, whose journal *Commonweal* gave space for back-to-nature ideas until its demise in 1890.

28 Galtung in fact sees Green movements as the 'fifth wave of modern movements'. In chronological order, these are: aristocrats, merchants, bourgeoisie, working class, Greens. So although he is pointing up areas of overlap between the programmes of socialists and Greens, he clearly sees Green movements as being distinctive enough to push modern societies beyond the institutional framework generated by socialist movements.

5 Twentieth Century Environmentalism

The Organisation of Twentieth Century Concern for Nature

Since the 1970s almost all industrialised societies have experienced the emergence of a range of new environmentalist organisations such as Greenpeace, Friends of the Earth and more recently the loose networks of Earth First!, and for the first time political parties based on a Green ideology and programme have been formed. The latter have achieved widely varying levels of success (Parkin 1989 & 1991; Müller-Rommel 1990).[1] The forms, activities, action repertoires, aims and ideologies of these new organisations have been cited by many commentators as evidence of a radical shift in the type of social movements which characterise (post)modern societies. The new environmentalism has been influential in supporting the new social movements (NSM) perspective in West European sociology, because it is seen as significantly different from previous social movements, particularly labour movements and a descriptive contrast between old and new has thus been generated.

In this chapter I contest the characterisation of the new environmental organisations which is used as evidence for the existence of new social movements by demonstrating significant continuities with previous environmental movement organisations. Whilst recognising some genuinely novel features, I attempt to explain these by locating the organisations within the context of the developing environmental movement as a whole. I contend that the failure to take a longer term perspective of the development of environmental organisations and activities has led to a distorted image of the new environmentalism as well as raising unrealistic expectations of it.

One of the problems which occurs when we fail to take seriously the prior existence of similar problematics such as the problem of society/nature relations is that this often leads to a quest for novelty at the expense of noticing significant continuities. As Pizzorno (1978: 291) has noted there is a danger that, '... at the start of a wave of conflict we shall be induced to think that we are at the verge of a revolution; and when the downswing appears, we shall predict the end of class conflict'. The misinterpretation of waves of collective action which is apparent in relation to contemporary environmentalism is only one aspect of what Elias (1987) has called the 'retreat of sociologists into the present', and as I have argued, has lead to a reliance on theories which portray static pictures of 'industrial' and 'post-industrial' societies, rather than focusing on the processes of industrialisation and urbanisation and the con-sequences and changing forms of resistance to these dominant processes.

For many commentators, the earlier phase of concern for nature, explored in the previous chapter, has little if any relevance for the understanding of contemporary radical ecology. There are several reasons for this. Firstly it is argued that early conservationist and preservationist sentiment was unrepresentative of the wider population, being confined to an upper-class elite with no intention to challenge the dominant mode of modernisation. In short, it was not popular. Secondly, despite these early stirrings of concern, environmental organisations have failed to make any impact on the way in which industrial societies have developed, their influence has been relatively insignificant until recently. Finally, some have argued that the new movement is so different from all earlier forms that the two are effectively different movements. Radical ecology movements are seen to present a fundamental challenge to continuing modernisation and to Western culture, especially in its Enlightenment guise. They are therefore part of broad postmodern cultural trends or the perceived shift from simple modernity to a more reflexive form of modernity (Beck 1992, 1994; Giddens 1991, 1994).

What these characterisations of old and new environmental movements do not take seriously enough in my view is the possibility that the contemporary organisations are part of a longer term development of environmentalism. A significant marker of the continuation of nature concern is the formation of new groups and organisations by successive generations. If we take the formation of new environmental organisations as evidence for the continuing development and indeed vitality of the movement across generations, then the evidence is that after the initial phase of organisation building which ended at the turn of the twentieth century, the fledgling environmental movement did not lose its way or rest on its previous achievements. A concern to protect the natural world, maintain open spaces in cities and towns and to regulate industrial development have been part of twentieth century environmental movement activity. If we look at the main national organisations which were founded throughout the course of this century, up to the formation of radical ecological groups, it is clear that with

Table 5.1   Twentieth century environmental organisations

Name of Organisation	Date of Formation
Society for the Preservation of the Wild Fauna of the Empire	1903
The Federation of Rambling Clubs	1905
Society for the Promotion of Nature Reserves	1912
The Forestry Commission	1919
International Council for Bird Preservation	1922
Council for the Preservation of Rural England	1926
Association for the Preservation of Rural Scotland	1931
Council for the Preservation of Rural Wales	1935
Ramblers Association	
Association of Bird Watchers and Wardens	1936
Ulster Society for the Preservation of the Countryside	1937
International Union for the Protection of Nature	1948
The Nature Conservancy Council	1948
The Civic Trust	1957
The Council for Nature	1958
The Conservation Corps	1959
World Wildlife Fund (now Worldwide Fund for Nature)	1961
The Conservation Society	1966
Committee for Environmental Conservation (CoEnCo)	1969
The Countryside Commission	1969
Friends of the Earth	1971
The Woodland Trust	1972
The Green Party (People Party in 1973, Ecology Party in 1975 and Green Party in 1985)	1973
European Environmental Bureau	1974
Greenpeace (U.K)	1977
The Green Alliance	1978
Wildlife Link	1979

the exception of the periods of the two World Wars, the development of the movement has been 'evolutionary' rather than disjunctive. Table 5.1 is a selective list of some of the more important organisations.

Again, these are only the most well-known national (and international) organisations and do not include the hundreds of small, local groups which now exist around the country.[2] Nevertheless, the conclusion must be that rather than a disjunctive history with an active period in the late nineteenth century followed by demise and resurgence in the 1970s, the history of the environmental movement at the organisational level is a fairly continuous one. Evans' (1992: 93) interpretation is probably closer to my own than NSM theories when he says that,

> The war years had interrupted the momentum of the voluntary conservation movement. Membership figures levelled out and the number of new initiatives dropped as Britain understandably turned its attention to more pressing matters. But, with the return to peace, the time was right to renew the thrust. Conservation fitted into the ideal of a brave new world very comfortably. Britain had pulled through again, and her people deserved to receive their promised land in good heart. Public access in search of a new knowledge of the countryside would rely upon its conservation and careful management.

This kind of interpretation of the history of the environmental movement as a fairly continuous one, conflicts with the self-understanding of many movement activists, and with NSM interpretations.

Creation of a Mass Movement

During the course of the twentieth century, membership of environmental organisations in Britain steadily increased until the 1980s, when there was a pronounced phase of growth, reflected in the enormous expansion of memberships. It is this transformation of environmentalism from an apparently elitist, reformist movement with its base in insider groups using established pressure group tactics, to a popular, radical mass movement using unconventional direct actions which challenge accepted notions of progress and development, which seems to have impressed NSM theorists.

For example, Kuechler and Dalton argue that the contemporary environmental movement is very different from the conservationist and preservationist groups of earlier times, at least in terms of their interests and aims. They see the difference between the old and new environmental movements as one of differing goals:

> The fundamental goal of [the environmental movement] today is different from that of the environmental movement at the turn of the century - reflecting a drastic change in the historical context. In the past, local solutions were sought. It was (or at least it seemed) possible to geo-graphically restrict the impact of environmental hazards. ... The establishment of parks, preserves, and sanctuaries seemed to be a viable tool to protect nature and wildlife and to provide recreation areas for the citizenry in the past. Obviously such local strategies are insufficient today. ... The fundamental goal of the movement today is not particularistic. It serves the very survival of the human species (Kuechler and Dalton 1990: 284).

On this view the new movement appears to be of a different kind to the range of single interest groups which made up earlier environmentalism. In particular, the perceived more radical groups such as Greenpeace and Friends of the Earth (and the Green Party) seem to be at the forefront of the new environmentalism with their supposedly non-class based demands, decentralised structures, anti-institutional focus and direct action campaigns. There may appear to be a clear divide between these groups and the moderate, lobbying styles of earlier elitist environmental organisations such as the CPS and National Trust. However, a closer investigation of the expanding movement reveals a more complex picture.

The environmental movement in Britain has been described as the largest social movement in the country, with an estimated combined membership of around four and a half million by 1990. This represents about 8% of the total population (McCormick 1991, 34).[3] The mass character of the movement is credited to the expansionary phase which began in the early 1970s and has a clear link to the aftermath of student protests across Europe and the USA which peaked in 1968. Lowe and Goyder (1983: 127) notice that 'The first executive director of FoE had been chairman of the National Union of Students Committee on the Environment, and many initial staff members and supporters had also been involved in student politics'.

Cotgrove's 1982 study also showed that students were significantly over-represented amongst members of FoE and the Conservation Society (8% compared to 1.4% in the total population), indicating something of a possible generational contrast between old and new groups. Membership of other environmentalist organisations also seems to be predominantly middle class.[4] Lowe and Goyder note that 'a sizeable majority of members' of the RSPB, the National Trust, the Conservation Society and FoE are middle class, but that some differences do exist between the groups. The RSPB being mainly lower middle class and the National Trust 'strongly upper middle class', with the Conservation Society and FoE 'predominantly' upper middle class. All tended to have 'higher incomes and much higher levels of education' (a majority of the members of FoE and the Conservation Society have degrees) than a sample of the general public (Lowe and Goyder 1983: 10-11). Only 5.4% of members of FoE and the Conservation Society were in manual work compared to 28.2% in the population as a whole, and there is no evidence of significant working class involvement in environmental organisations, though there have been a few instances of co-operation between trade unions and environmental groups.[5]

Best estimates of the growth of the most visible new groups, Greenpeace and FoE, reveal a rapid rise in membership throughout the 1970s and 80s, though the evidence is that this period of growth is now at an end. In 1980, Greenpeace had around 10,000 members, increasing to 50,000 by 1985, 320,000 in 1989 and around 400,000 at present. Figures for FoE show that membership stood at 2,000 in 1971, 12,000 by 1980, 27,000 in 1985, 120,000 in 1989 rising to 180,000 in 1990 (figures from McCormick 1991: 152, and Evans 1992: 113). With a combined membership of around 600,000 and the resulting high levels of income and public attention, there is clearly some validity in the suggestion that the new environmental movement has only emerged over the last three decades. However, this assessment needs to be qualified.

Firstly, in relation to both organisations, 'Only a minority of supporters have ever become active in local groups ... ' (Lowe and Goyder 1983: 126), which probably means that the number of active campaigners is relatively small. This would seem to be borne out by looking at the numbers involved in Greenpeace and FoE campaigns and public protests, most of which are of a symbolic kind (Melucci 1985, 1989). Although some demonstrations have involved several thousands, these tend to be anti-nuclear or peace protests which draw in peace campaigners, socialists, feminists and others, rather than being purely environmental protests. More typical are Greenpeace's direct actions against toxic dumping at sea, continued whaling and nuclear testing where a few committed campaigners can use the group's resource base to attract media attention and bring issues before the public. Similarly with FoE's campaigns, the goal has often been to ensure media attention rather than to involve large numbers of sympathisers and supporters:

> One example was a nine-foot high Coca-Cola can delivered to the American embassy in London as part of an international day of action to urge the US President to introduce legislation controlling throw-away cans and bottles. Such legislation, it was anticipated, would set an example for other countries to follow. The three television crews and two dozen pressmen and photographers sent to record the scene outnumbered the environmentalists (Lowe and Goyder 1983: 130).

As Pepper (1986: 138) has argued, 'Amidst all the talk of a 'new awakening', and gains in membership, there has been blindness to the fact that relatively few people are really 'waking up' to the environmental problems of the kind that groups like FoE, Greenpeace, CPRS or the National Trust are concerned with'. Secondly, we need to look more closely at how other, more established environmental groups have fared since the 1970s.

The National Trust's membership had been growing steadily during the course of the twentieth century to stand at 159,000 in 1967. But by 1980, partly on the 1970s wave of renewed interest in the environment as a political issue, the Trust had 950,000 members, 1,323,000 by 1985, and on October 1st 1990 the 2,000,000th member was recruited. The WWF saw its membership grow from 51,000 in 1980 to 202,000 in 1989, whilst the RSPB had 25,000 members in 1964, but this had risen to 300,000 by 1979 and 433,000 ten years later. Today the RSPB claims over 1 million members. The Ramblers Association doubled its numbers from 36,000 to 73,000 between 1980 and 1989, and the Royal Society for Nature Conservation grew from 140,000 to over 205,000 in the same period. Even the Council for the Preservation of Rural England, whose membership had remained static for a number of years grew from 27,000 to 44,500.[6] The Woodland Trust, which was formed in 1972 to, '...conserve, restore and re-establish trees and in particular broadleaved trees, plants and all forms of wildlife ...' (In Evans 1992: 138), had less than 1,000 members in 1979, but by 1989 this had risen to 65,000.

So, despite the fact that the highest growth *rates* during the 1980s were in FoE and Greenpeace, the most striking point to note from overall membership increase is that the overwhelming majority of new members drawn into the movement were joining either more moderate, single-issue groups and organisations or more significantly, organisations which pre-date the advent of the new environmentalism.[7] Indeed the National Trust itself now accounts for just under half of all members of environmental movement organisations in Britain, and as Dwyer and Hodge (1996: 23) have pointed out, '... over the whole period [since its formation] the *rate* of increase in growth has been remarkably constant; it has been exponential with troughs between 1915 and 1925, 1939 and 1945 and briefly in the late 1960s'. Increasing support for the National Trust would therefore seem to be relatively independent of phases of renewed interest and public activity.

On the basis of these figures it would seem that claims that the mass environmental movement represents a new oppositional force with the potential to replace the old labour movement (Touraine 1981; Olofsson 1988; Eder 1993) are extremely difficult to sustain.[8] The phase of renewed interest in nature and concern for environmental issues has not occurred in a political or organisational vacuum. It is precisely because the environmental movement pre-dates the 1970s resurgence, that this renewed interest and concern has been channelled as much (if not more) through existing organisations as newly formed ones. We will not understand the new environmentalism unless we discuss it in relation to the continuing development of the movement over a much longer period of time. Given that there is no simple correlation between new radical organisations and the creation of a mass movement, we must now examine whether these new organisations represent a break with the past in terms of their internal structures, policy programmes and styles of campaigning. This will then enable us to assess the claim that they are part of a raft of new social movements in the late twentieth century.

Globalising the Environmental Movement

Given the wide range of environmental organisations and the different levels on which they operate (local, national, international), generalisations about them are difficult. Some organisations are insider groups with contacts and interrelations with (and in some cases dependency on) government and ministerial offices. These include the National Trust, RSPB, RSNC and BTforCV.[9]   Others are outsider groups which shun formal links to government, jealously guard their independence and often campaign openly against government policy. These include FoE, Greenpeace and Earth First!. Some organisations are closed oligarchies with effectively self-perpetuating hierarchies, others are open oligarchies which allow members to rise to the top levels of the organisation, and a few (such as FoE) mix 'monologic' and 'dialogic' forms across local, national and international levels (Offe & Wiesenthal 1980; Bagguley 1992). Earth First! is the best known example of the other informal networks which are not formal organisations, preferring a radical individualistic approach which emphasises the individual's responsibility in ecological protest.[10] In addition, there are widely differing ideological allegiances and motivations amongst environmental groups. Some are amenity groups, campaigning for public access, others seek to restrict such access; some are conservationist, others preservationist; some are more concerned specifically with animal welfare or individual animal rights, others with nature writ large. Some take a human welfarist position, others see this as part of the problem which legitimises the destruction of nature. Despite all this, a few tentative general conclusions can be drawn from this study so far.

Firstly as Lowe and Goyder (1983: 50) point out,

If democracy implies that constituents have a real opportunity to select their leaders, most environmental groups are not democratic. These organisations are oligarchic in nature; in all but a few, the leaders cannot be realistically challenged. Many, though not all, have elections; but they are often not contested, and the primary source of nominations is the centre and not the grassroots. ... In the words of a staff member of one of the large wildlife groups, 'Essentially we appoint council members for their expertise and contacts. As in other conservation groups, the elections are a formality.' He could have added that environmental groups are not alone in this respect among voluntary organisations generally.

Although there have been *some* innovative ways of organising and campaigning in *some* organisations, the basic structural forms of most voluntary environmentalist organisations bear the stamp of their place within the long-term development of the movement as a whole, and this applies to the more recent groups such as Greenpeace, FoE, Wildlife Trust etc., as much as to older groups. The symbolic direct actions with which Greenpeace and FoE made their name are best seen as the creative use of the potential offered by new forms of visual media (television, video etc.) and not as symptomatic of qualitatively different types of social movement. Direct actions have also been one part of their initial attempts to carve out a place within the existing structure of movement organisations, rather than constitutive features of the organisations themselves. As I argued earlier, direct actions in defence of nature (though clearly of a limited kind) can be traced all the way back to the first environmental organisations in the late-nineteenth century. To some extent, the move away from simple direct actions, towards professionalism and strengthening of internal organisational structures reflects the success of FoE and Greenpeace in marking out their own space within the movement as a whole. Young (1993: 22) observes that,

> ... Greenpeace and FoE which were the media stunt *enfants terribles* of the environmental lobby in the 1970s have slowly changed their tactics. During the 1980s they deliberately shed some of their old image, and co-operated more with other groups. An example was concerted opposition to water privatisation.

This process of professionalisation (some would say, 'de-radicalisation', or 'assimilation' by the establishment), has opened up a gap within the movement for a more loosely organised direct action group which EF! and other loose networks currently fills, notably drawing some members away from the formerly 'radical' groups.

Secondly, in relation to the kinds of issues which the new groups are concerned with, it is evident that there are also continuities with those of the developing environmental movement. WWF, Greenpeace and FoE are part of a globalising phase of development in the environmental movement. As industrial capitalism has become a 'global system' (Robertson 1991; Wallerstein 1974, 1983, 1991; Sklair 1991), environmental issues and the concerns of environmental organisations have become internationalised. Industrial developments such as nuclear power plants, extraction of oil reserves, factory-ship whaling, world-wide transport systems, together with the scientific discovery (creation?) of global environmental problems such as ozone depletion, acid rain and pollution, climate change, extinction of species, and the emergence of international political institutions like the United Nations (including UNESCO and United Nations Environment Programme) and the European Union (including the European Parliament), have generated an international context for environmental action.[11]   Adam (1996: 86) has argued that the process of globalisation,

> ... implies social institutions and practices oriented towards global issues. The World Bank, the United Nations, the World Commission on Environment

and Development, the Campaign for Nuclear Disarmament and the Organisation of Petroleum Exporting Countries (OPEC), all expressions of this development, dissent from the traditional focus of sociological inquiry, and all transcend society as bounded by the nation state.[12]

The formation of 'global' environmental organisations such as Birdlife International, Earthwatch, FoE International, Greenpeace International, the International Union for the Conservation of Nature and Natural Resources, Wetlands International and the Worldwide Fund for Nature, also provides evidence of this process, as does the creation of the European Environmental Bureau, an umbrella organisation for 150 European environmentalist organisations, giving them a presence in the European Community.[13] However, the general tenor of this globalising environmental concern remains reformist, and can be seen as consonant with the values of the majority of local and national groups.

Thirdly, it would appear that the 1970s wave of environmental concern represents a generational contrast, with younger environmentalists attempting to establish their own organisations which embody a relatively new internationalist outlook. The new groups show a tendency to have younger members than the older ones, especially university-educated students, although it must be borne in mind that, as we showed earlier, the surge in membership from the 1970s was certainly not confined to the perceived new environmentalism, and it is likely that many young people have joined already existing environmental groups.

Finally, it is clear that the radical environmentalist organisations of the 1970s are not themselves ecocentric or Green. Dobson (1990: 14) is right to say that,

... organizations like Greenpeace and Friends of the Earth (which campaign in many fronts at the same time) stop short of being wholly Green. This is because, while many of their members might individually subscribe to the necessity for the radical changes in our political and social life referred to above, the organizations do not explicitly do so. I should warn at the same time against a too-hasty identification of Green parties with ecologism. Just because Green parties have views that cover the whole range of political and social life does not mean that they have Green views ... I suggest that Green parties typically draw their inspiration from the principles of political ecology rather than seeking to fully enunciate or enact them.

Though the available evidence does seem to show that the British Green Party is the repository for many people whose views can be said to be ecocentric in Dobson's sense of the term.

It should be clear that the evidence presented here does not support the characterisation of new social movements as a new bloc of social movement activity within contemporary industrialised societies. To characterise the diverse range of new movements as essentially similar is to fall into Touraine's trap of reading contemporary social movement activity as leading through practical necessity towards a new, unified oppositional movement. I do not think this kind of interpretation can be justified at present, though I accept though that there is a need for more research into the constitutive social movements of modern societies in order to reach firmer conclusions, and to draw out the different structural locations, motivations and forms of social movements.

Precursors of Contemporary Ecocentrism

So far, this chapter has concentrated on the development of environmentalism as an organised social movement attempting to intervene in and regulate (bring order to) the interaction between industrial societies and non-human nature. This movement has developed into a mass social movement increasingly as concerned with global environmental issues as with local and national ones. I also argued in Chapter Four, that although some recognisably 'Green' ideas and initiatives can be found in the late-nineteenth century, these cannot really be described as evidence of an ecocentric orientation in the present sense, because they were informed by a humanistic socialism or anarchism. These did not read ideal forms of social organisation from the needs of nature, but instead saw decentralisation and de-industrialisation as improving the quality of human relationships. So although they may have promoted some of the same solutions, their reasons for doing so differ significantly from today's ecocentric Greens, who try to develop a coherent non-anthropocentric or non-humanistic perspective. In the words of one well-known American radical activist and writer, 'My political position is to be a spokesman for wild nature. I take that as my primary constituency' (Snyder 1980, 49 quoted in Devall, 1990: 76).

In this section I shift the focus to examine what has variously been described as radical ecology, Green politics, ecocentrism and deep ecology.

In contrast to environmentalism, radical ecology rejects reform environmentalism, perceiving it to stop short of getting to the real causes of environmental damage. This is not to suggest that on occasion radical ecologists do not find themselves publicly arguing for conservation in managerial environmentalist terms, but in doing so, they remain convinced that this is politically judicious rather than expressing the real tenets of radical ecology (Dobson 1990). Greens trace the causes of environmental degradation to modernity's break with nature in several forms, for example through classical scientific methods, urban living and industrial development. I have argued that a radical ecology perspective does not characterise environmental organisations (Earth First! apart), but it is important to recognise that this does not exclude the fact that some people who join environmental groups do adhere to an ecocentric orientation, though more research is needed in this area to give us a better overall picture. An example of recent research is Bennie et al's recent study of the British Green Party (1995), which upholds the contention that a majority of its members share an ecocentric perspective and support quite radical Green policies.

Several commentators have also pointed out that many of the values, ideas and proposals for change of contemporary ecocentrics have a long history and can be traced back to romanticism (Eder 1990,1993; Worster 1985), utopian socialism (Pepper 1994, 1996: Ch.4; Gould 1988) and even to fascist movements (Graber 1978; Bramwell 1989). The appeal to nature in support of the political goals of both right and left-wing politics would seem to show that no consensus exists on the political import of knowledge about natural processes or of placing nature's needs (however these are perceived) above those of human societies.[14] Mannheim (1953: 162 [footnote]) observed that a 'philosophy of life' could lead in either direction noting that,

> As far as it is possible to judge at present, it has the tendency - when it regains political significance - to provide an ideological foundation for the modern eruptive activist currents (whether in a reactionary or progressive sense). This at any rate is true of the Bergsonian trend which provided the impetus both for Fascism and for the direct action of syndicalism ... .

It also implies that a politics of nature is just as likely to be a politics of the right as of the left, and although it is easy to see the links between contemporary Green Party politics and the left, particularly in the German case (Galtung 1986; Fogt 1989), there is also some evidence of links with the right in the kinds of authoritarian solutions proffered by Ehrlich (1962), Ophuls (1977) and Hardin (1977), who argue that authoritarian measures must be taken to fend off over-population and resource depletion.[15]

However, the acknowledgement that ecocentrism can be used as a platform for both right and left-wing politics should not be allowed to obscure the essential difference between anthropocentric and ecocentric orientations in environmentalism and radical ecology respectively. From the analysis so far, and anticipating my conclusion, I think that we must avoid an interpretation which suggests that environmental reformism is being radicalised, as the concern with nature broadens out towards concerns for a reconstructed global concept of a planetary nature. Despite an increasingly international dimension to environmental campaigning, the bulk of the movement's intentions remain reformist, and we must therefore reject the idea that radical ecological ideas are leading to the creation of a transformative mass movement.

The response of socialists and marxists to the re-emergence of radical ecology and the creation of Green political parties was initially hostile. For example, Enzensberger's (1974) influential essay accepted that radical ecology had the potential to attract a mass following but he argued that the ecologists' analysis was extremely confused, lacking the grounding of a class perspective. By the 1980s though, others recognised that some of the themes emerging within radical ecological thought bore a striking resemblance to aspects of earlier British socialism, long forgotten. In E.P. Thompson's introduction to Rudolf Bahro's *Socialism and Survival* (1982: 8), he noted that,

> Bahro's vision, which does not refuse the utopian mode ... is fresh and original. And yet, in a surprising way, it is traditional also. When I read the third and final section of *The Alternative*, I was astonished to find, on page after page, a reincarnation in modern dress of some of the essential preoccupations of William Morris in his socialist writings of the 1880s. Yet Morris's socialist essays were unknown to Bahro. It is encouraging to know that this vision, fresh and with new additions, wells up once again.[16]

More recently still, after surveying the ecocentric position and thinking through how best to address global environmental problems, Martell (1994: 199) declares, '...I reject capitalist and laissez-faire solutions to ecological problems and find myself coming more and more back to socialist political economy. I think state intervention, global co-ordination and political action by the green movement are necessary for resolving such problems'. The difficulty though, is that Greens have no trust in state intervention or global co-ordination, favouring decentralist solutions which offer more possibilities for participatory forms of democracy. A further difference is that the root of socialists' and Marxists' critique of ecologism lies in the latter's apparent anti-humanism, that is, their prioritising of the needs of nature as a whole. In particular, this change in priorities rankles with socialists like Weston (1986: 3) who says that, 'To think that whooping cranes are important (possibly more so than people) one has to be free of the more pressing human problems like that of poverty ... [W]hich is why green politics remains a middle-class phenomenon'. He goes on,

> Living as I do in a principally working-class neighbourhood, as part of a working-class family, I find it difficult to accept that the most important issues which society has to tackle are all related to 'nature'. And yet it is 'nature' - its protection and restoration - which motivates virtually all the actions of greens. Furthermore, despite all the arguments about the social benefits of ecological protection, this concern for 'nature' remains little more than a middle-class priority that is based upon a middle-class understanding of what 'nature' is (ibid: 2).

The lack of a class analysis leads to the mistaken belief that the new ecological problematic holds equal relevance for all social groups. For socialists this ignores the differential experience of environmental degradation, and the different ways of defining environmental problems. Greens offer no consistent, sustained critique of the human environmental problems of inner city decline for example. Further, Weston argues that the emergence of the Greens was only the latest manifestation of a populist political tradition, which gains strength when 'a previously independent group is undergoing fundamental change' (1986: 25). In this sense, Green politics is not novel. 'Far from being the 'new paradigm' which transcends the old political framework of left versus right, green politics is part of a long tradition in political thought - older, in fact than both liberalism and marxism, yet encompassing elements of both' (ibid.). Green politics is seen as closely related to the inclusion of 'non-productive' public sector workers, such as teachers, social workers, doctors etc., within the commercial constraints of capitalism from which they had previously been relatively free. This then feeds into the typically populist recourse to nature as the 'final trump card' (ibid.: 27) to support Green arguments in favour of de-industrialisation. Hence this focus on nature politics is not new, nor is it a particularly significant area of social struggle. There is therefore no possibility that radical ecology can develop into a transformative mass movement as it reflects the ideals of a specific fraction of the middle class.

Even so, many socialists have since seen the potential for bringing political-ecological ideas into a productive alliance with socialism in order to develop a thoroughgoing 'eco-socialist' perspective concentrating on the way capitalism destroys local, national and global environments of both human and natural kinds, rather than accepting the Greens' focus on non-human nature.[17] Many socialists argue that this inevitably leads in the direction of a reform environmentalism, from which Greens cannot really distance themselves.

> Apart from some cosmetic measures to protect wildlife, the pressures upon the environment are as strong today as ever; despite a decade and a half of lobbying and campaigning, that 'right' of capital to pass on its costs to society and the environment is just as entrenched. Its radical image and its recent expansion hide the fact that modern environmentalism has failed to live up to its early promise; it has remained tied to the same narrow concern for wildlife protection from which its founders had hoped to escape (Weston 1986: 12).

This reformist character is ineffective in preventing the forces of capital from continuing to use the natural environment with impunity. Part of the reason for this is that radical ecology has no real strategy for social change, apart from 'ecological enlightenment' through education to change people's attitudes towards nature. Pepper (1986: 125) argues that this amounts to no strategy at all because:

> ... it assumes that social change will come about largely through people changing their ideas and values. As the *FoE Supporters Newspaper* editorial (Autumn 1985) put it: 'FoE is seeking to bring about change at a deeper level - change in people's attitudes and values.' As such, these sentiments are largely hogwash, for they presume that there can be a miraculous creation of the ecologically - conscious human being via some cathartic, unspecified revolutionary experience.

What will bring about this experience is unclear, but some Greens still argue that this shift in attitudes will not occur until environmental damage has advanced to crisis proportions, and despite some commentators' assertions that the catastrophist environmental writing of the early 1970s was a brief phase which has long been surpassed, it is quite clear that contemporary radical ecological works are still replete with references to 'the ecological crisis'.[18] As such, this perceived crisis still forms a key motivation for Green activists and is seen in the kind of analysis put forward by eco-radicals like Goldsmith (1988: 216-7) who argues that,

> At present there is considerable disenchantment with the benefits of modern industry, while conventional wisdom is losing much of its credibility. It is but a question of time for this disenchantment to yield total disillusionment, and for conventional wisdom to become correspondingly discredited in the face of the ever more obvious failure of the expedients it prescribes for solving our worsening problems. ... At some point, panic will set in and people will grope about frantically for an alternative set of solutions. The most attractive is likely to be the most radical - the one which provides the best vehicle for expressing the reaction to the values of industrialism. The ecological philosophy best answers these requirements.

So, although socialists and some radical ecologists acknowledge a need for more co-operation, it is difficult to see how this could be brought about without compromising the ecocentrism of the Greens. If 'ecologism' really does constitute a new political ideology (Dobson 1990), then any accommodation towards an eco-socialist position will be seen as an unnecessary assimilation of ecologism into an old ideology. More significantly, the basis of ecologism's originality is, as the term suggests, the privileging of nature's ecology in any analysis or political project, as opposed to the anthropocentric or human welfare orientation of socialism. This clearly draws on the science of ecology, which in some interpretations, lends strong support to the arguments of eco-radicals. For example, Clapp (1994: 7) argues that 'Ecologists, with geologists and economists, have shown the limits of man's power and the truth of the adage that, browbeat Nature as you may, she will have the last word. In ecology man is a powerful and disturbing influence but not necessarily the most important figure, or the most highly esteemed'.

It is differences in perspective of this kind, which seek to re-orientate our understanding of the place of human beings in nature, which lie at the heart of Eckersley's recent ecocentric critique of Habermas's work for example (1990), and which, more than anything else, bonds Greens together.[19] In the words of Earth First!, the organisation itself can almost be reduced to its key belief, 'There are no members of Earth First!, only Earth First!ers. It is a belief in biocentrism, or Deep Ecology, and a practice of putting our beliefs into action' (Anti-Constitution 1992). Because radical ecological ideas have re-emerged outside of existing socialist and labour movements, ecocentrism has become an article of faith and a source of the crucial beliefs which differentiate Greens from all other forms of 'grey' politics. Socialists could not support the sentiments of Earth First! founder Dave Foreman (Foreman & Haywood 1989: 14-17) when he says that, 'John Muir once said that if it ever came to a war between the races, he would side with the bears. That day has arrived ...'. Now we need a better understanding of this ecocentric bond and its historical antecedents.

Recognisably ecological ideas have a conflictual history containing both 'imperialist' and 'arcadian' strands, extending back beyond the emergence of the discipline of scientific ecology.[20] In fact Worster (1985: xi) argues that '... one might very well cast the history of ecology as a struggle between rival views of the relationship between humans and nature: one view devoted to the discovery of intrinsic value and its preservation, the other to the creation of an instrumentalized world and its exploitation'. This seems to strengthen the argument we saw in Chapter Three that modern culture is Janus-faced, alternating between modernism and romanticism (Eder 1993; Szerszynski 1996), and despite attempts to play up the originality of the radical ecology position, in fact its main tenets can be found in earlier periods.

For example the focus on holism, intrinsic value in nature, and the primary importance of the needs of nature (the 'nature-knows-best' principle), can all be uncovered in the English Romantic movement in the late eighteenth and early nineteenth century (for instance in Wordsworth), and amongst American 'transcendentalists' such as Thoreau and Emerson,[21] as well as in the organic 'bio-dynamic' agriculture of Rudolf Steiner in the 1920s and '30s (Pepper 1996: 125). In the midst of the 1970s counter-culture, Musgrove (1974: 65) observed that 'Nineteenth century Romanticism was strikingly like the contemporary counter-culture in its explicit attack on technology, work, pollution, boundaries, authority, the unauthentic, rationality and the family'. Similarly, philosophies which see in the organisation of nature a 'vital principle' or 'natural spirit' can be traced back to at least as early as the seventeenth century 'Beginning with Henry More's *Anima Mundi* and on into the revival of arcadianism, these ancient ideas were revived to counter the mechanistic science developed in the

Newtonian era' (Worster 1985: 81). It has also been noted that the revival of vitalist philosophies during the 1880s fed into support for nature conservation and protectionist sentiments. Allen (1978: 202) goes so far as to say that the influence of vitalism was 'immense and crucial' in this respect 'even though few of those who then rushed in can have been conscious of owing their inspiration to it specifically'. This dialectical relationship between cultural trends, radical ideas and organised environmentalism in the 1880s lends support to the thesis of counter-cultural waves reviving environmental movements, and can be seen in the contemporary period, as evidenced by the enormous rise in membership of all environmental organisations over the last thirty years on the wave of counter-cultural critique from the late 1960s.

Szerszynski finds two main strands in romantic forms of ecology, the 'expressive' and the 'traditionalist' (1996: 120). Expressivist ecology is characterised by attempts to reconnect individuals with nature and their authentic or pre-social state of being, as in Rousseau, Wordsworth and Thoreau, but it is also apparent in today's ecocentric attempts to experience and explore the ecological self (Fox 1990; Naess 1988, 1989; Griffin 1978; Eckersley 1992; Devall 1990: Ch.2).[22] Traditionalist ecology instead promotes a more collectivist solution which re-embeds people 'in a concrete community and substantive tradition' (Szerszynski 1996: 120), and can be found in Carlyle, Ruskin and William Morris, but is also evident in Murray Bookchin's recent ecoanarchism (1980, 1982). This strand promotes the idea that some forms of social organisation (anarchistic small-scale communities) just are more harmonious with the natural world than modern social organisation, even if the former are not self-conscious attempts to be so. It is evident that modern ecocentrism contains both of these romantic strands to varying degrees, and a few examples will illustrate how closely current radical ecological ideas are to earlier forms.

Mid-nineteenth century American transcendentalists claimed that 'Nature ... enjoyed its own morality which, when understood, could lead the sympathetic and responsive human being to a new spiritual awareness of his own potential, his obligations to others, and his responsibilities to the life-supporting processes of his natural surroundings' (O'Riordan 1981: 3). Thoreau (quoted in Worster 1985: 79) was quite clear that nature was not a lifeless world, the mere background to human life: 'The earth I tread on is not a dead, inert mass, it is a body, has a spirit, is organic, and fluid to the influence of its spirit, and to whatever particle of that spirit is in me'. This means '... that all nature is alive, and that whatever is alive has a claim on man's moral affections' (ibid: 85). From here it is a short step to Naess's (1988: 4-7) ideal of 'biocentric egalitarianism in principle' in which human beings are seen as just one species in the 'web of life', and have no legitimate claim to special rights or to treat other life forms as inferior (animal rights activists today describe the latter position as 'speciesist'). Thoreau (quoted in Worster 1985: 93-4) also felt this equalitarian attitude whilst on his forays into American woodlands, 'I believed that the woods were not tenantless, but choke-full of honest spirits as good as myself any day, - not an empty chamber in which chemistry was left to work alone, but an inhabited house, - and for a few moments I enjoyed fellowship with them'.

A love of nature, and ideas of the equal worth of natural entities, can easily lead to the view that the value of these entities lies in themselves, in their own properties, rather than in the human mind. This is the idea of intrinsic value which exercises deep ecologists today, but it can also be found in English romantic poets like Coleridge and Shelley who sought to expand the boundaries of morality beyond human beings. 'Nature has her proper interest; and he will know what it is, who believes and feels, that every thing has a life of its own', (Coleridge quoted in Thomas 1984: 91).

The notion of value as residing in nature is also evident in Ralph Waldo Emerson's essay on *Nature* (1836), in which he says, 'Such is the constitution of all things ... that the primary forms, as the sky, the mountain, the tree, the animal, give us a delight *in and for themselves*' (quoted in Pepper 1996: 199). Intrinsic value theories are currently part of the attempt by deep ecologists to produce a Green value theory which could be used to give the defence of nature a firmer philosophical basis.

The current ecocentric 'transpersonal ecology' strand (Fox 1990), which advocates the development of the ecological self through attempts to promote the experience of ourselves as part of nature, bound inseparably with it, is also prefigured in Thoreau. He expressed a desire to commune with nature as an antidote to the modern society/nature dualism. 'I to be nature looking into nature with such easy sympathy as the blue-eyed grass looks in the face of the sky' (quoted in Worster 1985, 78). Contemporary ecofeminists have been prominent in pursuing this kind of strategy. The following from Susan Griffin (1978: 40) would not have been out of place in the mid-eighteenth century, 'We know ourselves to be made from this earth. We know this earth is made from our bodies. For we see ourselves, and we are nature. We are nature seeing nature. We are nature with a concept of nature. Nature weeping. Nature speaking to nature of nature'.

It is clear then that romantic-inspired ecocentric ideas have a long history, but what could mark the contemporary period out as in some sense new, might be that these ideas now include some genuinely new extensions and that these have become more widespread amongst the population at large and within established environmental organisations, thus opening the possibility that the romantic side of modern culture could become culturally dominant (as in Eder 1993: Ch.7). If evidence for the latter could be demonstrated, then we may well be moving towards a new epoch. The rest of this chapter will assess whether there is any real evidence for this interpretation at present.

Ecocentrism: The Deep Ecological Ideological Bond

Kuechler and Dalton (1990: 280) have argued that the characterisation of contemporary new social movements as a bloc *is* warranted because peace, feminist and Green movement core members share an 'ideological bond' which unites them, despite their evident differences.

> This ideological bond has two major traits: a humanistic critique of the prevailing system and the dominant culture, in particular a deep concern about the threats to the future of the human race, and a resolve to fight for a better world here and now with little, if any, inclination to escape into some spiritual refuge. Our current social order is perceived as *inhumane* in various ways: as fostering a "survival of the fittest" mentality on the level of individual interaction, as pursuing a course of mindless waste and exploitation with respect to the use of natural resources, and as relying on domination backed by military strength on the level of international relations.

This characterisation seems to ignore some significant precursors. A 'humanistic critique of the prevailing system' has been a recurring theme in the opposition to the development of modern societies, and which Brand describes as a recurring 'modernization critique' (1990: 28). This recurrence may be linked to the long-term economic waves of capitalism (Dicken 1992), thus periods of explicit humanistic cultural critique are not entirely new. Also, the notion that activists show 'little inclination to escape into some spiritual refuge' does not fit some versions of eco-radicalism well at all. In particular, the deep ecology philosophical strand of eco-radicalism (Naess

1973, 1988; Devall 1990; Devall and Sessions 1985; Fox 1984, 1990) together with some variants of ecofeminism (Griffin 1978; Spretnak and Capra 1984; Spretnak 1986, 1993; King 1990) emphasise the importance of developing a Green spirituality, which at the far end of the spectrum moves into new age beliefs about the future development of humanity and its relationship to nature. Rudolf Bahro's (1986: 98) position has moved in this direction. He says for example that 'The accumulation of spiritual forces ... will at a particular point in time which can't be foreseen exceed a threshold size. Such a 'critical mass', once accumulated, then acquires under certain circumstances a transformative influence over the whole society'. Whilst Spretnak and Capra (1986: 50) argue that:

> We feel that deep ecology is spiritual in its very essence. It is a world view that is supported by modern science but is rooted in a perception of reality that goes beyond the scientific framework to a subtle awareness of the oneness of all life, the interdependence of its multiple manifestations, and its cycles of change and transformation. When the concept of the human spirit is understood in this sense, as the mode of consciousness in which the individual feels connected to the cosmos as a whole, the full meaning of deep ecology is indeed spiritual. [23]

Similarly, the perception of the modern social order as inhumane cannot be sustained as a new feature of NSMs. Late nineteenth century utopian socialists like William Morris and Edward Carpenter (among others), clearly shared this perception of modern capitalist industrialism as a system which was dehumanising and destructive of the 'beauty of nature' and human potential, and which pitted 'worker against worker'. Whilst John Ruskin (1905: 159) argued that,

> You must either make a tool of the creature, or a man of him. Men were not intended to work with the accuracy of tools, to be precise and perfect in all their actions. If you will have that precision out of them, and make their fingers measure degrees like cog-wheels and their arms strike curves like compasses, you must unhumanise them.

I think that Kuechler and Dalton's attempt to justify the theory of new social movements in terms of a shared ideological bond is unsatisfactory. However they do provide some insights into the nature of contemporary radical ecology. For them, core members and their beliefs and ideology form the basis of the unity of social movements, rather than any other identifiable aspects such as interaction between individuals or the creation of movement organisations. They believe that ' ... the core members and their shared beliefs - their ideological bond - are the essence of a social movement, [and] that the organizational manifestations are an epiphenomenon. As a consequence, the "newness" of social movements is largely dependent upon the nature of this ideological bond' (Kuechler and Dalton 1990: 282).

This idea of an 'ideological bond' as the fundamental basis of social movements is not in itself a new one, something similar was stated explicitly by Heberle (1951: 24). He argued that 'The constitutive ideas are those ... most essential to the movement' and which '... form the basis of its solidarity', though in fact, he was trying to discern what constitutes the ideological differences between social movements, not the bond which is common to them all. Much of my discussion has been arguing against the latter position, which seems to reduce social movements to beliefs and ideas, in the same way that some resource mobilization theories want to reduce movements to 'issue cleavages' (Zald and McCarthy 1987).

As I have already argued, a better explanatory framework is provided by locating the 'structural focus' (Bagguley 1992) of social movements and their constituent organisations as forms of resistance to dominant social processes in modern societies. There is an institutional continuity of the environmental movement over time, and it is precisely the formation and continued existence of environmental movement organisations which effectively carries this movement and its complex of ideas and beliefs forward over time. This then provides a focus for new generations with similar sensibilities and feelings for nature, even if this legacy is appropriated negatively, leading to generational shifts and the formation of new organisations as part of the movement's development and expansion. However, in relation to the contemporary Greens, I think that the notion of a shared ideological bond does give us a grasp of what it is that holds people together in the absence of formal, enduring ecocentric organisations. I suggest that the ideological bond which ties loose networks of eco-radicals together is precisely an ecocentric orientation to action, which Pepper (1996: 329) describes as,

> ... a 'mode of thought' which regards humans as subject to ecological and systems laws. Essentially it is not human-centred (anthropocentric), but centred on the natural ecosystems, of which humans are reckoned to be just another component. There is a strong sense of respect for nature in its own right (bioethic) as well as for pragmatic reasons. Ecocentrics lack faith in

modern large-scale technology and society, and the technical, bureaucratic, economic and political elites.

This ecocentric orientation provides eco-activists with a shared sense of identity and purpose. As Pepper notes, an ecocentric orientation is a fundamental constitutive feature of what Dobson (1990) describes as the political philosophy of ecologism and we must now look more closely at the main features of this perspective in the current period.

Many researchers have been struck by the ideological diversity within Green thinking. For example, Bennie et al (1995: 219) note that,

> Any student of green politics quickly realises that 'greenness' itself has become a major conflict point in the politics of green semantics. The many shades of green may express themselves openly in different factions of the green movement, vociferously berating each other - often in terms of the other side being not green enough.

The existence of shades of green in relation to radical ecology has often been noticed, but there is a tendency to play up this diversity and consequently to ignore the obvious areas of agreement among the various positions. In particular, at the core of Green thinking, there is an ecocentric orientation, and a concerted attempt to oppose human-centred modes of thought from this position. The ecocentric perspective argues that human societies must be sustainable in relation to their practices as part of, or embedded within a global or planetary nature. Eckersley (1992: 49) argues that 'Ecocentrism is based on an ecologically informed philosophy of *internal relatedness*, according to which all organisms are not simply interrelated with their environment but also *constituted* by those very environmental interrelationships'. This then feeds into an ecocentric criticism of shallow environmentalism as a promethean approach which tries to manage the natural world by providing nature reserves, setting aside areas of wilderness and monitoring environmental damage.

In this vein, the originator of the Gaia Hypothesis, James Lovelock, argues that the idea of a human stewardship of nature is patently unrealistic, since in the long run 'Gaia' - his name for the global system of nature - is in control. Lovelock's (1988: 152) hypothesis states that '... the physical and chemical condition of the surface of the Earth, of the atmosphere, and of the oceans has been and is actively made fit and comfortable by the presence of life itself'. In short, the Earth resembles a self - regulating organism. He declares, '... thank God we are not the stewards of the Earth: this stewards of the Earth business is nonsense' (quoted in Bunyard, P and Goldsmith, E eds) 1988: 166).[24] Though it is often referred to in support of an ecocentric perspective, Lovelock's work has a somewhat ambiguous relationship to radical ecology, as his argument does not necessarily support the view that human activity is destroying the planet. In fact, the Gaia Hypothesis seems to focus our attention on the deleterious effects on human societies. Lovelock seems to swing between radical ecological pessimism and environmentalist optimism. For example the following passage conflicts with eco-radical assumptions about population levels and the kind of technologies which should be supported, and seems to place him in the technocentric camp (O'Riordan 1981).

> The European, American, and Chinese experience suggests that, given wise husbandry, twice the present human population of the world could be supported without uprooting other species, our partners in Gaia, from their natural habitats. It would be a grave mistake, however, to think that this could be achieved without a high degree of technology, intelligently organized and applied (Lovelock 1979: 121).

This is precisely the sort of enlightened self-interest justification for environmentalism which the majority of moderate environmental organisations base their arguments on, and does not necessitate a new philosophy of nature or attempts to wrangle with the problems of intrinsic value theories of natural environments.[25]

For ecocentrics the modern assumption that humans could concentrate on rationally building society with no sense of natural limits is a product of the Enlightenment optimism embedded in the practices of modern science, nicely summed up in Condorcet's (quoted in Lively 1966: 75) comment that '...we have good reasons for believing that nature has set no limits to our hopes'. It is partly because of the ecocentric re-introduction of the Malthusian idea of natural limits that some researchers have deemed radical ecology to be a postmodern phenomenon, part of the wide-ranging attack on scientific certainties and modernisation (Hannigan 1985: Ch.10), though the ecocentric advocacy of the natural grounding of human beings, based on an intuitive grasp of their natural affinity with the rest of nature, sits uneasily with the typical postmodern suspicion of foundations and essences, and the very possibility of unmediated access to reality. Nonetheless, the identification of nature as a reality set against the artificiality of human constructions is a key motivating force for ecocentrics.

Edward Goldsmith's conceptualisation of the society/nature relationship makes a clear distinction between the 'real' world of nature and the 'surrogate' world of human products and consumer goods, and is a good example of the way ecocentrics try to privilege the 'otherness' of nature.[26] Goldsmith (1988: 185) is critical of the way that modern societies and science perceive the natural world as simply the backdrop to human activity, instead he sees nature as the source of all value.

> If the world were a lifeless waste, as is the moon, there could be no industrialization. If it has occurred at all, it is that over the last few thousand million years the primaeval dust has slowly been organized into an increasingly complex organization of matter - the biosphere, or world of living things - or the 'real world' as we might refer to it - which provides the resources entering into this process. Industrialization is something which is happening to the biosphere. *It is the biosphere, in fact - the real world* - that is being industrialized ... In this way, a new organization of matter is building up: the technosphere or world of material goods and technological devices: or the *surrogate world.*

The problem is that the building and expansion of the surrogate world takes place at the expense of the real world, via the extraction of resources and return of waste products from production processes as pollution. Unfortunately, Goldsmith is working with the very same dualism of society/nature which ecocentrics purport to be transcending, and which they identify as wrong thinking. Perhaps this shows just how deeply embedded in the mental structures of modernity radical ecology is (Szerszynski 1996).

In contrast to Goldsmith, the promethean technocentric perspective is summed up by Gellner (1986: 39), who argues that 'Mankind is irreversibly committed to industrial society and therefore based on cumulative science and technology. Only this can sustain present and anticipated population levels. No return to agrarian society is possible, without mass starvation and poverty'. Radical ecologists of course, argue that world population levels need to be controlled and ultimately reduced in order to provide for a decentralisation strategy which would create sustainable communities. In the words of two British Green Party members, 'The explosion of human numbers is the greatest long-term threat to the future of human and non-human inhabitants of the earth. While nuclear arsenals present grave potential dangers, the predominant crisis of overpopulation is with us today' (Irvine and Ponton 1988: 17). Again, this is an issue (like the notion of an ecological crisis) which has been part of Green thinking since the 1970s and continues to exercise concern. There is a clear echo here of Malthus's fears of overpopulation and consequent food scarcity[27] which formed part of the background for the introduction of the new Poor Law in 1834 which '...was not directly inspired by him, but many of its defenders were 'Malthusians' who wanted restraint on family size to be enforced in workhouses...' (Briggs 1984: 338). In the 1970s and '80s the emphasis was on introducing modern methods of contraception to developing countries as a way to slow down population growth. Aware of the increasing sensitivity of the population issue, the British Green Party's (1992: 9) Election Manifesto noted that '...population is not just a Third World issue. People in the rich industrialized countries consume more than 80 per cent of the world's resources', but it is significant that they propose no concrete measures to tackle this apparently pressing problem apart from the statement that 'We must address the issues of reducing our own population and our own consumption levels' (ibid: 4).[28]

The concern with (over) population is an example of the shift in emphasis which lies at the heart of the ecocentric reorientation. Eckersley's (1992: 28) recent work is one of the clearest attempts to explain and develop a thoroughgoing ecocentric orientation. In a section titled 'Ecocentrism Explained' she argues that,

> ... an ecocentric approach regards the question of our proper place in the rest of nature as logically prior to the question of what are the most appropriate social and political arrangements for human communities. That is, the determination of social and political questions must proceed from, or at least be consistent with, an adequate determination of this more fundamental question. ... ecocentric political theorists are distinguished by the emphasis they place on the need for a radical reconception of humanity's place in nature. In particular, ecocentric theorists argue that there is no valid basis to the belief that humans are the pinnacle of evolution and the sole locus of value and meaning in the world. Instead, ecocentric theorists adopt an ethical position that regards *all* of the various and multilayered parts of the biotic community as valuable for their own sake.

I think this is an accurate rendering of a general ecocentric perspective which makes plain the basic challenge to existing anthropocentric or at least humanistic political ideologies such as socialism, marxism, liberalism and conservatism. To the extent that these ideologies develop social and political theories which take the natural world as merely the backdrop to human activity and human conflicts, then they will be deemed unsatisfactory by ecocentric theory. This is because they place no value on nature in-itself, and hence fail to call into question the necessary relationship between human beings and the rest of the natural world. A similar criticism can also be levelled at the environmentalist perspective, in the sense that environmentalist arguments are couched in terms of the value of conservation and preservation *for* human beings, as a form of enlightened *self*-interest. The problem is that this argument is ineffective because if self-interest can be shown to lie elsewhere, then an attitude of care towards the natural world will be sidelined. As Eckersley (1992: 53) says:

> Although the anthropocentric resource conservation and human welfare ecology streams of environmentalism adopt a general ethic of prudence and caution based on an ecologically enlightened self-interest, they differ from an ecocentric perspective in that they see the ecological tragedy as essentially a *human* one. Those belonging to the ecocentric stream, on the other hand, see the tragedy as *both* human and nonhuman. ... Such a general perspective may be seen as seeking "emancipation writ large".[29]

What Eckersley (ibid: 91) means by 'emancipation writ large' is '... the maximization of the freedom of all entities to unfold or develop in their own ways'. She goes on to say that,

> What is new about an ecocentric perspective is that it extends the notion of autonomy (and the interactionist model of internal relations on which it is based) to a broader and more encompassing pattern of layered inter-relationships that extend beyond personal and societal relations to include relations with the rest of the biotic community. This means that the nonhuman world is no longer posited simply as the background or means to the self-determination of individuals or political communities, as is the case in most modern political theorizing. Rather, the different members of the nonhuman community are also appreciated as important in their own terms, as having their own (varying degrees of) relative autonomy and their own modes of being (ibid: 55).

The idea that the extension of the idea of autonomy to other non-human entities is a new feature of ecocentrism, ignores romantic precursors and I do not think that Eckersley's claim to novelty can be upheld. Nevertheless, the most significant feature of political ecology is the insistence on an ecocentric orientation to theory and politics which marks it out from modernist, humanistic, anthropocentric orientations and ideologies. We should not lose sight of this. As Eckersley (1992: 70) herself says,

> Whatever label is ultimately adopted, however, a general ecocentric emancipatory theory must accommodate all human emancipatory struggles within a broader, ecological framework. That is, it must be able to provide the context for establishing the outer ecological limits within which the different needs of human emancipatory movements can be addressed and harmonized in order to ensure that the interests of the nonhuman world are not continually sacrificed in the name of human emancipation.

In this way an ecocentric orientation provides fertile ground for the development of a distinctive political ideology which effectively cuts loose from modern ideologies and tries to carve out a new space in opposition to them. Ecocentric ideologies perceive that they pose a real challenge to existing ideologies and an examination of the nature of this challenge to political ideologies follows.

Ecocentrism in the Green Party

As I noted earlier, similar versions of what we now describe as Green or ecological ideas and arguments can also be found in earlier periods. Gould's historical reconstruction of Green politics in late nineteenth century Britain sees that in this period Green politics was about 'values and industrialisation'. That is, Greens attempted to 'reassert traditional values' against commercialism, and to expose the dark side of continuing industrialisation in order to provoke opposition to it. This recognition shows that reflection on the consequences (side effects) of industrial processes is evident even in the period Beck (1992) labels simple modernity. Gould (1988: ix) argues that 'Those traditional values may be transposed from a work on the sociology of current environmental politics, significantly without violation', and that Greens 'challenge conventional world-views and propose the creation of a different society' (ibid., vii).

However there is one way in which contemporary radical ecological ideas differ from some earlier ones. Because ecocentrism defines itself in opposition to anthropocentric social and political theories, progressive humanistic social movements find it difficult to reach an accommodation with it. Whereas radical concerns for nature protection in the late-nineteenth century were tied to anarchist and socialist movements, and hence placed importance on the way contact with nature and its preservation were beneficial for humans, in contemporary radical ecology, there is a serious attempt to devise a political theory which effectively breaks with this humanism. Although some links can be uncovered between radical ecology and the new left for example (Fogt 1989; Boggs 1986), a thoroughgoing ecocentrism must prioritise the protection of natural diversity and integrity of nature over social class-based demands. Martell (1994) argues that although radical ecology adds something new to the political analysis of modern societies, in its own terms it is incapable of prescribing necessary social arrangements. This goes back to a point I made earlier, that historically, recourse to nature has been the focus for both left and right-wing political programmes. It is possible to try to generate an ecocentric orientation to politics, but much more difficult to see what a form of social organisation based on ecocentric principles would look like. Martell (1994: 160) is right to say that,

> Traditional political theories are challenged by ecology. Ecology requires that they are adapted to take into account natural limits and non-humans. ... However, ecology cannot provide a new paradigm through which a political theory can be constructed on green grounds. Dealing with environmental issues involves drawing on old conservative, liberal, socialist and feminist analyses.

This may of course be no bad thing, but it does mean that the idea of the birth of a new political ideology of ecologism becomes hard to sustain.

One attempt to argue the case for an ideology of ecologism is in Dobson (1990), whose study has become a key reference point for researchers in this field. For Dobson, a Green political ideology or ecologism, is a genuinely new ideology which could not have existed in previous historical periods. In part, this is because the kinds of evidence which radical ecologists draw on have only become available as recently as the 1970s. What he means by this is that '... the gloomy future predicted for us [by ecologists] would have no persuasive purchase if damage to ecosystems had not reached levels that can sensibly be argued to be globally disruptive' (1990, 33). Scientific research into global warming for instance, whether or not this phenomenon actually is causally linked to industrial activities, has helped to legitimise the arguments of radical ecologists and has helped to create a supportive cultural climate for the development of an ecological ideology which, without such kinds of support, would have been literally unintelligible.

It has often been said that the origins of contemporary radical ecology (and hence of ecologism) can be found in Rachel Carson's influential book, *Silent Spring* in 1962, which drew attention to the ecological dangers of the widespread use of modern chemical pesticides. But there were other factors such as nuclear weapons testing, concerns about the long-term consequences of rising population levels (particularly in developing countries) and worries over the depletion of natural resources which also fed into the creation of Green parties and new movement organisations and groups (Atkinson 1991: 15).[30] Dobson (1990: 35) argues however, that it is only in the 1970s that a new ideology becomes visible so that '... in 1962, ecologism (and therefore the possibility of being Green) did not exist, and that Rachel Carson's book and the period in which it was written are best viewed as part of the preconditions for ecologism'. Dobson suggests that ecologism really comes into being with the publication of the 'limits to growth' thesis of Meadows et al in 1972, in which the authors' computer modelling and extrapolation of current trends of resource use pointed to a societal collapse in the 21st century. This is because the notion of absolute natural limits to ever expanding economic growth is the fundamental principle which lies at the heart of the new ecocentric perspective and which is an 'unsurmountable fact of life' (Dobson 1990: 80). It was the *Limits* report for the Club of Rome which formed the material for Edward Goldsmith's *Ecologist* journal's *Blueprint for Survival* (1972) which was adopted as the British Green Party's manifesto.[31]

The point of trying to locate the moment at which ecological ideas begin to crystallise into a new ideological position is to demonstrate that the radical ecology movement today is not simply a modern version of old ideas, but does introduce something genuinely new into social and political theorising. As Dobson (1990: 35) puts it,

The final point of historicizing the ideology is that it enables us to emphasize the novelty of its analysis. It has been remarked that, despite its claims to the contrary, the Green movement's perspective is merely a reworking of old themes ... This interpretation fails to take full account of the historically specific nature of ecologism. For it is precisely the ideology's point that, while the terms of its analysis are not new in themselves, the fact of them being posited here and now gives those terms a novel resonance.

For example, in the context of globalising economic processes, scientific research into global ecological problems, and the failure of established political movements to incorporate the ecological problematic, nature politics takes a radical turn away from simple environmentalism which is unable to shake off its localised ameliorist approach to the destruction of nature. Although Dobson is right to point out that Green ideas have emerged in a different social context from earlier periods, this does not mean that ecologism forms a coherent political ideology with an identifiable social constituency of support. Indeed, Greens often argue that the issues that concern them are of concern to everyone, and that it is precisely this universalist character which makes the Green position so distinctive.

It is clear that there is a concerted effort across several academic disciplines to develop a coherent and comprehensive ecocentric perspective as the basis for progressive politics, and the extent of this very attempt is a new feature in the present period. However, it must be re-iterated that this radical side of nature politics has not made significant inroads into the mass environmental movement which remains reformist in intention. There is no evidence that radical ecological proposals for the transformation of society have been adopted by environmental organisations. In the next section I want to look at the British Green Party, which should be the organisational base for building support for radical ecology.

The Green Party

Spretnak and Capra's influential *'Green Politics'* (1984), saw the emergence of Green political parties as part of a new vision of reality which they argued was becoming widespread in Western industrialised societies. They characterised this new movement in the following way:

> The emergence of Green politics in many countries is ... an ecological, holistic, and feminist movement that transcends the old political framework of left versus right. It emphasizes the interconnectedness and inter-dependence of all phenomena, as well as the embeddedness of individuals and societies in the cyclical processes of nature. ... Green politics rejects all forms of exploitation -

of nature, individuals, social groups, and countries. It is committed to non-violence at all levels. ... Green politics, in short, is the political manifestation of the cultural shift to the new paradigm (Spretnak and Capra 1984: xvi-vii).

This new paradigm was inspired by an ecological perception of the unsustainable nature of the practices of modern industrialised societies which were destroying natural systems, and therefore the basis of all life on Earth. This section will show however, that the history of the British Green Party gives little support to the idea that a widespread cultural shift to a 'new paradigm' is underway.

The first Green political party was the Values Party in New Zealand in 1972, formed from local citizens groups. However, the British Green Party was the first European Green political party. It began life as 'People' in 1973, in the aftermath of *The Ecologist* journal's publication of the *'Blueprint for Survival'* (1972), which the new party adopted as its manifesto in the 1974 General Elections.[32] The *'Blueprint'* was a radical document which proposed to make localities self-sufficient and to adopt a policy of de-industrialisation in order to stave off global ecological catastrophe. It was therefore clear from the start, that the Green Party would attract ecological radicals. It is probably fair to say that in 1972 the gap between the analysis of eco-radicals and that of existing environmentalist groups could hardly have been greater. The mass of environmental activists did not (and by and large, still do not) support the Green Party, which appeared to be something other than an environmental organisation.

The Green Party's programme, centred around the ideological position of ecocentrism, tried to show that this could embrace many political issues, so that,

> The theory that green parties and the green movement are somehow about 'single issues' and thus have no separate ideological dimension has never had any currency. Any serious observer of the green movement in its various manifestations quickly grasped that there was something more at stake than simple singular environmental issues. This manifested itself not only in the emergence of self-proclaimed ideologues of the new 'green politics' but also in comprehensive political programmes of green parties which addressed virtually every issue there could be - not just 'environmental' ones (Bennie et al 1995: 217).

A more appropriate name change occurred in 1975, when 'Ecology Party' was adopted. Although Ernst Haeckel is commonly associated with the first scientific use of the term 'oecology' in the 1870s, to refer to the systematic study (*logos*) of the home or household (*oikos*), it was not until the 1960s that 'ecology' came to be associated with the activities of nature conservation and preservationism which had previously been brought under the general term 'environmentalism' (Williams 1987: 110-11). In this sense the changing use of the term 'ecology' was one way in which those who perceived themselves to be radicals attempted to demarcate themselves from environmentalists. Ecological concern acted as a device for demarcation between old and new with the consequent implication that this also indicated a more radical politics of nature. Something of a similar process had taken place after the Second World War, when use of the term 'conservation' had gradually been overtaken by 'environmentalism' (Williams ibid; Hays 1987: 2). It would appear that changes of this kind reflect generational shifts within the broadly based environmental movement, and mark more or less distinct 'phases' of nature concern through which new issues are brought within the remit of the movement as a whole. A final change occurred in 1985, when, partly to fall in line with other European Greens, the Ecology Party became the 'Green Party'.[33] With the more readily identifiable name of the Ecology Party, individual membership rose from 500 in 1978 to over 5000 by 1980, then as the 'Green Party', membership continued to rise, reaching a peak of 18,523 in 1990 before falling away sharply to 10,300 in 1991, and 5,500 in 1993.[34]

The electoral history of the British Greens has been a chequered one, and the party has always performed better at the local rather than the national level. In 1993 the party had 23 district councillors, one county councillor and over 100 councillors at parish level (Young 1993, 38). Its best result at local level was gaining 8 per cent of the poll in 1990. Success at this level probably reflects the Greens' ability to capitalise on concerns surrounding development planning, which has a more direct impact on localities compared with national and international politics. It may also be a result of the greater interest of party members in 'grassroots' issues, and hence more effective campaigning.

Although the Green Party fielded progressively more candidates in national elections from 1974 to 1992, in the 1997 General Election the party seriously considered not contesting the election at all before eventually deciding to field 71 candidates in selected seats.[35] Some decentralists questioned whether the party's finances should be 'wasted' when it was widely perceived that they could not succeed electorally. This may seem strange for an electorally concerned party, but decentralist Greens have always argued that the party exists in order to 'bear witness' and to maintain a presence for Deep Green ideas, rather than to try to win elections. This does mean however, that the party becomes another movement organisation and has to compete with, say, Earth First! or even Greenpeace for support, and it is not clear why a political party should be the best form of organisation for radical ecology ideas. Earth First!s loose networks could be seen as more consistent with Green ideology.

Table 5.2   Summary of Green Party performance in British General Election 1992

No. Seats contested	Total votes	% vote per seat	Avg. votes	Best result (%)
257*	169, 835	1.3	660	3.8% (1420 votes, Islington North)

* includes 4 Welsh constituencies (Monmouth, Newport East, Torfaen and Ceredigion and North Pembroke) in which the Green Party and Plaid Cymru fielded one joint candidate. Results do not include these constituencies.

Source: calculated from General Election results

In common with Green parties across Europe, the British Greens perceive they have a better chance of success in elections for the European Parliament, rather than in national elections. It was the European Election of 1989 which seemed to have marked a turning point.[36] In it, the party fought all 79 seats, gaining 14.93 per cent of the vote (2,292,696 votes in total) and saved all their deposits. Their highest share of the constituency vote was 24.5 per cent.[37] However, due to the British 'first-past-the-post' electoral rules, no Green Party MEP's were elected. Under a system of proportional representation the party could have expected to gain 12 out of the 79 British seats. Nevertheless, membership expanded rapidly in the wake of this result, the government published its 1989 White Paper on the environment, and the main political parties developed their own 'ecological' policies (Young 1993, 37-8). The Green Party was apparently unable to deal with their overnight

Table 5.3 Green Party performance in national elections 1974-92

Year	Seats Fought	Average % of Poll	Highest % Vote
1974	5	1.8	3.9
1974	4	0.7	0.8
1979	53	1.5	2.8
1983	108	1.0	2.9
1987	133	1.4	3.6
1992	257	1.3	3.8

Source: Adapted from Young 1991, 37. 1992 figures calculated from Election results.

success though, and membership fell rapidly after 1990. At the following General Election in 1992, support for the Greens was back to previous levels at around 1.3 per cent. In terms of votes per constituency, the 1992 performance was slightly down on 1987 (660 votes compared with 670 in '87), but more than 10 per cent down on the position in 1979 (755 votes) (Porritt and Winner 1988, 76-7). The 1992 result suggests that if candidates had been fielded in every constituency, the party would have polled around half a million votes. Given that membership of the voluntary environmental movement stands at approximately 4.5 million, even allowing for the possibility of overlapping memberships, the Green Party does not seem to attract the regular support of environmentalists in national elections (Rüdig and Lowe 1986).[38] This may be because the party is perceived as proposing radical changes which environmentalists do not perceive to be either necessary or feasible.

It appears that a turning point for the Green Party was in the factional disputes following the 1989 European Election which eventually effectively split the party. This split centred around an electoralist group, Green 2000, who wanted to bring the party's organisation and internal decision-making processes closer to that of conventional parties, and a decentralist or anarchist group, arguing that an exclusive concentration on electoral success directed efforts away from grassroots campaigning and extra-parliamentary action.[39] The Wolverhampton Conference in 1991 saw the success of a motion on organisational change proposed by the Green 2000 group, but later wrangling between the 11 member Executive, dominated by electoralists, and the 28 member Regional Council, dominated by decentralists determined to stop the process of change, eventually led to the resignation of six Executive members, including the well-known Sara Parkin. Some of the consequent media coverage conveyed the idea that this marked the end of the Green Party, but though reduced in numbers, the Party fielded 71 candidates in selected seats in the 1997 general election.

Bennie et al's (1995) study of the party, carried out after the acrimonious split identifies four major dimensions of Green ideology within the British Green Party. These are:

1. Left-anarchism, which argues for social justice, party decentralisation and non-violent direct actions. Bennie et al. argue that there is no statist, centralist, reformist eco - socialist group within the British Greens (unlike in Die Grünen in Germany and Agalev and Ecolo in Belgium).

2. Deep Ecology or 'biocentrism', which concentrates on individual responsibility, and comes close to American 'New Age' thinking with its emphasis on personal lifestyle changes.

3. Electoralists, who continue to fight for a more realistic strategy and organisational structure and a single party leader, which they think would enable more media attention and coverage and hence further the growth of the party.

4. Finally, they noted a group who were in favour of electoral pacts against the Conservative Party, and are therefore more prepared to compromise and negotiate with non - Greens in comparison to left-anarchists and deep ecologists.

This study suggests that in comparison with environmental organisations, the British Green Party seems to attract a higher proportion of ecocentrics, who share a belief in the value of nature in-itself. Some 95 percent agreed with the statement that 'Plants, animals, streams and mountains, the earth as a whole, have intrinsic value independent of their appreciation by humans' (Ibid. 223). More research of this kind into the attitudes of members of environmental organisations would begin to show us how far these sentiments have spread within the wider movement.

The main problem that faces electoralists in the Green Party is that many decentralist and deep Greens are opposed to any involvement in the institutional structures of existing formal grey politics. Decentralists favour grassroots campaigning and consciousness-raising, fearing that the Green Party will be assimilated into formal politics and lose its radical edge if it becomes more focused on electoral competition. In this sense, they see the party as a means with which to promote Green values and ideas, not as a serious electoral competitor. So although the Green Party does seem to be home to many decentralist ecocentrics, its internal structures militate against conventional measures of success in electoral competition. Complaints that the party fails in national elections miss the point somewhat, because many party members do not see this as part of its role. It is also clear that the links between the Green Party and reform environmental organisations hardly exist, with no formal support for the party in elections, and the relatively small number of votes for the Greens in national elections shows that there is no simple commonality of interest between Greens and the mass environmental movement.

There are a number of reasons why the British Green Party has not been successful in electoral terms, especially at national level. Firstly, the electoral system makes it extremely difficult for 'third' parties to push through. Secondly, after the Greens' success in the European Election in 1989, other mainstream parties successfully portrayed themselves as having a 'Green' agenda of their own, thus competing directly with the Green Party for votes (Young 1993). Thirdly, potential Green supporters who had no taste for becoming involved in the existing channels of interest mediation, which reformist environmental groups offered, may have been drawn to organisations such as Greenpeace which they perceived as being more radical, rather than the Green Party. This may help to explain the low levels of Green Party membership, but does not account for the lack of environmentalist support for the party. Even those who support organisations which they perceive to engage in radical direct actions (like Greenpeace) might also see the symbolic benefit of a large Green vote. Finally, Young (1993: 39-40) notes that the party's 'radical image' itself, internal factional disputes and the lack of a clear leadership probably account for its inability to hold on to new members. This is a strange comment. If potential 'Greens' were joining direct action groups because of their radical image, then it is unclear to me why they would see the party's radical image as a deterrent to involvement. Nonetheless, given the mass membership of environmental organisations it is still surprising that the Green Party has consistently failed to do better in elections. If the Party *was* the 'political wing' of the wider environmental movement we would expect the two to be mutually supportive and to forge closer links. There are a number of reasons why this has not happened.

Firstly, many environmental organisations are (at least in part) registered charities which gives them financial advantages and tax concessions. Charitable status also precludes any formal political involvement, hence formal support for the Green Party would threaten this position. Nonetheless this does not account for the lack of electoral support for the Green Party from individuals. Secondly, most environmental organisations pride themselves on their independence from political parties, which they see as necessary for attracting new members and in order to be able to speak out on any issues of concern without being tied to a specific policy programme. Thirdly, we have to question seriously whether environmentalists support the kinds of radical policies of the Green Party. In his address to the 1989 Green Party conference, Jonathon Porritt (then Director of Friends of the Earth) warned that '... the Green movement, including Friends of the Earth, would never specifically endorse the Green Party' (quoted in Yearley 1991, 96). More research is clearly needed in the area of connections between environmental organisations and the Green Party, but I would suggest that one of the main reasons for the small numbers of Green Party members in relation to that of many environmental organisations, and the poor performance of the Greens in elections is that a radical ecology perspective is not widespread in the wider environmental movement. This would provide an explanation for North's observation that 'I have hardly ever met any serious informed environmentalists who are members of the Green Party. I don't mean that there are no environmentalists in the Green Party, or that there are no Green Party members who take the environment seriously. But if I go through the list of *professionals* involved with the environment, they are just not members of the Green Party' (cited in Porritt and Winner 1988, 18).[40]

Environmental activists are reformists, working within the institutional framework of modern industrial societies in order to regulate and reform it. They do not promote ecocentric ideas for the de-industrialisation of society or for the anarchistic decentralisation of social organisation. Rather than being mutually supportive, radical ecology and environmentalism are in a state of constant tension, with environmentalists proposing practical measures for nature conservation, whilst radicals promote significant social change. This is particularly evident in current criticisms of environmentalism by radical ecologists, and shows why environmentalists do not routinely support the Green Party. Rüdig et al's (1986) research into Green Party membership found that a majority of members had had no previous involvement in environmental organisations, whilst McCormick (1991, 123) argues that,

> Because Green politics is much more than environmental politics, it does not follow that there should be much overlap between the Greens and the environmental lobby. Nor indeed is there. There is much evidence that many environmentalists have shunned the Greens, and certainly there have been few formal or informal links between the party and the environmental lobby.

More research into the levels of support for deep ecological positions and Green Party policy proposals within the membership of environmental organisations would enable us to draw firmer conclusions but on the basis of the present evidence we must conclude that there has been no mass 'Green' radicalisation of the environmental movement. Given this assessment, there is no basis for the conclusions reached by disjunctive new social movement theories of the 'transition to a new age' and so on in the development of the environmental movement. These radical conclusions are posited because NSM theories concentrate on the minority who propound radical ecology ideas, taking them as constitutive of the mass environmental movement, but this is an exaggeration which is poorly supported by empirical studies. In this way we can see that, to the extent that radical ecology movements are seen as ideal-typical 'new social movements', then NSM theories provide inconclusive support for theories of post-industrialism.

Development or Disjuncture?

In this chapter I have been arguing that the most significant new aspects of contemporary radical ecology are the attempts to develop an ecocentric ideology and a political programme based on this. In the wider context of nature politics which also includes long-standing reformist forms of environmentalism, this ideology remains a cultural undercurrent rather than part of the mainstream. For radical ecology activists, the importance of an ecocentric 'ideological bond' is heightened by their suspicion of formal organisation fearing establishment as hierarchical bureaucracies. Given that there is little evidence for the existence of widespread support for ecocentrism within established environmental organisations, and that the location of ecocentric beliefs seems to be restricted to the Green Party and some loose networks such as Earth First!, we have to conclude at this stage that it is unclear whether this particular perspective has a long term future.

I find it difficult to agree with Kuechler and Dalton (1990: 285) that,

> ... the new movements can rely on a stable and ever-growing support base. Consequently, the movements' goals are likely to stay on the political agenda for some time to come. Even if the movements as such will lose momentum, we expect that they will have a longer-lasting impact: key goals will be absorbed by the larger segment of sympathizers who will provide permanent stimulus for society to change in the direction of the new movements' visions. In this sense, the recent emergence of the new movements could mark the beginning of a new age.

I also find it hard to concur with Sklair (1994: 213) when he says that '... the traditional 'back to nature' and conservation movements that previously spoke for and nurtured the environment are being transformed as a consequence of the relentless insertion of the whole world into the global capitalist system'. These interpretations of new movements marking the start of a new age, and transforming established environmental organisations in their wake find little support in this study. The available evidence shows that the mass support for nature politics throughout the twentieth century, including the expansionary 1970s phase to the present, has fed into increased membership for all environmental organisations, most of which do not show high levels of support for the ecocentric ideological bond, and where support for this bond is evident, for example within the Green Party and Earth First!, the number of activists (and supporters) is relatively small. The apparently radical direct action organisations of the 1970s such as Friends of the Earth and Greenpeace do not show support for this ideological bond either, and over time both organisations have undergone a change in the direction of professionalism and establishment rather than striving to remain part of the non-established radical ecologists. This is clearly reflected in the antagonisms between these groups and EF! as well as the refusal of Greenpeace and Friends of the Earth overtly to support the Green Party (in common with all other reformist environmental organisations).

Contemporary radical ecology has benefited from the counter-cultural wave which spread across most Western societies from the 1960s, and which promoted a return to nature. Although this wave has occurred in a different context to previous ones, namely where a growing awareness of global nature and problems which occur at this level, this does not mean that radical ecology has become the most significant orientation. The concerns for nature which the counter-culture helped to propound have been mediated through pre-existing environmental organisations all of which are reformist in orientation. In chapter 7, an alternative framework for understanding environmentalism and radical ecology will be formulated to demonstrate its efficacy in explaining the state of contemporary nature politics and to throw some light on what we can reasonably expect from it in the future. Although this is not intended to be the word on the subject, I think that it has more explanatory potential than those I outlined earlier, and opens up interesting areas for further research.

Notes

1 I will discuss the Green Party later as it is clearly a special case in the organisation of environmentalism, with little overt relationship to other environmental groups.

2 McCormick (1991: 4) estimates that there are '... around 150 organizations which can be described as national, regional or local environmental interest groups ...'. Even this is in all likelihood an underestimate, as many 'groups' are relatively invisible and are really informal networks of people (Melucci 1989).

3 This claim seems to ignore trades unionism, which has almost double the membership of environmentalism, and takes no account of the possibility of overlapping membership of environmental organisations. It also combines both environmental and radical ecology organisations as well as many organisations which have only a tenuous link to nature politics. For example, Lowe and Goyder's much used work includes the Pedestrians' Association and Camping Club as part of the movement (1983: 81).

4 Porritt and Winner (1988: 182) admit that, 'As it happens, the stereotype of a typical environmental activist as a university educated, middle class professional is pretty close to the truth'. If this is the case, then it is of course no longer a stereotype.

5 Most notably between dock workers and environmental campaigners to prevent rainforest timber being brought into the country.

6 The Council for the Preservation of Rural England was founded in 1926 to oversee increasing urban developments, in particular its emergence was stimulated by the extensive house-building between the wars.

7 As mentioned earlier, it is also worth remembering that *local groups* had been expanding in numbers and membership since the late 1950's. McCormick (1991: 33)

points out for example that, '... the number of local amenity societies increased sixfold between 1958 and 1975. By 1977 they had a total membership of 300,000'.

8   Klaus Eder (1993: 118) has recently argued that,

'The answer to the question of whether there is one new social movement representing *the* new social movement which is replacing the old labour movement as a historical actor, has been left open by Touraine. A good candidate for this has been the environmentalist (or ecological) movement ... Therefore, instead of continuing to talk of 'new' social movements, the time has come to give these new social movements a name. Any term from environmentalism, ecological movement, life politics movement might serve as a possible candidate for name giving. They all denote the same problem: the nature-society relationship, or 'the question of nature".

It is exactly this interpretation of new social movements, which collapses quite different movements together, that I am arguing against in this study.

9   An estimate of 23% of groups reliant on government was made in 1983 by Lowe and Goyder (42).

10   Dwyer and Hodge (1996: 211) point out that older organisations like the National Trust and the RSPB are of course, major landowners, unlike FoE and Greenpeace, and that this leads them to become involved in negotiations and compromises, rather than pursuing issues based on strict principles. They are therefore likely to appear more moderate in relation to the issues they campaign for, and the ways in which they campaign.

11   Lowe and Goyder (1983: 163-5) note that the International Office for the Protection of Nature (1928) and the Advisory Commission for the International Protection of Nature (1923) failed precisely because no international body existed which they could lobby, whereas the International Council for Bird Preservation (1922) became established due to the fact that it acted as a co-ordinating body for national organisations to lobby national governments. In this respect, it was not really pursuing international issues. (Ripley 1973).

12   Adam (1996: 88, quoting Albrow 1990: 9) points out the centrality of technological development in the globalisation process, particularly as this relates to global communication and transport networks in order to demonstrate how 'global time' is '...fundamental to an understanding of globalisation as 'all those processes by which the people of the world are incorporated into a single world society'.

13   The EEB started out with 39 constituent organisations in 1974, including the Civic Trust, FoE, CPRE, Conservation Society amongst the British members. The rise in membership shows the increasing perceptions of the importance of an international presence among national environmentalist groups.

14   The possibility of the symbolism of nature leading to support for the far right is well-demonstrated by the proponents of organic farming between the two World Wars, when leading British figures in the organic farming movement such as Rolf Gardiner, Lord Lymington and Edmund Blunden expressed Nazi sympathies (Conford 1988: 1-19).

15   The conservatism of appeals to 'nature' is summed up in the following from one of the founders of Greenpeace, when interviewed before setting sail to disrupt nuclear

testing, 'Our goal is a very simple, clear and direct one - to bring about a confrontation between the people of death and the people of life. We do not consider ourselves to be radicals. We are conservatives, who insist upon conserving the environment for our children and future generations of man' (Metcalfe quoted in Hunter 1979: 12).

16 Thompson's reference to *'the alternative'* here, is Bahro's *The Alternative in Eastern Europe* (1978), which earned him a jail sentence, from which he was released after two years. He then moved to West Germany (sic), where he joined the Green Party.

17 Eco - socialist works include those by A. Gorz (1980, 1985), F.O. Wolf (1986), B.F.Frankel (1987), M.Ryle (1988) and D.Pepper (1992). Although the early socialist responses to Green political theory and analysis tended to be negative, some common ground is now evident, as in Eckersley (1992) and Martell (1994).

18 Perhaps the widespread perception of an ecological crisis is different from catastrophist writing in the 1970's in the sense that its use has spread to many areas of debate as well as to many social scientists, who now seem to use the term as if its meaning was self-evident. For example, as I noted earlier, Eder (1993) uses the ecological crisis as part of his explanation for the rise of a new nature politics, whilst ecological crisis forms the backdrop to theories of the creation of high consequence socially produced risks, in Beck (1992, 1994) and Giddens' (1991, 1994) recent theorising.

19 Eckersley's attempt to show that Habermas's critical theory remains rooted in the human-centred assumption that 'the emancipation of human relations need not require or depend upon the emancipation of nature' (1990: 768), makes clear the efforts of radical ecologists to produce a 'post-marxist' discourse (Boggs 1986a).

20 For a discussion of this issue in relation to the USA see Schmitt 1969.

21 Pepper argues that all three tenets were part of Ernst Haeckel's own ecocentrism (1996: 185).

22 Sociologists justifiably question this idea of a pre-social state of an original human relationship to nature, arguing that 'man is inconceivable outside social relations or severed from biological nature' (Kilminster 1991: 88; see also Moscovici 1976). The romantics' recourse to natural man as a critique of their perception of modernity's attempt to constitute man beyond nature, reproduces the very modern dualism they claim to abhor.

23 Dobson (1990: 70) argues that '... the differences between the philosophy of deep ecology and its political manifestation are symptomatic of a failure of the philosophy to make itself practical'. He also notes that '...the West German Green Party (sic) ... is not really Green at all ..', and that '... the less visible but more fundamental manifestations of the Green movement are greener than the West German Green Party(sic) ...' (ibid: 5). What he seems to be meaning here is that Green is more of an attitude or belief system, closer to my own interpretation of what constitutes the unity of ecocentrics.

24 Although many radical ecologists often refer to Lovelock's work and the Gaia Hypothesis in order to show a) the relative insignificance of the human species in relation to the Earth as a whole, living system and/or b) support for the fundamental deep ecological concept of the delicately balanced interrelatedness of all life; in fact, Lovelock has often been critical of radical ecologists for interpreting his work in this way. His more recent idea of the need for 'geophysiology', as the 'medical' science of 'planetary health' (1991: xvii) is probably closer to the approach of modernist

environmentalism than the prescriptions of radical ecologists and seems to contradict his own earlier dismissal of human 'stewardship' of nature. Whether or not this is the case, it is clear that Lovelock and Margulis (his partner in developing the hypothesis) expended a lot of energy in the late 1960's and early 1970's trying to find conventional 'scientific' outlets for publishing the Gaia Hypothesis (L.E.Joseph 1990).

25 The idea of a 'living Earth' also has a long history which can be traced back to at least the Renaissance period and vitalist philosophies, which perceived that 'The Earth was another living being among humans' (Pepper 1996: 130). It should be noted however that Lovelock intended his thesis to be the basis for a scientific research programme.

26 Goldsmith founded *The Ecologist* journal in 1969 and continues to edit it. He was one of the authors of the *Blueprint for Survival* (1972).

27 Malthus's, *Essay on the Principle of Population* was published in 1798.

28 The issue of global population levels has been a concern of ecological politics since the catastrophist writers of the late 1960s and early '70s (Borgstrom 1969, Ehrlich 1972 are typical examples of this phase).

29 Eckersley (1992: 42) identifies 4 major streams of reformist environmentalism. These are:

1. Resource conservation - this approach is 'tied to the production process and based on husbanding of 'resources.' 'Resource conservationists therefore sees nature as objects, things or raw materials to be used for the benefit of human beings'. Friends of the Earth would fit this description with its concentration on promoting the wise use of natural resources.

2. Human welfare ecology - argues in favour of the creation and maintenance of a 'safe, clean, human environment'. This leads human welfare ecologists to argue (for example) for the creation of nature reserves, open spaces in cities and for public access to areas of 'wild' nature as part of the benefits for human beings. This approach is therefore anthropocentric (or at least 'humanist') rather than ecocentric.

3. Preservationism- As the name suggests, this approach argues for the preservation of wild nature in its original (natural) state, free from human interference. This has been historically more prevalent in the USA where large tracts of wilderness have been the focus for preservationist activity. Eckersley suggests that preservationism, suitably radicalised, could lead into a thoroughgoing ecocentric position by encouraging a sense of awe and wonder at the vastness of wild nature.

4. Animal liberation - Although it steps 'unambiguously over what might be called the 'great anthropocentric divide', animal liberation is too closely tied to an individualistic utilitarian philosophical position (Singer 1975; Regan 1983), and as such fails to become fully ecocentric.

This is a fairly comprehensive typology of the main varieties of reformist nature politics, though I do not agree that animal rights arguments are so far removed from ecologism, particularly the individualistic arguments in favour of developing an ecological self. Nevertheless she is right to note that the first three approaches have more in common with each other than with the radical ecology perspective.

30 Influential works in this period include Leopold 1949; Bookchin (1962); White (1967); Borgstrom (1965), (1969); Ehrlich,P and Ehrlich,A (1970); Commoner (1966), (1972); Marcuse (1964). Though all of these can be said to have been influential in raising issues and concerns relevant to the development of radical ecology, the period up to the 1970 is seen by Dobson (1990) as laying the pre-conditions for the 'new' perspective rather than outlining it.

31 At this time the Green Party went by the name of 'People'.

32 There were two General Elections in this year. Only five candidates were fielded in February and four in October.

33 Porritt notes that Conference motions to change the name to Green Party in 1983 and '84 had failed, and that part of the reason for eventually adopting the new name was to 'put all the other major parties on the run' (Jones cited In Porritt 1988: 61) by showing that Green policies went far beyond what the other parties could consider, though the success of the *Die Grünen*, in the 1983 election probably had just as much influence on the change of name.

34 Figures are collated from S. Young 1993, 37; J.McCormick 1991, 121 - 22, and Frankland 1990, 7-28.

35 From 'Greens will brave disaster at the polls', In *The Guardian* newspaper, September 21st 1996, 6. As one Conference speaker protested, 'This whole argument is about resources. We can spend it all at General Elections, and charge in like the Light Brigade and get blasted.' However, others thought that a refusal to stand in the General Election would damage support for the Greens in local elections.

36 Though as Frankland points out, in the by-election in Vauxhall on June 15th 1989, the party gained 6.1 per cent and saved its first ever deposit (1990, 15). Given the 1992 results, this probably says more about the vagaries of by-elections than of the party's future electoral prospects.

37 It must be noted here though, that in Britain, European elections are perceived as 'secondary' to national elections with a subsequently lower turn-out of voters. In 1989 only around one-third of the electorate voted. McCormick argues that Green voters were probably more committed to vote than supporters of other parties, but also notes that there was an increasing protest element against Margaret Thatcher's leadership which fed into support for the Greens at this particular time (1991, 122 - 123). Whatever the reasons, this spectacular success has not been repeated.

38 Rüdig and Lowe (1986) argue that the British Green Party has consistently failed to attract the support of other 'new social movement' activists and supporters (such as C.N.D. for example).

39 This basic division is a characteristic feature of all Green parties and can be traced back to the Greens' intention to break new ground in terms of organisational structures, such as the annual rotation of leaders, direct democracy at the party conference etc. In the (then) West German *Die Grünen*, this division is between 'realos' and 'fundis' (Hulsberg 1988), but the source of the disagreement is much the same. It is also of course, related to the ideology of ecologism and its preference for decentralisation and the dispersal of power.

40 Richard North was environment correspondent for *The Independent* newspaper.

6 Industrialisation and Nature Politics

Introduction

One of the major claims put forward by radical ecologists is that the advance of 'industrial civilisation' is the root cause of environmental destruction which has led us to an 'ecological crisis' of global proportions. As the editors of *The Ecologist* (Goldsmith et al 1972: 15) see it, 'The principal defect of the industrial way of life with its ethos of expansion is that it is not sustainable ... we can be certain ... that sooner or later it will end'. The consequences of industrialisation are nicely brought out in a Greenpeace campaigning leaflet which tells us that, 'Planet Earth is 4,600 million years old'. It continues:

> If we condense this inconceivable time-span into an understandable concept, we can liken Earth to a person of 46 years of age ... Modern man has been around for 4 hours. During the last hour man discovered agriculture. The industrial revolution began a minute ago. During those sixty seconds of biological time, Modern man has made a rubbish tip of paradise (Greenpeace - 'Against All Odds', 1990). [1]

One of the points Greenpeace is trying to convey here is that destructive industrial civilisation is a very recent development (at least in a biological or even, geological time-scale). But from the perspective of post-industrial society theories, working within a different (human) time-scale, industrial societies have existed for 250 years or so (from the time of the Industrial Revolution in Britain) and are now in some senses 'traditional' societies whose basic structures are in the process of transformation into something quite different which is genuinely post-industrial. Although there are some differences between key post-industrial theorists, I think that the general picture they all paint has diffused into sociology's basic assumptions about the nature of social change in the contemporary period, and underlies research into many areas of modern societies.

This chapter begins a re-envisioning of the industrialisation process in Britain in order to contribute to a critique of post-industrial theory, in so far as this theory claims novel insights into the emergence of environmentalism and radical ecology, together with postmaterialist concerns for the natural world. Towards this end I look in more detail at British industrialisation, and attempt to use this survey as a starting point for the production of a more realistic picture of the time-scale involved in this process. This is a necessary first step in the endeavour to produce a more rounded account of the emergence and growth of the modern environmental movement in Britain, which will allow us to make sense of the history of organised environmental concern and the recent rise to prominence of a radical ecology perspective.

Industrialisation in Historical Perspective

It is not my intention to produce a comprehensive survey and comparison of historical accounts of British industrialisation.[2]   The main purpose of this chapter is to show the utility for our understanding of the emergence of organised environmentalism in Britain, of making a distinction between early recognitions of the potential for industrial development (for example in Saint-Simon) and the later acceptance of industrialisation as a permanent and normal part of modern societies. In short, this is the difference between possibility and reality, and will help us to account for the timing of the early phase of environmental movement organisation in the late nineteenth century as part of the attempt to regulate and shape industrial and urban development. To this end I draw on a number of historical sources and accounts which help to bring out this contrast.

David Landes (1969) has distinguished three senses in which the term, 'Industrial Revolution' can be and has been used by analysts in various disciplines. These are as follows [I have changed Landes's order of presentation to my own purposes]:

Meaning 1:   Any phase in human development which involves widespread technological change or the development of new tools and methods of working on nature. On this definition it is possible to speak of an 'industrial revolution' of the thirteenth century, sixteenth century, eighteenth century and so on.

Meaning 2: The specific technological and associated social, demographic and economic changes which took place first in Britain between 1750 and 1830 and which subsequently spread throughout the world via emulation, diffusion, force, and of course as politically planned developments. In this sense we can speak of an industrial society as one in which manufacturing industry takes precedence over agriculture for the first time and a numerical majority of the working population is involved, either directly or indirectly in the production of material goods. A long term shift from rural to urban living also takes place.

Meaning 3: In the broadest sense, the Industrial Revolution was also an 'evolutionary' social development of the human species as such. Here, the closest parallel would be with the Neolithic Revolution which brought about settled communities and agriculture. Industrialisation in this sense is the systematic replacement of human and animal labour with that of machines.

I will take issue with aspects of this categorisation later, but for now I want to use it to discuss the characteristic features of post-industrial theories.

The three meanings Landes identifies now co-exist and have given rise to certain confusions. In particular there has been something of a neglect of industrialisation in sense three in much recent post-industrial theorising. In human world-historical development we should not be too eager to dismiss the processes and significance of industrialisation. McNeill (1979: 425) puts the issue into perspective in the following passage:

It seems likely that the change in ordinary everyday experience and habit implied by wholesale flight from the fields will alter society as fundamentally as it was altered when men ceased to be simple predators and began to produce their food. If so, it is difficult to overemphasize the historical importance of the industrial revolution and impossible to believe that the social organization and styles of life that will eventually prove to be best attuned to industrialized economies have yet clearly emerged.

As an evolutionary development of potentially global proportions, industrialisation has been a very long-term process, traceable to developments much earlier than the British Industrial Revolution, at least to the thirteenth century and most probably even earlier (Goudsblom 1989). In its modern sense, industrialism can be distinguished from capitalism in the following way:

> ... if capitalism means a competitive economic system, in which commodities are bought and sold on national and international markets, and in which wage labour also becomes a commodity, it is distinguishable from industrialism. By industrialism we can understand a certain type of production process, linked directly to specific modes of social organisation. Industrialism presumes the applying of inanimate sources of power to production technology, and thus represents a prime medium of the interaction between human beings and the material world ... (Giddens 1990: 20).

One of the crucial consequences of industrialisation for Giddens is the production of a 'created environment'. What he means by this is broadly similar to many radical ecologists' identification of the key problem of modernity, namely that the creation of a 'surrogate world' of material products and urban environments is only made possible by degrading and diminishing the 'real world' of nature or the biosphere (Goldsmith 1988). This distinction is a fundamental one in radical ecological discourse and cannot be understated as a source of motivation for ecological activism. The real world is ultimately a finite one, and there are therefore natural limits to the human exploitation of natural resources. The artificial world of humanly created environments cannot exist without the real world of nature, but the reverse is not true. Greens argue that this means we must start to privilege the real world over the artificial one and force those who would intervene in the former in order to expand the latter to explain and justify their actions.

The idea that industrial societies distance people from a real connection with nature is not only asserted as fact, but is seen as a key reason for the adoption of destructive attitudes to the natural environment in Western societies (Jones 1987). In Green discourses, there is an inevitable tension between industrial processes and the natural development of ecological systems.

> Industrialization is something which is happening to the biosphere. It is the biosphere which is being industrialized. In this way, a new organization of matter is building up: the technosphere or world of material goods and technological devices: or the surrogate world. ... the surrogate world ... is in direct competition with the real world, since it can only be built up by making use of resources extracted from the latter, and by consigning to it the waste products this process must inevitably generate (Goldsmith 1988: 185).

Industrialisation and its technological capacity for transforming nature has led to large-scale urbanisation and the distanciation of modern human groupings from an immediate, everyday reliance on, and interaction with the rest of the non-human material world. In this sense it is industrialisation which brings about a change in the relation of humans to the non-human natural world and in turn, fundamentally affects their conceptions of nature and the relative value attributed to it. The effects of connecting industrialisation with capitalism should not be understated. Polanyi (1967 [first 1944]: 42) clearly recognised the potentially destructive consequences of this historical phenomenon long before the re-awakening of ecological concern during the 1970s, 'Machine production in a commercial society involves, in effect, no less a transformation than that of the natural and human substance of society into commodities. The conclusion, though weird, is inevitable; nothing less will serve the purpose: obviously, the dislocation caused by such devices must disjoint man's relationships *and threaten his natural habitat with annihilation*' [emphasis added].

Given the world historical significance (Wallerstein 1979, 1983) of the wide-ranging changes wrought by capitalist industrialisation, it is clear that Landes's meanings 2 and 3 are closely connected. Although industrialisation as an evolutionary development may be traceable to events and trends over a much longer period of time, it seems that the eighteenth century Industrial Revolution intensified the spread of these trends, leading to the creation of recognisably industrial or industrialised societies. To speak of post-industrial societies as representing changes of this magnitude is therefore surely misleading, and Calhoun is right to suggest that theorists of disjunctive changes, particularly those who see the social condition of postmodernity as a new era, overstate their case.[3] He thinks that 'Though changes are real and major, they do not yet amount to an epochal break. Indeed, many of them reflect continuing tensions and pressures which have characterized the whole modern era' (Calhoun 1993: 75). Even the perceived 'information revolution' which has been said to be in progress today, can easily be seen as an industrial development in Landes first meaning, not as a development taking us beyond industrialism in sense three. We can be said to be living today in an 'informational society' (Landes' meaning one) in the same sense that previous generations could be said to have lived in 'steam societies' or 'electrical societies'. But these technological developments are part of longer term scientific - industrial developments (meaning three). That is,

No less than such situations [that is, of heavy industry], the notion of industrialism applies to high technology settings where electricity is the only
power source, and where electronic microcircuits are the only mechanised
devices. Industrialism moreover, affects not only the workplace but
transportation, communication, and domestic life (Giddens 1991: 55-6).

So, while post-industrial society theories make some valid points in
relation to meaning 1, they tend to push the significance of post-industrial
developments too far, often arguing that these undermine notions of an
industrial society (meaning 2) and of industrialisation as an 'evolutionary'
social development (meaning 3) (as in Toffler 1981). In doing so I think they
claim far too much for post-industrial change. Indeed, many of the specified
changes such as the development of information technologies, increasing
numbers of people working in services and so on, can themselves be seen as
continuations of the long-term process of capitalist industrialisation.

Structural Bases of Environmentalism and Radical Ecology

Let me state as clearly as I can the linkages which have become
commonplace in discussions of the emergence of widespread concern for the
natural world, that is between environmental politics in the broadest sense,
post-industrial theories and the idea that (post)modern societies are
undergoing a shift towards postmaterial values. In doing so, I must also state
one of the central arguments of my study. This is that environmental and
Green protests, organisations and movements whose primary aim is to
challenge some or all aspects of the relationship between industrialised
societies and the non-human world, are not new phenomena of the late
twentieth century. Much of the rest of the investigation paints a clearer
historical picture of this claim. The idea that these movements and
organisations are new is given sociological validity by the apparent
convergence of two sociological theories which are widely referred to in
discussions of new social movements.

Firstly, Ronald Inglehart's postmaterial values thesis points to the post-
scarcity socialisation of the post-Second World War 'boom' generation as an
explanation for the spread of values which are potentially at least,
antagonistic to expanding conspicuous mass consumption (1977, 1990).
Secondly, the post-industrial society thesis argues that (post)modern
societies have moved from an industrial to an informational basis of

production, which has marginalised the capital/labour conflict and generated a variety of non- or cross-class issues (environmentalism is the best example), and a corresponding range of new social movements (Bell 1974; Touraine 1971, 1981; Gorz 1980, 1985).

Clearly these two theories of social and cultural change can be brought together as an explanation for the rise of environmental and Green movements. With the historical problem of resource scarcity seemingly resolved in the advanced mass consumer societies, the concerns of protest movements turn away from material and distributional issues towards postmaterial ones, in particular those which affect the perceived quality of everyday life including the condition of local and valued environments. As with all theories which try to make distinctions between levels or hierarchies of needs and wants, the postmaterialist thesis runs into the problem of how to draw boundaries between basic and higher level needs.[4] The problem here is not simply to identify which needs are basic and which constitute higher level needs, but also to explain what criteria can be used to decide when basic needs have actually been met.[5] What seems to have happened in postmaterialist arguments is that the emergence of apparently new issues and movements has been taken as evidence that basic needs have been met, at least for significant numbers of people.

Post-industrial society theories seem to give postmaterialist ideas a social-structural base. A key proposition of these theories in relation to the emergence of new social movements is that industrialised societies are being transformed into post-industrial ones in which service sector employment is becoming the dominant form of work. Employed either outside the industrial manufacturing sector or only indirectly in relation to production processes, large groups of people, particularly those groups defined by Eder as the new middle class (1993), perceive themselves as having little or no stake in expanding economic growth and the extension of human control and use of the natural world and its resources. Concerns now begin to move towards public access to information resources, democratisation and control of what happens in localities rather than 'old' issues such as wage bargaining, wealth redistribution, employment rights and economic progress, which were focal concerns of the labour movement. Surveys of environmental and Green organisation members seem to lend support to this kind of theory. All tend to show that high proportions of Greens and environmentalists are not employed directly in industrial occupations, have been through or are in higher education and display recognisable postmaterial values.[6] Environmental and Green movements would therefore seem to be typical new social movements.

It should be noted though that despite the linkage which is often made between postmaterial and post-industrial arguments, the two can be seen as simply different forms of evidence. For example, whilst I am happy to acknowledge that Inglehart's European-wide survey of changing values provides some convincing evidence for the emergence of different priorities and interests amongst large sections of most Western European populations, it does not necessarily follow that these are due to significant large scale social structural changes in the types of employment in these nations. Even if there is evidence for postmaterial values, this does not necessarily imply post-industrialisation. It is more likely that more people are now turning to 'post-scarcity', quality of life concerns as a result of the general spread of increasing affluence and mass consumerism since the 1950's, and the creation of expanded welfare provision (Shils 1972: 277). Postmaterialist changes of this kind may be part of the explanation for the increasing memberships of environmental organisations, though this does not also involve conceding the validity of post-industrial or new social movement theories. Environmentalist attitudes and interests may be linked as Inglehart's work suggests, to perceptions of plenitude and the elimination of scarcity, and to hierarchies of needs, interests and concerns (Maslow 1954), but in my view they are not dependent on post-industrial or postmodern cultural change, nor are they rooted in the rise to prominence of a new middle class.

To take seriously the evidence of early (before their time?) forms of Green ideas, environ-mental organisations and movements in Britain (and elsewhere) in the latter part of the nine-teenth century poses a problem for post-industrial theories *as explanations* for the rise of a late-twentieth century politics of nature, and challenges the thesis that we are currently experiencing a radical break with industrial societies. Whilst rejecting the idea that a self-conscious nature politics is unique to post-industrial societies, I think we should be equally careful not to see it as a constant or a universal feature of all societies.[7] A better way of looking at this issue is to see nature politics as part of the variety of '... visions and values (that) have come to be loosely grouped together under the name of 'modernism", that is, '...(the) amazing variety of visions and ideas that aim to make men and women the subjects as well as the objects of modernization, to give them the power to change the world that is changing them, to make their way through the maelstrom and make it their own' (Berman 1983: 16). Environmentalism and Green politics, though long neglected, were part of industrialising modernity and have been present in varying degrees of visibility and significance since nineteenth century *fin de siècle* modernism.

Institutional Dimensions of Modernity

Giddens has recently attempted to develop a typology of the multi-dimensional character of modernity in which he identifies four 'institutional dimensions of modernity' which 'in the real world intertwine in complicated fashion, but which for analytical purposes should be kept separate' (1990: 20). This last point must be borne in mind as all attempts at categorisation of social phenomena run the risk of appearing too neat. They may appear to bring a spurious sense of order to what is in reality much more complex, messy and intertwined. This much we can admit at the start. The use of a typology here is intended as an aid to understanding, not an exhaustive description of reality. Giddens' four institutional dimensions of modernity are: capitalism, industrialism, administrative power and military power. Each institutional dimension is partly constitutive of what we call 'modernity', but at the same time can be seen as an arena of conflict or a space for the creation of opposition to dominant institutions. The potential at least, exists for the emergence of social movements aiming to reform or transform the institutional complex itself.

In this context, we can say that movements which spring up and disappear when their immediate policy aims are met can legitimately be called 'political movements'. Movements which arise at the level of changes in attitudes and lifestyles can be termed 'cultural' (or counter-cultural) movements (Musgrove 1974, Roszak 1969), but my approach in this work is to use the term social movement to describe only those movements which endure over time, generate organisational forms which carry the movement forward, and which actively attempt to (re)shape or redirect dominant social processes. Leaving to one side the sociologically well-established and theorised conflict between Capital and Labour which constitutes capitalism, Giddens identifies the three other institutional complexes and their oppositional social movements:

Institutional Complex	Corresponding Social Movement
Industrialism (& urbanisation)	Ecological (Counter-Cultural)
Administrative Power	Civil & Human Rights
Military Power	Peace (& Anti-Nuclear)

I have included urbanisation with industrialism to emphasise the point that industrialisation leads to a created environment, and have used Giddens' own term 'ecological' to stand for the diverse range of activities and organisations which today constitute and have constituted nature politics. It is sufficient at this point to note that 'ecological' is probably not a wholly adequate term and would not have been used by earlier environmental activists.[8]

This four-fold characterisation of modernity can certainly be criticised for its selectivity. For example, Bagguley makes a good case for the inclusion of feminist movements which organise in opposition to changing structural forms of patriarchy (1992). It is also evident that these are not hard and fast distinctions between social movements, anti-nuclear movements have also demonstrated concern for the natural environment for example. However, I do not wish to take criticisms of this typology any further here. What is of interest to us is the importance which Giddens attributes to ecological movements as the main opposition to industrialism. In doing so, he seems to be in agreement with some of the theorists writing from within the contemporary environmental and Green movements. As we saw earlier, Jonathon Porritt, former Director of Friends of the Earth and Green Party spokesperson, has been one of the most vociferous opponents of what he also calls industrialism. Porritt (1984: 43-4) argues that the 'two dominant ideologies' of the modern world, namely capitalism and communism, have more in common with each other than we previously thought. So much so in fact that he believes that '... the similarities between these two ... are of greater significance than their differences, and that the dialectic between them is therefore largely superficial'.

Porritt is not arguing a contemporary version of the convergence theories of the 1950s however, and does recognise that there are 'many differences' between capitalism and communism (as ideologies), but from a distinctively ecological perspective both 'insist that the planet is there to be conquered', and are dedicated to 'industrial growth, to the expansion of the means of production, to a materialist ethic as the best means of meeting people's needs, and to unimpeded technological development' (ibid.). In this sense, capitalist and communist ideologies are antagonists, but antagonists within one overall world-view, or as Porritt puts it, 'one all-embracing 'super-ideology', which, for the sake of convenience, I intend to call industrialism' (ibid.), and which promotes economic growth as the route to progress.

With this conceptualisation in mind, it now seems possible to make some sense of the oft-repeated claim amongst radical ecologists that Green politics 'is neither left nor right, but in front' (Pepper 1996: 40). From the Green perspective, the political tags of 'left' and 'right' refer to two ideological camps within the underlying framework of assumptions of industrialism, two ways of organising industrial societies. Because Greens are opposed to further industrialisation and seek a radical transformation of industrial societies, they see themselves as outside this conventional political spectrum. In its more extreme manifestations, this argument comes close to mystical New Age ideas, as expressed in the work of Capra (1983: 466) who says that the conventional politics of left, right, socialist, fascist are,

> ... in the process of disintegration. The social movements of the 1960s represent the rising culture, which is now ready for the passage to the Solar Age. While the transformation is taking place, the declining culture refuses to change, clinging ever more rigidly to its outdated ideas ... As the turning point approaches, the realization that evolutionary changes of this magnitude cannot be prevented by short term political activities provides our best hope for the future.

Capra sees a clear break between an old politics of class conflicts and distributional issues, and a new politics concerned with the central question of nature/society relations. This is quite close to the sociological theories of Beck and Eder, and also to Touraine's post-industrial thesis, but again, I think that there is a lack of historical perspective here which distorts the analysis towards an awareness of novelty at the expense of recognising longer term developments and continuities.

In terms of Giddens' institutional complexes of modernity, we can say that analytically there is no necessity to try to place Greens on the left or right, as these labels apply to capitalism and its direct oppositional social movement, organised labour. In reality of course, there are often complex interrelations and (dis)agreements between many political, social and cultural movements which tend to efface some of the apparently fixed boundaries between them. Nevertheless, if we accept that ecological movements arise primarily in response to industrial development and not in opposition to the social relations and organisation of capitalism, then the terms left and right may simply be inappropriate in any definition of the specifically Green position.

The discussion up to this point has looked for aspects of the self-identification of environmentalists and Greens which find an echo in Giddens's sociological, analytical (and admittedly speculative) typology. However, in relation to the rest of this study, we can usefully identify three main problems raised by the above.

1. Giddens sees that ecological movements arise in opposition to industrialism, but post-industrial and new social movement theories seem to ignore the environmentalist forms which existed before the late1960s, and which go back as far as those of the late nineteenth century when local communities were uprooted, local environments degraded, and urban and industrial development proceeded at a previously unprecedented rate. This neglect serves the purpose of marking out a break between old and new, but does not help us to see the links between these, nor does it allow for a sense of social process in the long-term development of environmentalism.

2. There is something strangely incongruous between the expectations of post-industrial and new social movement theories, and the Green critique of modern societies. Whilst the former use the rise to prominence of environmental and Green movements as evidence of a real shift away from industrialism, the latter continue to argue that it is precisely the continuation of industrialisation processes and their increasingly global spread which threatens natural environments and even the biosphere itself. It appears then, that theories of disjunctive social change fail to take seriously the critique which forms a key motivation for Green activists, and that they therefore underestimate the central importance of industrialisation.

3. One further question is that, at some point people caught up in the early industrialisation process become aware that the process is, to all intents and purposes, irreversible and begin to pursue measures to control its future development, in short to reform it. This realisation is demonstrated by the creation of a series of interlinked environmental organisations in

the late nineteenth century which sought to regulate and control industrial development.

Questions of the kind outlined above require a reorientation of our view of social movements. The lack of a historical perspective on the emergence and development of social movements, particularly in recent new social movement theories, has contributed to the general notion that social movements are somewhat unusual, spontaneous, and sporadic forms of highly visible collective behaviour.[9] The longer term process sociological approach of the 'Elias School' would seem to provide a better overall perspective which may provide a more adequate orientation to the study of social movements. For example, Johan Goudsblom (1989: 22) argues that 'It may not be a bad rule of thumb and not an unsound research strategy to assume that for any given trend a counter-trend may be found, operating in the opposite direction', this is often because '... changes which are beneficial to some people are almost bound to be harmful to others. Even if those others are small in numbers or weak in power, they are nevertheless likely to put up some resistance and this resistance then constitutes a countervailing tendency'. In his own work, Goudsblom is concerned with very long term trends in human history as a whole such as 'the increasing differentiation between human groups and all other mammals', or 'towards higher production of food in increasingly more concentrated areas ...' (1989: 23). Nevertheless, the basic principle of trends or social processes giving rise to resistances and countervailing tendencies is suggestive of a more adequate perspective on social movements in the sense in which Giddens uses the term. If, as many have noted, social movements are 'anti-systemic' (Pakulski 1991: 32), this is because in some respects, the dominant trends in society or the institutions which are constitutive of it are developing in a different direction from the way the adherents of the social movements would like.

Goudsblom's rule of thumb is useful for students of social movements because it shifts the research emphasis. Instead of finding social movements as unusual phenomena, we should perhaps expect to find some forms of resistance to dominant trends or processes which may then develop into collective social movements with their own distinctive organisations and memberships. Of course, this may not happen. Resistances may remain at the level of individual beliefs and ideas and never develop into collective forms of resistance expressed for example through public demonstrations, networks of people or organisational forms which endure over time. The formation of oppositional organisations is dependent on the kind of 'political opportunity structures' in societies (Kitschelt 1986, 1990). At the most basic level, a democratic polity which provides a focus for lobbying and legislative change is more conducive to wider participation for social movement activists than in authoritarian systems where such activism is prohibited. Although, as Melucci has pointed out, because resistance is not publicly expressed does not mean that there is none, it may be that there are informal networks of activists which are 'submerged' in everyday life (1989).

The Creation of an Industrial Society in Britain

In this section I begin to question some common-sense assumptions concerning the industrialisation process in Britain. In particular I will call into question the time-scale involved in the production of the world's first modern, industrialised society, in order to show that organised environmentalism emerged around the point at which the process of industrialisation began to be sensed as irreversible, and the experience of living in an industrial society became widespread.

Krishan Kumar (1986: 132) notes that, 'It is a widespread assumption, certainly among sociologists, occasionally even among historians, that the making of the industrial society was basically a nineteenth century phenomenon: more or less completed by the mid-century in England ...'. This historical perspective seems to draw its apparent validity from two events which occurred in the same year, 1851, and which appeared to signify the logical endpoint of two large scale social processes: industrialisation and urbanisation.[10] The Great Exhibition of 1851 and the Official Census of the same year were widely perceived at the time, and have been interpreted since, as marking the beginning of a new era not only in Britain but in human 'world history'.

The Great Crystal Palace Exhibition of 1851 has been seen as marking the 'apogee of England's career as the 'workshop of the world'' (Landes 1969: 124), whilst the census showed (amongst other revelations) that for the first time, over half of the population now lived in 'urban locations'. England it seemed, had entered a new era, and become a radically different type of society. Many Victorians thought that the rest of the world would have to follow. At the Exhibition, England won almost all of the scientific, technological and industrial awards, demonstrating to other aspiring nations its superior knowledge and creativity (this was to be short-lived however, at the Paris Exhibition sixteen years later, England won only one in ten of the awards) (Read 1979: 13). Prince Albert's Mansion House speech in the previous year had set out the optimistic interpretation of the meaning of the Exhibition. England would provide the rest of the world with '... a new starting point from which all nations will be able to direct their further exertions'. This meant that,

> ... man is approaching a more complete fulfilment of that great and sacred mission which he has to perform in this world. His reason being created after the image of God, he has to use it to discover the laws by which the Almighty governs his creation, and, by making these laws his standard of action, *to conquer nature to his use*; himself a divine instrument (quoted in Golby 1986: 2 [emphasis added].

This statement from a speech in the mid-nineteenth century seems to speak from and to a different world. The strong anthropocentrism expressed in the idea of 'conquering nature' to human ends has been one of the main targets of attack from within contemporary ecocentric or biocentric and radical Green circles (Ehrenfeld 1981; Eckersley 1992). However it would also not have fitted well with the expressed aims of late nineteenth century conservation and environmental protection organisations such as the Commons Preservation Society (C.P.S.) or the National Trust, so that even in the late nineteenth century, some groups of people were beginning to perceive strongly human-instrumental sentiments to be misguided.

The confident tone expressed by Prince Albert can, at least in part, be attributed to the return of relative social stability after a period of sometimes violent protests surrounding Chartist agitation. England's escape from the revolutionary upheavals which had beset other countries in Europe during the 1840s owed much to the severe punishments handed out to Chartist leaders and organisers, several of whom were hanged and many more transported. When the much feared demonstrations against the Exhibition failed to materialise on its opening on the 1st of May, it seemed to confirm to some that class conflict was not inevitable. Thomas Babington (later Lord) Macaulay's diary for this date records his contempt for the pessimists: 'There is just as much chance of a revolution in England as of the falling of the moon ...' (cited in Golby 1986, 3). *The Times* remarked that on one day alone, visitors numbered 109,915 (in Best 1985: 253). What the Crystal Palace display symbolised for many was not only England's scientific and industrial prowess, but a veritable model of the 'modern' industrial society at peace with itself, proud of its achievements and the envy of Europe.

Nevertheless, Kumar is unhappy with this picture of England as a fully-fledged and essentially 'completed' modern industrialised society by the time of the 1851 Great Exhibition, and a distinction can be made here which is crucial for our inquiry, between *the process* of industrialisation with its principle of replacing human and animal labour by machine, and the crystallisation of industrial trends into *the accomplishment* (or widespread perception of accomplishment) of an urban, industrialised, modern society. This distinction is important because it allows us to differentiate between a series of connected developments and processes, such as urbanisation, industrialisation, bureaucratisation, democratisation, and to take account of the uneven and extended time-scale of the spread of these processes across society.

If the Great Exhibition symbolised England's place as the 'workshop of the world' then it should also be stated that England was indeed literally a place of small workshops rather than large manufacturing plants and factories. What seems to be *the* characteristic form in which industrial work took place, the mass-production factory, did not become dominant until well into the twentieth century. In 1851, census returns from the cotton industry revealed that almost two-thirds of the production units employed less than fifty people, and this was in the most advanced sector of industrial production, textiles. Most 'factories' were in reality little more than small or 'medium-sized' workshops where Adam Smith's famed extended division of labour, as well as the mechanisation of production were strictly limited. Firms such as Horrocks, Miller & Co., which employed 700 spinners and 6000 handloom weavers in their four mills as early as 1816 were in fact the exception not the rule. In 1851, mechanised industries in England (including the coal industry) employed less than two million people. This was only about one third of those employed in the non-mechanised sector (Mingay 1986: 25-6).

The population of England and Wales grew by 150 per cent during the first half of the nineteenth century, with most of the increase being attributable to the growth of towns and 'urban' areas (Purdue 1987: 61). Yet despite this, the census showed that the number of farmworkers stood at an all-time high of 1,284,000 male and 199,000 female agricultural workers. These figures are underestimates of the rural workforce and do not include the variety of other members of agricultural service workers such as blacksmiths, millers, carriers, thatchers and other tradespeople as well as independent hedgers, stone-wallers and drainers, and a large number of country-house servants. What we may deduce from this is that, although urban centres were growing in this period, bringing with them new forms of work, the growth of population created the need for more food production and hence traditional farmworking continued to be a major provider of employment, whilst the actual number of agricultural workers had increased.

Similarly, patterns of employment continued to exhibit traditional rural influences based around the seasonal nature of work. During spring and summer, families would leave the towns to look for work in the countryside, returning to the town in the autumn and winter. As Samuel points out, the distinction between the nomadic life and the settled one was by no means hard and fast, "Tramping' was not the prerogative of the social outcast, as it is today; it was a normal phase in the life of entirely respectable classes of working men ...' (Samuel cited in Dyos and Wolff 1973: 152)

It was also not unusual for a workshop to find a majority of its labour force absent for the first day and a half of the week, during spells of hot weather, on traditional holidays, or on the arrival of a fair in the town (Mingay 1986: 33). The disciplined, rationalised use of time, characteristic of industrial capitalist production, and an integral part of the internal social control of the factory which enabled the expansion of productivity, clearly could not exist in this climate, and it was not until the turn of the century that what we now know as 'scientific management' techniques came to be explored.[11] In addition, most working class protest before the 1880s in England (and elsewhere) came not from Marx's industrial proletariat attempting to overthrow the whole capitalist edifice, but rather from groups of supposedly 'pre-industrial' workers: artisans, small traders and farmers who were engaged in a defence of their independence against the forces and the principle of capitalist industrial organisation which threatened to reduce them to wage labourers (Kumar 1986: 146-9). At the time when Marx and Engels were calling the proletariat to revolutionary action, this class actor had not yet arrived on the stage to be able to play its part. As one commentator has remarked, 'Marx's conception of a revolutionary proletariat is a composite which corresponds to no known historical reality' (Lubasz 1970: 289), at least not by the mid-nineteenth century. The early forms of workers' unions leading to the Chartists' 'People's Charter' in 1838 were different from those in the late-nineteenth century which took place in a period '... when industry had come to be taken for granted and when labour had its own set of institutions' (Briggs 1984: 276).

So, the widespread acceptance that England was an industrialised society in any real sense in the first half of the nineteenth century, and that there was a widespread experience of it as such, is somewhat misleading and '... even in the narrowest sense, Britain's industrialisation did not mature until late into the second half of the nineteenth century, over a hundred years after Watt had invented the steam engine (1769); while many developments associated with industrialisation did not come to fruition until our present century' (Kumar 1986: 143-44).

The industrialisation process and its basic principle of replacing human and animal labour with that of machines can certainly be traced back to 1760 and maybe even before, but the experience of living in an industrialised society did not become a commonplace until the late nineteenth and early twentieth centuries. In a passage worth quoting in full, Briggs reminds us that the introduction of the principle of industrialism was only gradually adopted during the second half of the nineteenth century. He notes that,

...there were many economic activities that by 1860 were still relatively little touched by invention: in a labour force which was more specialized than that which had existed in1780, only three out of ten people were employed in activities that had been radically transformed in technique since 1780. Nor was human strength completely obsolete, as boilermakers of later generations would testify. There were also large numbers of out-workers, sub-contractors and, at the base, casual workers, including 'wandering tribes' of migrant labourers; and there were more domestic servants than operatives in the textile industry, more males engaged in building and construction than in mining and quarrying and more still engaged in agriculture, horticulture and fishing than in construction and mining combined (Briggs 1984: 261-2).

In fact, the crystallisation of perceptions of English society *as* an industrial society only occurred after 1860. 'A person born in the eighteenth century and formed within its characteristic attitudes would have found the Britain of 1865 still a society whose structures and institutions were tolerably familiar and understandable', but 'The years between the 1860s and the First World War transformed Britain more swiftly and more profoundly than any other comparable era. British society became urbanized and suburbanized, secularized, democratized ... in a word, it became 'modern''

(Shannon 1974: 11). If the process of industrialisation only began to crystallise into a recognisably permanent industrial society after about 1860, and this view is consistent with the other authors I have cited in this chapter, then post-industrial theories appear to limit the life-span of such societies to a very short period of just over one hundred years. I think this is an unrealistic picture of the significance of industrialisation which fails to do justice to the historical significance of this development for human societies world-wide.

During the first half of the nineteenth century, the population of Great Britain grew by 150 per cent to stand at 20,817,000 in 1851, of which, 51 per cent were deemed by the official census to be living in 'urban' locations (Best 1985: 23-4). This has been taken as indicating the turning point in the process of urbanisation, as for the first time the urban population exceeded the rural. Not only was this seen as the triumph of industry over agriculture, but also as that of town over country and modernity over tradition, in short

Table 6.1   Urban population in England and Wales 1841-81

	1841	1851	1861	1871	1881
Urban areas:					
Over 100,000	7	10	13	17	20
20,000 - 100,000	112	141	160	196	235
Urban as % of total pop.	48.3	54.0	58.7	65.2	70.2
Urban Population as % of total:					
areas over 100,000	20.7	24.8	28.8	32.6	36.2
50-100,000	5.5	5.8	6.1	5.5	7.3
20-50,000	6.8	7.0	7.5	9.6	9.4
10-20,000	5.3	6.4	6.6	6.6	6.6
2,500-10,000	10.0	9.9	9.8	10.5	10.5

Source: Adapted from Best 1985: 24.

as a progressive development. When examined more closely though, there are quite large differences to be found in the nature and character of the officially designated 'urban areas' which seriously question the idea of mid-Victorian Britain as a largely urbanised society as we understand that term today.

Total population in England in the 1851 Census was 16.9 million (Briggs 1984: 336). Of the 54 per cent (8,619,000) deemed to be living in an urban region, only 24.8 per cent lived in the seven areas which each had a population exceeding 100,000, and of these one, London, accounted for 2,685,000. At the other end of the urban scale, around 10 per cent lived in towns with populations of between 2,500 and 10,000 and a further 46 per cent still lived in smaller settlements than these. Of course, as Table 6.1 shows, the trend was flowing against the latter, but the extent to which these much smaller villages, hamlets and towns shared the same characteristics as the much larger urban areas at this time must be open to question.[12] Even many of the new 'industrial' settlements maintained a 'distinct continuity with earlier rural patterns' (Kumar 1986: 136). In the Midlands and the North, towns grew through the linking of self-sufficient, independent industrial villages which recruited their labour force from the surrounding rural area, thus retaining a strong rural influence even into the second half of the century. The enormous growth of population during the first half of the nineteenth century meant that towns were more numerous and gradually of an increasing size, yet the distinction between 'town' and 'country' was still obvious. Even the newer industrial towns were relatively distinct and did not expand outwards into the countryside. 'Nature' and 'society' co-existed, but seemed to inhabit different spheres, though this situation was to change after the turn of the century when the term 'urban sprawl' came to be used to describe the increasing colonisation of the countryside by a more thorough-going and expansive urbanism.

Much more important to Victorians than the actual size and spread of the new industrial towns was their recognisable differences from traditional rural villages. Urban areas and industrial villages were thought to promote different values and a wholly different culture from that of traditional rural England. Polanyi notes that 'The industrial regions of that age resembled a new country, like another America, attracting immigrants by the thousands' (1957: 91). They therefore represented to many a seemingly different world of *Gesellschaft* relations, elected local government, modern inventions such as gas and (later) electricity, higher wages (important with the onset of agricultural depression in the 1870s), and beset by a raft of new social problems.[13] This aspect of the industrialisation process has no real parallel in theories of post-industrial society, suggesting again, that any post-industrial transformation is of a lower order than that which occurred during industrialisation. The contention that a post-industrial transformation is as significant a change as modern industrialisation is, in my view, simply untenable.

Significantly, negative views of the emerging 'new world' were not confined to rural landowners and workers, but were also held by a sizeable section of urban dwellers themselves, many of who felt that the countryside promoted higher morals than the emerging towns and cities, 'The tone of much Victorian literature and art is anti-urban and anti-industrial ... for many eloquent Victorians, the country rather than the town was home' (Purdue 1987: 63), although of course not literally. The reasons for this are complex, but a theory of phases of modern experience within the overall process of industrialisation might be an aid to understanding the paradox. To develop a model of this kind would take us beyond the scope of this work and away from its central issues, but Berman's (1985) ambitious reading of phases of modern experience shows the sort of shifting structures of experience during the transition towards modernity. His model divides the modern experience into three phases as follows:

Phase 1. ... from the start of the sixteenth century to the end of the eighteenth ... [People] grope, desperately but half blindly, for an adequate vocabulary; they have little or no sense of a modern public or community within which their trials and hopes can be shared.

Phase 2. takes in the nineteenth century [and] ... begins with the great revolutionary wave of the 1790s. [When] ... a great modern public abruptly and dramatically comes to life.

Phase 3. In the twentieth century, our third and final phase, the process of modernization expands to take in virtually the whole world ... [and] as the modern public expands, it shatters into a multitude of fragments, speaking incommensurable private languages; the idea of modernity, conceived in numerous fragmentary ways, loses much of its vividness, resonance and depth, and loses its capacity to organize and give meaning to people's lives. As a result of all this, we find ourselves today in the midst of a modern age that has lost touch with its own modernity (Berman 1985: 16-17).

Our main concern in this phase model is with Berman's 'Phase 2' which covers the nineteenth century. He notes that the main distinguishing feature of this phase is that,

> ... the nineteenth century modern public can remember what it is like to live, materially and spiritually, in worlds that are not modern at all. From this inner dichotomy, this sense of living in two worlds simultaneously, the ideas of modernization and modernism emerge and unfold (ibid: 17).   .

The major intellectual figures in Berman's discussion, Marx, Baudelaire and Nietzsche, produced their most vivid modernist imagery in the later decades of the nineteenth century. Similarly, much late nineteenth century sociological work on industrial societies relied for its effect on contrasting what was emerging with what was being lost. Tönnies' description of the changing balance between *Gemeinschaft* and *Gesellschaft* relations (1887) and Durkheim's (1893) theory of a new source of 'organic' social solidarity rooted in the extended division of labour, replacing the previous 'mechanical' form, both describe aspects of a world which was in the process of becoming 'modern'.

So, whilst Hobsbawm (1968: 46) may be right to state that 'If the sudden, qualitative, and fundamental transformation, which happened in or about the 1780s was not a revolution then the word has no common sense meaning', we must still insist that it was not until the latter decades of the nineteenth century that perceptions of England as a modern, urban, industrial society became widespread, and the extension of democratic rights to all social groups would have to wait even longer to be accomplished. So, the 'characteristic processes of the nineteenth century, the urbanization, the mechanization, the development of factories had begun, but they had not penetrated as deeply into the life of the community as perhaps we are apt to think. Very much what had existed in 1851 was in fact closely akin to what had existed in 1800 ...' (Kitson Clark 1970: 118). Hobsbawm himself argues later that 'A fully industrialized economy implies permanence, if only the permanence of further industrialization', but that this stability was noticeably absent until after 1850, before which time no one could be sure of the industrial system's future.

> It might collapse. It might be overthrown. It might be an episode and not an epoch. It was too young to have established its permanence by sheer duration, for as we have seen, outside a few pioneer areas, even in textiles the main weight of industrialization occurred after the Napoleonic Wars. At the time of the great Chartist general strike of 1842 every adult person in, say, Blackburn could remember the time when the first spinning factory and powerloom had been introduced in the town, less than twenty-five years earlier (Hobsbawm 1968: 119-21).

He goes on to explain that it is only after mid-century that Britain began to become 'fully industrialized', and capitalism began to expand across the human world, a point also made accurately by Polanyi (1967: 89):

> No one had forecast the development of a machine industry; it came as a complete surprise. For some time England had been actually expecting a permanent recession of foreign trade when the dam burst, and the old world was swept away in one indomitable surge towards a planetary economy. However, not until the 1850s could anybody have said so with assurance.

It is only after the mid-nineteenth century that state intervention to control, regulate and shape modern development began to take off significantly, when the realisation began to dawn that industrial development was becoming permanent and that industrialisation was not uniquely tied to a single technology or event but was in fact a long-term process of interconnected developments. The historian G.D.H. Cole describes the 1870s as 'By far the most active period for social legislation of the entire nineteenth century' (cited in Polanyi 1967: 217), whilst Polanyi dates 'the collectivist period' from 1870, and correctly in my view, includes attempts to protect 'open spaces' from development in this category.[14] This rather later endpoint of the perceptions of 'becoming modern' helps us better to understand why organised forms of 'environmentalist' resistance to industrialisation and its potential for transforming nature did not appear until the late nineteenth century. Rethinking the extended time-scale of British industrialisation and perceptions of it, can help us to understand why environmentalism as an organised social movement is not a product of a post-industrial transformation, but is rather a modern product which is structurally rooted in the response to ongoing industrialisation and urbanisation.

Conclusion

The modification of our understanding of the history of modernity and one of its main constitutive features, industrialisation, which is necessitated in this chapter is a fundamental part of the structural basis of the emergence of the origins of an organised politics of nature, which can be traced back to the 1860s in Britain. The new industrial society which began to efface traditional relationships, structures of authority, work patterns etc., came to be associated with the concept of 'society' or 'civilisation' as such. Bolstered by an increasingly active and interventionist nation-state, the emergence of modern society came to be seen by many critics as an artificial construct, the product of humanity removed from a natural world of necessity. The other side of this perception was that some Green and environmentalist critics of modern industrial society came to identify *with* nature and *against* society. As Raymond Williams says, 'The 'state of nature', and the newly personified idea of Nature, then played critical roles in arguments about, first, an obsolete or corrupt society, needing redemption and renewal, and, second, an 'artificial' or 'mechanical' society, which learning from **Nature** must cure ... ' (1987: 223). These have been recurring themes and are evident in the arguments of contemporary radical ecology.

Early environmentalists and nineteenth century Green thinkers used a number of arguments and strategies in this vein. They sought to preserve natural areas from development and to create open spaces in urban locations so that people could be brought daily into contact with the 'divine' and 'authentic'. Some went further. They demanded a return to nature and the land, and in some cases the overthrow of restless, destructive modern society itself. Significantly for example, William Morris sub-titled his utopian socialist novel *News From Nowhere* (1890), 'an epoch of rest', expressing a weariness with the continual changes wrought by the experience of modernity. This Green strand of thought also inspired a number of experimental small-scale communes based on the idea that humankind needed to be kept in close association and direct interaction with the natural world in order to be really 'healthy' (Hardy 1979).[15]

We are now in a position to add flesh to the bones of Giddens' typology which identifies 'ecological movements' as the main source of opposition to industrialism. Recognisably Green ideas concerning society/nature relations can be found in the late nineteenth century (and before), and in this way, it is evident that movements concerned with the 'right' relationship between society and the natural world are not constitutive features of a new post-industrial state of society, but go back to the maturation phase of industrial societies themselves. The environmental movement has been a feature of British society since the 1860s, and that a 'politics of nature' has long been a somewhat neglected part of what Berman calls modernism.

Despite our reservations concerning its selectivity, Giddens's analytical typology of institutional complexes of modernity does enable us to hold apart reformist and transformative social movements without collapsing them together under the master concept of social class, for example reading all environmental and radical ecology movements as products of the 'new middle class'. Therefore a typology of this kind can be an aid to understanding as well as enabling us to ascertain the structural location of environmental movements. As Bagguley argues, we should '... take seriously the critique of social relations by social movements' (1992: 42), something which most explanations failed to do with regard to 'early' nineteenth century environmentalism.

Notes

1   This does not mean that Greenpeace is a radical ecological organisation however, I argue that it is not. What it does highlight is the way that environmental organisations make use of more radical arguments in order to enhance their own image in the eyes of potential supporters.

2   Most of these are in fact economic histories. See for instance, Hobsbawm, E.J. (1968): *Industry and Empire: an Economic History of Britain since 1750*, Mathias, P. (1969): *The First Industrial Nation*, Checkland, S.G. (1964): *The Rise of Industrial Society in England, 1815-1885*, and Cipolla, C. (Ed) (1973): *The Industrial Revolution*.

3   The distinction between post-industrial society and postmodernity seems to have become blurred in recent times, Kumar preferring to see postmodernity as encompassing post-industrial changes but going beyond these to describe 'epochal social change' (1995). Nonetheless, the main features attributed to post-industrial societies seem to be taken for granted assumptions in postmodern theories, as in Lyotard (1984).

4   Maslow's psychological theory of a hierarchy of needs (1954) and Marcuse's idea of a distinction between 'true' and 'false' needs (1964) are fairly representative of this kind of approach. For a sustained critique of the theory of levels of needs see Heller & Feher 1988, Chapter 3.

5   An even more radical view is taken by Baudrillard who argues that the very idea of 'scarcity' and its overcoming is not universal but is rather the product of capitalist

development (Baudrillard *The Mirror of Production* 1975). 'The problem of scarcity is a modern invention' (Gane summarising Baudrillard's discussion in Gane 1991: 102).

6   See for example, Cotgrove & Duff 1980, 1981, 1982; Lowe & Goyder 1983; Bennie et al 1995.

7   I am concerned here with the formalisation of a politics of nature in modern societies. I do not mean to imply that only modern societies have (or generate) a 'problem of nature', the question of whether such a problematic can be found in other types of society is not addressed in this study.

8   Giddens' own use of the term 'ecological' is however, consonant with the use of this term amongst Green activists today.

9   Ironically the best-known theorist of new social movements, Alain Touraine, was attempting to bring the study of social movements into the centre of sociological theory.

10   There is possibly a third factor here, namely the experience of the railways. Most major cities and large towns were either served by 1852 or authorised to be so (see Simmons 1961: *The Railways of Britain*), helping to generate the sense that a new modern age of steam power had arrived (see also Kellett 1979: *Railways and Victorian Cities*).

11   There is evidently reason to be sceptical of the time-scale envisaged by Michel Foucault (1975) when trying to pinpoint the formation of the 'carceral society' in the early years of the nineteenth century.

12   Best (1985: 24) himself notes that 'The official mid-Victorian definitions of 'urban' and 'rural' were indeed calculated to make the 'urban' sound, at any rate to a modern ear, more intensely so than it often was'.

13   The problems experienced by landowners in this period are outlined in Bence Jones 1882.

14   The Parliamentary Report of the Select Committee on Open Spaces in London was published in 1865 and in the same year, the Commons Preservation Society (C.P.S.) was formed.

15   For a good empirically based discussion of recent Green communal experiments, including the Findhorn community in Scotland, see Pepper 1991.

7 Towards a Socio-Historical Explanation of British Environmentalism

Environmentalism and Radical Ecology: A Conceptual Distinction

Throughout this study my intention has been to use the case of British environmentalism and radical ecology (as far as possible) to provide a critique of current explanatory frameworks in our understanding of social movements. In particular I questioned the assumptions behind, and social-structural models used by new social movement (NSM) theories. The NSM characterisation of the new environmentalism is really only a description of a minority strand within the wider environmental movement, and yet NSM theories see this as a decisive and radical shift providing evidence of post-industrial forms of social movement.

We can certainly accept some distinctive features in the present situation, for instance the shift towards the internationalisation of environmental organisations and the formation of distinctive Green political parties (Müller-Rommel 1982, 1989b; Müller-Rommel and Poguntke 1989; Parkin 1989), with their attempts to devise a broad political programme based on ecocentrism.[1] It is important to note that these new aspects do not fit the NSM characterisation, and are better understood as part of the longer-term development of the environmental movement as a whole. Indeed I contend that NSM theories have presented us with a distorted picture of both the new and old environmentalism which fails to deal satisfactorily with the organised movement's development and growth. In addition, my reconstruction of organised environmentalism has served its own ends in terms of remembering just how long the 'nature' has been the focus for the activities of social movements throughout industrial modernity.

At the start of this inquiry I began with the distinction between environmentalism and radical ecology and which has shaped the form of debate both within and outside of the movement in the contemporary period (and before). This has proved to be a simple but useful device for understanding the different motivations for action in defence of nature, but I now want to explore this distinction further to show how the radical perspective provides a constant reference point for a critique of practical reform-oriented environmentalism which will set the scene for constructing a processual framework for understanding both contemporary activism and the development of the environmental movement over time.

One way to deepen our understanding of the different analyses of environmentalists and radicals is to show the way in which they conceptualise the society/nature relationship. That is, to look at the way they perceive society/nature relations at a high level of abstraction. Evernden (1992: 101) notes that both environmentalism and radical ecology '... share at least one assumption: that there *is* a thing called nature that needs our help. Both are in that sense at least, obvious inheritors of the long tradition of nature-thinking'. I think that they do both work with a dualistic conception of society and nature, but this dualism takes different forms.

Environmentalism sees nature and society interrelated though relatively distinct realms, with the main thrust of its efforts directed at regulating or managing the interchange between them, particularly as industrial societies make heavy demands on natural resources. Environmentalists try to bring a rational order to society's use of nature. The society/nature problematic lies at the border between human societies and nature. In so far as industrial

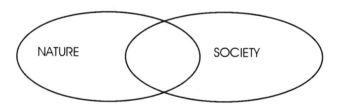

Figure 7.1 Environmentalism

development and technologies have become the main source of damage to nature at this border, then environmentalists seek to curb their effects by preserving important wildlife habitats, ensuring nature reserves and so on. In short, by controlling the effects and spread of industrialisation. A representative question environmentalists might pose is, how can we best use nature's resources to human advantage without exhausting them?

Economic growth is not perceived as a problem in itself, as different forms of technological development can quite radically alter the potentially damaging effects of continual growth. For example, switching to solar power to replace the widespread use of non-renewable sources of energy, could enable more economic activity not less (Lewis 1994). Increasingly however, the internationalist emphasis of contemporary environmentalism has shifted this whole problematic to levels above the nation-state, raising concerns about global problems and advocating international action and agreements to deal with these. Even so, the dualistic approach to society/nature relations still holds, but the concept of 'society' must be expanded to mean 'global human society' or some such term. Nevertheless, the problem is essentially similar; industrial development must be regulated and rationally controlled. This is clearly a technocentric approach to environmental problems (O'Riordan 1981), though it does not follow that it is also an unconcerned cornucopian one (Cotgrove 1982).

For radical ecologists however, the environmentalist perspective misrepresents society/nature relations. This is evident from Fig. 2, where societies are firmly located within the bounds of a limited, finite natural world. In this conceptualisation, the problem is subtly different. The concentration here is on establishing what is society's proper place within the

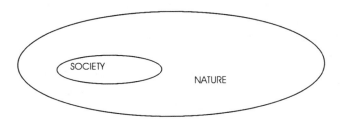

Figure 7.2 Radical ecology

natural world. The problem now is not how we can best use nature's resources to human advantage, but what is the form of social organisation which most effectively prevents the disruption of natural processes? Radical ecologists see natural systems as existing in a fragile state of balance, such that every human intervention unpredictable effects, hence the slogan 'tread softly on the earth', in order to minimise damage. The needs of nature come first, and humans must learn to live in ways which will fit into these. Bookchin's (1980, 1982) anarchistic social ecology sees small, decentralised, largely self-sufficient communities as the ideal social form which best fits nature's needs and does least damage, but it is also possible to see attempts to explore the ecological self in this way, as a form of 'practice' (Devall 1990, Ch.2; Devall and Sessions 1985) which encourages individuals to appreciate their place in nature, promoting the perception that damage to nature is damage to the self. This is the best form of nature defence according to transpersonal ecology (Fox 1990; Eckersley 1992).

An example of the way the two conceptions lead to different proposals can be seen in the issue of energy use. From an environmentalist position, Lewis argues for a 'decoupling' of human economic activities from nature (as far as possible) (1994: vii) in order to prevent further damage. This does not mean that humans can somehow survive without nature, but that the more that economies can be moved away from a reliance on organic, natural processes, fossil fuels and so on, replacing these with synthetic alternatives, the more nature protection will be possible. As he says, 'Our future lies not in abandoning technology, but in harmonizing it to a new environmental vision' (ibid: 15). In environmentalist terms, if taken seriously, the radical ecological proposal for a genuine return to natural living would lead to more ecological problems not fewer, 'If most Americans were to feel a need to devote a month every year to communing with nature in a wilderness area, the immediate result would be a massive loss of true wilderness' (ibid: viii). Lewis suggests that if nature is to be protected in the future, then high-technology solutions to environmental problems will be necessary.

For their part, eco-radicals this is no solution at all, because technological solutions still involve industrial production and are subject to the same criticisms as all other industrial technologies. Human societies exist and are dependent on a finite natural world, so the very idea of de-coupling is an unrealistic one. Industrial production methods and patterns of consumption which involve increasingly global transportation systems can never be sustainable in a finite natural world, so the solution must be to scale these down in a return to more self-sufficient, less energy intensive forms of life. Devall (1990: 83) gives an example of this:

> I try to base my own style, as much as possible, on products produced in my own bioregion. I buy milk and cheese from local dairies, salmon and other seafood in season (not frozen) caught in local waters, beer from a local

brewery, house furnishings made by local craftsmen and artists. Rich experience does not have to be expensive.

The similarity with Edward Carpenter's advocacy in the 1880s, of a return to simple lifestyles in tune with natural cycles is striking, and shows not only the prefiguring of current debates, but also the longevity of the reformism versus radicalism axis in the history of nature politics.

These conceptual distinctions help to create a clearer picture of just what the points of departure are for environmentalists and radicals. The important point is that radicals argue their analysis and the solutions they offer go beyond a now outdated ameliorist environ-mentalism. In a critique of this idea, Goodin (1992: 43) argues that,

> Implicit in the shallow/deep dichotomy [environmentalism/radical ecology] is, in effect, an assertion that the deeper view of the matter contains all the truths of the shallower view, plus some additional ones as well. The truth of the matter is, of course, otherwise. The shallow view is in no sense a proper subset of the deep one. Rather, the two are simply *different* views. Which is the right view is, therefore, a genuinely open question.

To an extent, this can be seen in the conceptualisations described above.[2] Radical ecological thought offers an alternative conception of the society/nature relationship from which a critique of moderate environment-alism can be mounted. The two are therefore in conflict over what is the best approach to society/nature relations. They start from different positions, produce different arguments for nature protection, and consequently offer different solutions. The problem identified in this work is that although it is the case that the radical ecology perspective has shaped much recent academic debate with its call for exploring the ecological self, decentralising society, de-industrialising and living closer to nature, it is a mistake to think that the wider environmental movement is being transformed in this radical direction.

In the same way that revolutionary socialist groups berate the Labour Party and trades unions for pursuing reforms within the capitalist system instead of working to overthrow it, a similar relationship is at work in the politics of nature, where the working out of practical, pragmatic reforms will always be subject to radical attacks, whilst the specific character of radicalism is affected by the successful initiatives which alter the terrain on which the reform/radical axis stands. This gives environmentalism (and other social movements) an immanent dynamic and direction towards the gradual widening and expansion of its concerns.

The identification of global environmental problems and the shift to an international level of organisation has helped to generate a context which is favourable to the radical ecological conception of nature as a global ecosystem. This globalisation of environmental concern is one reason for the assumption among NSM theorists that the radical ecology strand has permeated the mass environmental movement (Sklair 1994), but we saw in Chapter Five that the evidence for this position is weak. Similarly, Eder's (1993) reading of the creation of a mass environmental movement as signifying the social-transformative potential of nature politics is not borne out here.

The rest of this chapter constitutes an attempt to introduce some of the elements of social process in long-term development of environmentalism as an alternative to reading off new social movements from large scale, disjunctive social-structural change, and therefore to fill in some of the gaps in the thesis. This explanation foregrounds social processes, but also identifies a series of connected phases which help us to capture significant moments marking transitions to expanded levels of environmental concern and organisation. Towards this end I want first to examine a recent attempt to use a model of phases in the explanation of the trajectory of post-1968 environmentalism. This will help to show the potential utility of such a model, but in my critique of this particular attempt I will be able to demonstrate why a longer-term perspective is vital.

Phase Models and Social Process

Andrew Jamison's recent argument attempts to use a series of connected phases to explain the direction of recent environmental movement activity (Jamison 1996). In this sense his work is much close to my thinking on the way the environmental movement has developed over time.[3] It should be noted at the start however, that Jamison does not make use of the distinction between environmentalism and radical ecology in this discussion, preferring instead to use environmentalism, ecology and Green as synonymous expressions. I will point out where this becomes particularly problematic. However, from the analysis he produces it becomes clear that his concern is with internationalist environmentalism and its concerns.

Jamison argues that the environmental movement has passed through a series of connected phases which have followed a clear direction, from a period of general ecological awakening, through a flurry of social movement activity, and finally to the incorporation and integration of the movement's 'knowledge interests' within the wider society (and hence the de-radicalisation of the movement itself).[4] He sees the movement's chronological development in the following way (Jamison 1996: 227):

Period	Phase	Emphasis
pre-1968:	awakening	public education
1969-74:	organisation	institution building
1975-80:	social movement	political controversy
1981-86:	professionalisation	environmental assessment
1987-	internationalisation	incorporation / integration

What Jamison is trying to show here is that there was a direction to the recent development of environmentalism, and this is one of the main advantages from his model of phases, which facilitates a move away from positing static social states towards a more dynamic model of change. Jamison argues that from a period of generally increased awareness of environmental problems emerged a phase when organisation-building was considered important and which led to he formation of the Green Party, Greenpeace, Friends of the Earth and others. This activity politicised environmentalism, bringing it into contact with formal politics and the state. At this stage a genuine social movement was created which was able to publicise its knowledge interests and force the rest of society to take notice. In doing so, the environmental movement attracted the interest of professionals in the state administration, political parties and scientific establishments who incorporated ecological issues leading to the eventual professionalisation of movement organisations. At this point the ecological message became assimilated into the wider society, and this marked the normalisation of environmentalism and the de-radicalisation of environment-alism as a social movement.

As an heuristic model, there are some distinct advantages to this kind of approach. It is able to capture shifts of emphasis in the development of the movement which are seen as specific phases of activity. The model also shows an awareness of changes in the form of organisation over time, and hence avoids seeing social movements as characterised by one specific type of organisational structure or campaigning style, as in NSM theory's emphasis on loose networks. The theorised shift from a loose form (the social movement phase) to a more professional and bureaucratic one (the professionalisation phase) which relies more heavily on science-based, rational argument would seem to fit the actual development of groups such as Friends of the Earth and Greenpeace much better than NSM theory. However, there are some problems specifically related to Jamison's broader thesis concerning the knowledge interests and cognitive praxis of social movements (Cramer et al 1987).

Jamison's account is rooted in his wider theory (with Ron Eyerman) of social movements as relatively short-lived episodes of 'cognitive praxis' which become less effective when their message (in this case of global ecological damage) is incorporated by more powerful established groups (business, political parties, governments) and effectively becomes deconstructed into its component parts (Jamison 1996: 240-43).[5] The idea of cognitive praxis involves three dimensions:

1. The production of a new worldview or *Weltanschauung*: the cosmological dimension.
2. The identification of new issues and social problems to be solved: the technological dimension.
3. The generation of new organisational settings in which the previous two dimensions are developed: the organisational dimension.

When these three elements come together, a social movement is created which is capable of pursuing its knowledge interests into the wider society.[6] Jamison (1996: 239) says that,

> Social movements for us, are conceptualised as 'cognitive praxis'; and this cognitive praxis is an integrative activity, bringing together new world-view assumptions, or ideas about reality, with the identification of new problems or issues in innovative organisational settings ... our argument has been that social movements become cognitive actors when the three dimensions are integrated into a cohesive cognitive praxis ...Such integrative praxis exists only for short periods; other social actors eventually grow interested and try to incorporate the various component parts of the social movement's knowledge interests into their own cognitive praxis.

In relation to environmentalism he says that '... the global environmental discourse represents the environmental movement's coming in from the cold, its incorporation into established political routines and, as such, its demise, at least temporarily, as an activist, outsider movement' (ibid: 225). For Jamison therefore, between 1975 and 1980 radical ecology *was* a social movement, but in the 1980s and '90s it has been deconstructed into its three component parts. The World Wide Fund for Nature (W.W.F.) continues to promote the ecological worldview, business corporations take an interest in producing ecologically sound products and technologies without any adherence to the ecological worldview, and finally, formerly radical organisations such as Greenpeace have lost their radical edge, gradually becoming more bureaucratic and populist, no longer promoting significant social change.

One problem with Jamison's approach from the perspective of my argument in this book is that he only considers post-1968 developments, describing the previous period as one of 'awakening'. I think that this comes much too close to endorsing a new versus old interpretation of environmentalism. I have been arguing against this as it fails to explain the origins of environmental concern, nor does it enable us to see the way that an internationalist environmentalism concerned with global problems has developed over a longer time-scale. This aspect of the contemporary movement does have some clearly discernible forerunners. Secondly, the definition of social movement is limited to a conception of movements as producers of knowledge, and although this is part of what they do, it is insufficient to reduce movements to this function. Environmental movement organisations continually work to try to regulate industrial development, and in doing so they are repeatedly drawn into contact with scientific research and knowledge production, and political decision-making. It is not satisfactory to restrict the movement's knowledge producing function to a brief five year span (1975-80). Thirdly, we need to remember that social movements and their constituent organisations also form emotional communities of feeling (*Gemeinde*) and mutual solidarity, tied in to processes of personality formation. That is, a movement is also '... a form of affectual solidarity that allows, through the creation of distinct lifestyles, shared symbols and solidarity, a revalorization of self-identity' (Hetherington 1993: 768). This is one of the reasons for looking deeper than simply the most public, visible aspects of movement activity. To see social movements as fleeting periods of cognitive praxis is to miss out on the activities of actors submerged within the networks of everyday life (Melucci 1989), including those within and between movement organisations. Environmental organisations offer resources and sites for the construction of self-identities and as such are more than just knowledge producers.

By focusing only on visible actions and the knowledge producing aspect of the environmental movement, Jamison is led to the misleading conclusion that the life of the movement is very short-lived. I think that this rather weakens the potential gains of adopting a model of phases. If movements only really exist at one particular period or phase, then at other times they are not really movements at all, but loose aggregates of individuals, unrelated organisations or simply collections of ideas, and this makes social movements rather unusual features of social life. Like Alain Touraine, I think social movements are a much more important part of social life than that, and I would argue that even after the incorporation/assimilation of parts of the movement's ideological position and knowledge interest by other social groups, and after changes to the form of environmental organisations, the latter continue to defend their gains and work towards advancing environmentalist interests.

The organised environmental movement continues to oppose uncontrolled industrial development, as it always has done, but it now does so on a number of different levels, local, national and international, while its range of concerns has steadily grown over time. To see how this has occurred, we need a longer-term developmental model of the history of environmentalism.

In this study I have concentrated on the growth of the organised environmental movement over time as a standpoint from which to criticise the old versus new framework which is embodied in new social movement theories, and to make the case for moving beyond this. The critical intent of the research has meant that I have been particularly concerned to point out some neglected similarities of environmental concerns and continuities, for example of organisational forms within the movement from its origins in the 1860s. However, environmental concerns and activities have expanded over time, and environmental organisations now operate on a number of levels. This section presents the expansion of environmentalism though a model of connected phases.

The identification of a series of phases in the long-term development of environmentalism is not intended to be read as implying that each phase forms a distinct period with its own exclusive characteristics. The phase model here acts as a means of orientation (Goudsblom 1989: 16) which enables us to capture for analysis some of the main developments of environmental concerns as they have expanded over time, and also helps to raise some questions concerning the mechanisms and social processes which have brought about this expansion. I think that the social processes need to be brought into the foreground with specific phases seen as 'moments' within these. Goudsblom (1989: 17-18) explains why this is important:

> At first sight, there appears to be a fundamental difference between 'processes' and 'phases': the former seem to be dynamic - characterised by movement - whereas the latter seem to be static. At closer range, however, it is clear that processes of transformation seldom stop at a particular juncture; the normal course, certainly for social processes, is to continue in one form and direction or another, even when a new 'stage' has been reached. Every 'stage' or 'phase' is a passage in an ongoing movement; it consists of minor processes and it forms a part of larger processes.

The identified phases of environmental concern and organisation should then be seen as part of a process of widening environmentalist concern and action. Before I get into an extended discussion of the three main phases and the transitions between them, it is important to specify some of the elements of social process through which new developments have been generated. I do this through the identification of a number of axes around which changes are produced that push the movement to new levels of concern and organisation.

The Reformism/Radicalism Axis

In Chapter Three, Eder's (1993) thesis of the history of modern culture as internally divided between a dominant modernism and subordinate romanticism was seen to be useful in so far as it sensitises us to the kinds of recurring 'pendulum-swing' (Mannheim 1953: 124) between these two traditions in the history of social protest, in the form of anti-science movements (Toulmin 1972) for example, or in the flowering of alternative counter-cultures, both of which draw on the cultural tradition of romanticism (as in Brand 1990). Where Eder's thesis falls down however, is in the attempt to construct an interpretation of contemporary culture as marking a decisive shift towards reversing the two sides as romanticism becomes dominant and modernism is subordinated. The evidence from the history of environmentalism presented here does not support such an interpretation of disjunctive social and cultural change.

Nonetheless, it is evident that the environmental movement has developed partly through the dialectical interplay between romantic ideals of a return to nature, the benefits of a life lived close to the land and so on, and the rational, modernist attempt to reform the existing society. Even though environmental reformists reject the solutions offered by radicals, they nevertheless make use of radical arguments as part of their own propaganda, and can be seen to exhibit signs of radical influence in taking forward the identification of problems and translating these into practical proposals for reform. In particular periods the utopian radical horizon continues to be a source of inspiration and motivation which brings new activists into the movement, and its analysis can be seen to be pulling the environmental movement into different areas of concern. In this way the submerged and occasionally highly visible romantic side of modern culture has provided a continually accessible repository of radical ideas and modes of argument about society/nature relations which enables critics of current environmental practices to instigate new issues. The radical critique has been a spur to new developments, consistently berating existing organisations for their limited aspirations and goals. In the late-nineteenth century, and again in the late twentieth century, this has been particularly influential in propelling environmentalist interests into a new phase, of organisation-building and internationalisation respectively.

The Problem Identification/Practical Implementation Spiral

Since the formation of the earliest organisations, the kinds of initiatives pursued by the environmental movement have undergone a process of expansion, gradually moving environmentalism into the preservation and conservation of larger areas of nature. Part of the social process underlying this expansion of concern is internal to the movement itself, and can best be described as an expansionary spiral, which starts with the identification of an environmental problem, followed by attempts to formulate and implement practical solutions. Once implemented, the general form of the solution can be applied to other problems, whilst the new situation becomes the starting point, at a different level, for the identification of problems at a higher level, thus leading to a gradual expansion of environmentalist concerns over time in the general direction of a larger conception of nature.

I shall outline this expansionary process in the next section, but to make the abstract analysis a little more concrete, part of my general argument is that the recent shift towards international environmentalist organisation and the identification of global concerns is best seen as part of the more extended and gradual process of the expansion of environmentalism which began in the late nineteenth century. In this sense, the wide range of issues which concern groups like Friends of the Earth and Greenpeace, and which seems to mark them out as very different from single-issue environmentalism, is a product of the long-term development of environmentalism which had begun much earlier than the 1970s, and formed part of the expanding spiral of environmental concern. And although this internationalisation has clearly had an important impact on previously established environmental organisations in terms of the way that the protection of nature is now seen as best served (many environmentalists now support the policy of 'sustainable development' for example), I think that a longer-term explanation is an advance on theories which de-contextualise contemporary shifts, and therefore fail to see that contemporary developments are the culmination of longer-term processes of change.

State Involvement: Established/Outsider Relations

A further factor which needs to be considered is the involvement of the national state in environmental management and conservation, particularly after the Second World War. This is an important development because once state conservation bodies are formed, many voluntary movement organisations become more involved in lobbying for legislative change, take part in public inquiries and so on, whilst others may decide to stay outside established channels. Not only does this push environmental organisations towards professionalisation in order to be taken seriously and to facilitate the presentation of a 'good case', but formal and informal channels are opened up with state bodies and individuals within these, which enable environmental organisations to become more established and to provide a clear focus for their campaigning effort.

The other side of this development is that it leaves the established organisations open to the radicals' charge of complicity with the state in maintaining the status quo. This is apparent in the way that radicals in the 1970s perceived themselves to be part of a genuinely new movement, entirely separate from earlier environmentalism, but can also be seen in the environmentalists' own suspicions of the radical Green Party. With the advent of more internationalist organisations, radicals could argue that the national groups were tied too closely to the nation-state, thus preventing them from organising and campaigning at a level adequate to deal with newly identified global problems.

Since the 1960s the creation of an international political context for environmental campaigning has influenced the campaigning strategies of environmental groups, particularly those which concentrate on global issues. The European Union's Environment Programme and the United Nations Conference on Environment and Development process (U.N.C.E.D.), are examples of the way that changes in the external political context can offer both opportunities for participation and 'dangers' of incorporation for environmental organisations. In this way, the potential at least, exists for this context partially to constrain and shape the organisations' aims and forms of campaigning (Tarrow 1994).

In the final section I shall explore some of the ways in which these mechanisms and processes have worked at various times to bring about the shape and content of the contemporary environmental movement. I cannot hope to construct anything like a comprehensive account here, but I think enough can be achieved to demonstrate that this kind of social process approach has more explanatory power and better accounts for the actual development of environmentalism than the alternatives already discussed.

The Long-Term Development of Environmentalism

The discussion which follows covers some important developments, particularly where environmentalist interests shift to a new level, both in terms of content and practical efforts, and in their organisational forms. The identification of these phases is shown schematically in table 7.1. It should be remembered that all of the dates in this table are intended as signposts to mark out some of the main developments and extensions of organisational focus, they are not intended to be the definitive points of radical changes.

Table 7.1   Phases in the long-term development of British environmentalism

Period	Phase	Content & focus	Campaigning levels
1500-1860	Pre-history	Changing sensibilities, non-utilitarian attitudes to the natural world	-----------
Phase 1 1860-1900	Organisation-building	Open spaces protection, aesthetic appreciation, public access to nature, national historic buildings	Local/National
Phase 2 1900-1960	Expansion & state involvement	Nature reserves, habitat protection, rural life & countryside, national forests, international nature	National/Local (International)
Phase 3 1960-1990	Mass membership & internationalisation	Resource conservation, anti-nuclear, nature as 'the Earth', sustainable development	Global/Local (National)

In Chapter Four I discussed Thomas's (1984) and Elias's (1982) ideas concerning the gradual shift in attitudes towards the natural world over a long period of time, from the early modern period in Britain. They both argue that alongside the idea of nature as machine to be understood and controlled (Merchant 1982), was a gradual but discernible shift in sensibilities in favour of the aesthetic appreciation of natural beauty and wilderness. These two underlying attitudes to nature form part of the characteristic tension in modern culture between modernism and romanticism identified by Eder (1993), and although this area of study is enormously complex and many of the conclusions drawn from it must be considered as tentative, there is some agreement amongst different authors that the characteristic modern dualism of society and nature also stems from this period (Kelsen 1944; Collingwood 1945; Capra 1983).[7]

Rather than seeing the natural world as simply made for humans, who were able to do with it as they saw fit, concerns began to be raised for the welfare of animals and people came to appreciate 'wild' nature rather than seeing it as unproductive and in need of cultivation. These shifts in sensibilities and attitudes can be seen as producing the 'conditions of possibility' for organised environmentalism, and also gave impetus to animal welfare campaigns (the Society for the Prevention of Cruelty to Animals (S.P.C.A.) was formed in 1824) as well as being part of the artistic and literary romanticism of the late eighteenth and early nineteenth centuries.

I want now to explore some of the main features of each environmentalist phase as this will help to make explicit the developmental framework which has so far been implicit in the study. It should be noted that the phases are defined primarily by changes in the scope of the concerns and actions of environmental organisations, the levels at which environmental campaigning is pursued, and the relationship of a particular phase to the longer term development of the movement overall.

The period between 1860 and 1900 saw the creation of the first series of formal environmental organisations. A number of factors contributed to their formation apart from the spread of non-utilitarian attitudes to nature. More immediately important was a growing awareness of the unhealthy conditions of urban environments, industrial pollution of the air and rivers, and concern at the enclosure of common land for building. All of these had been evident for some time, but what had changed to provoke concerted action was the growing recognition that industrialism was a permanent state of society, to all intents and purposes irreversible. The early environmental reformers sought to prevent the industrial system from swallowing up nature and even national historical memories as embodied in buildings of national significance. The preservation of buildings of historic interest, creation and maintenance of open spaces in cities, protection of areas of natural beauty (such as the Lake District) and common land (and the right to roam freely on it), were founded on the principle that they improved the quality of life for people. As environmental interests began to be formally expressed and pursued at the local and national levels, a commonality of interest was created and environmental organisations in this period carried their concerns forward into the twentieth century.

This first phase of environmental organisation, which saw the creation of (amongst others) the Commons Preservation Society (1865), National Trust (1895) and the Society for the Protection of Birds (1889), can partly be seen as an attempt to turn radical proposals for re-connecting humans and nature, such as communal living, de-industrialisation, and simple lifestyles, in short the overthrow of existing society which was expressed by sections of socialist and anarchist thinking, into more moderate efforts at bringing people into contact with nature through practical conservation. And although environmental organisations did not seek to put radical ideals into practice, they were not wholly immune from these. A telling illustration of the interrelationship between reformism and radicalism lies in Octavia Hill's (cited in Gaze 1988: 18) comment that Ruskin '... was a visionary whose teaching could not always be taken literally'.

The thoughts of Ruskin and William Morris on the need to preserve natural beauty and historic buildings, Carpenter's practice of living simply as an alternative to Victorian over-civilisation and the socialist Clarion movement's love of the open-air were all motivating factors for many early environmentalists, who made use of ideas of the human need for natural beauty and the preservation of oases of nature in order to raise funds and attract interest, but they translated these ideals into a more limited conservationism which the C.P.S. showed could achieve real successes. This phase laid the organisational foundations on which twentieth century environmentalists continued to build, and as such, marks the point of departure for later forms, which are difficult to fully understand without appreciating their development from these earlier initiatives.

The period from 1900-60 is an extended one because, although environmental activity did not stop during the Two World Wars, its momentum was interrupted.[8] Taken as a whole though, this period consolidated and expanded the earlier concerns, new organisations were regularly formed, the state became involved in conservation, and the first signs of an international focus for environmental campaigning became visible. A few specific features of this phase will fill in the picture. A National Trust was established in Scotland in 1931, along the same lines as the original organisation. The Council for the Preservation of Rural England (C.P.R.E.) (1926) and Council for the Preservation of Rural Wales (C.P.R.W.) (1935) were created to monitor urban planning and development in an intense period of house-building which extended the boundaries of urban living. The idea of preserving open spaces was broadened into a concern to establish larger areas set aside for wildlife and nature, which led to the creation in 1912 of The Society for the Promotion of Nature Reserves (S.P.N.R.) (now the Royal Society for Nature Conservation), and whereas the S.P.N.R. researched and listed possible nature reserves, the R.S.P.B. began to purchase and maintain its own reserves in 1930, as had the Norfolk Naturalists' Trust (N.N.T.) which showed the way practically, by acquiring fifteen reserves by 1941 (Evans 1992: 55). County trusts on this model spread across the country in the post-war period. In 1929, C.P.R.E. also began to argue for the creation of National Parks, supported on public access grounds by the Federation of Rambling Clubs, and it was campaigning to persuade government of the need for National Parks which led to the Derbyshire direct action 'mass trespasses' of the 1930s. Ten National Parks were designated between 1951 and 1957.

If we take the whole period, from the first organisational phase which began in the1860s, through to the 1960s, we can see that the environmental movement has continually expanded its range of concerns. A specific example of this process can be seen in the way that attempts to preserve natural areas has expanded from public parks and open spaces in cities, through the protection of wildlife habitat and creation of nature reserves, to the creation of National Parks in the 1950s (Fig.3), all the way to today's identification of global environmental problems. In the late-nineteenth century, environmental reformers sought to preserve important buildings, public parks and open spaces in cities, and to encourage the appreciation of nature, partly through campaigning for public access. After the turn of the century these concerns began to broaden out into arguments in favour of larger areas in the form of nature reserves and the protection of wildlife habitat, as well as more explicit concern at the loss of the countryside and forests and woodlands. It seems increasingly the campaigning focus became national rather than local in this period. That is, although local initiatives

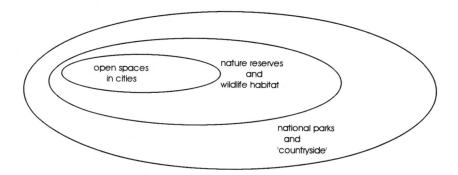

Figure 7.3 The expansion of nature conservation: open spaces to National Parks

continued, environmentalism came to be seen as best served by a planned national strategy for conservation. Examples of this were the founding of a series of nature reserves, the creation of the Nature Conservancy (1948) and its research into national sites of special scientific interest (SSSI's), and the establishment of National Parks in the 1950s. In a sense, the defence of nature was coming to be defined in national terms, and in order to achieve this, recourse to arguments about the need for state intervention to protect the natural world gained force.

The first state sponsored conservation body in Britain was The Forestry Commission, formed in 1919, ostensibly to address the problem of a shortage of timber reserves after the First World War, and as part of its brief was to be profitable, it came into conflict with voluntary conservation groups who saw the profit motive as threatening to take precedence over conservation. The first real national state body charged with nature conservation was The Nature Conservancy (NC), created in 1948. Its aims were threefold: 1) to provide scientific advice on the conservation and control of flora and fauna, 2) to establish and manage nature reserves, including 'physical features of scientific interest', and 3) to organise and develop research and scientific services related to the above. A specific example of this new role was the NC's listing and notification of sites of special scientific interest (SSSIs), such as those which contain rare or endangered species. In addition there has been the creation of the Countryside Commission (1969) and the Department of the Environment (1970). With the involvement of the state in conservation, a new focus was created for criticism and lobbying, and new organisations could begin to perceive themselves as 'outsiders' working to force through a more radical agenda. As we saw previously, the origins of a more internationalist approach to environmentalism can also be traced to this period, in particular after 1948 with the creation of the International Union for the Conservation of Nature.

To the extent that the counter-cultural wave of the 1960s revived ideals of a return to nature (Musgrove 1974; Brand 1990), it can be seen as providing support for a new internationalist environmentalism concerned with global issues and for the creation of a radical ecological perspective, though it also fed into peace, anti-nuclear and other social movements. However, an internationalist focus was being discussed as early as the 1920s in relation to the protection of migrating birds, and later in the formation of the International Union for the Protection of Nature (I.U.P.N.) in 1948, it is clear that the environmental movement was moving gradually towards adding an international level to its local and national campaigning, recognising the logic of international co-operation and agreement to protect the natural world writ large.

Nevertheless, it is not really until the 1960s that an international environmentalism became visible at the organisational level, with the formation of the W.W.F. (1961), F.o.E. International (1971), and later Greenpeace International (1977), and the current interest in global environmental issues does represent the coming to fruition of the earlier projects. Even so, local and national organisations have continued to be formed, but the shift towards an international level of organisation and concern has been founded on the identification of a whole range of new global environmental problems.

Between 1960 and 1990 environmentalism became a genuinely mass movement with huge increases in the membership of all environmental organisations. This was a period when the movement 'went public' and old organisations launched new campaigns. In addition international governmental bodies began to take an interest in global environmental issues and thus helped to create a climate of interest, necessary for recruiting members. The National Trust launched Enterprise Neptune in 1965, an attempt to acquire funds to buy large areas of coastline to prevent further development. The W.W.F. was launched with much media interest in 1961 to raise funds for the I.U.C.N., and 1970 was declared European Conservation Year. In 1971 the United Nations Educational, Scientific and Cultural Organisation (U.N.E.S.C.O.) launched its Man and the Biosphere programme to investigate the global use of resources, and a year later the UN Conference on the Human Environment took place in Stockholm, and the E.E.B. was formed to co-ordinate the efforts of national environmental groups within the European Union. The World Commission on Environment and Development was set up in 1983, leading to the Bruntland report, *Our Common Future* (1987), and the 1992 United Nations Conference on Environment and Development (U.N.C.E.D.).

Also at this time, catastrophist environmental writers performed the function of popularising potentially disastrous global problems such as rapidly expanding populations, global resource depletion and pollution of the air and seas, as well as continuing concerns over nuclear power and weapons production. F.o.E. (1971) and Greenpeace (1977) began to attract public attention to these problems with their media presence, and the British Green Party oriented its 1974 programme around 'saving the planet'. It is in this period that nature came to be defined in planetary rather than national terms, and a global environmental problematic was widely accepted, bringing environmentalists into closer contact (and sometimes conflict) with the World Development Movement. The very scale of these problems seemed remote from newly interested environmentalists, and the slogan, 'think globally, act locally' was popularised to stand for the idea that responsible individual action could be a valuable contribution to solving problems which are global in scope.

In this period with its internationalised focus, counter-cultural critique was able to feed more readily into support for radical ecology which seemed far removed from reform environmentalism. The student movements of the 1960s and the wave of counter-cultural protest in many Western societies occurred within a context of greater affluence, where postmaterial concerns had spread further. So, whereas the romantic movement of the late eighteenth and early nineteenth centuries was largely confined to relatively small groups of artists, writers and bohemians (Brand 1990), in the 1960s the potential reservoir of counter-cultural support was much wider (Shils 1972: 276-79; see also Musgrove 1974). Ecological radicalism in the form of proposals for small-scale decentralised communities in close contact with the natural world, and arguments for propagating an ecological self in touch with the rest of nature, gained credence at this time. It may even have seemed that the whole environmental movement was being transformed in the direction of a mass radical social movement against industrial society. But as I have argued, I do not think that this kind interpretation can be supported today when the intense period of counter-cultural critique has faded,[9] student radicalism has ended, and radical ecology remains a minority orientation. Nevertheless the environmental movement's shift to a new level of campaigning and the creation of an organisational focus above the nation-state was facilitated by the radical analysis and interpretation of society/nature relations as a global problem, and in this sense the dialectical interplay of moderate and radical elements in the contemporary period has worked to create a genuinely mass-based environmentalism.

Conclusion

In so far as the emergence of distinctively new, potentially socially transformative Green or environmental movements is used as evidence in support of post-industrial theories (Touraine 1971; Eder 1993; Lash and Urry 1987; Hall and Jacques 1989), then these theories find little support here. The lack of fit between the main assumptions of new social movement theories and the reconstruction of the long-term development of the organised environmental movement raises some serious questions in relation to the NSM interpretation. There is therefore a need for the NSM thesis to be examined more closely in relation to other social movements, in order to test its ability to account for the specific history of women's movements, peace movements, civil rights movements and so on. This would help to throw both the analysis and explanation of environmentalism in this study, and NSM theories into wider relief, and give us a better overall picture of social movements in general.

The explanation developed in this book is not intended as either the final word on the analysis of environmentalism, nor is it the fully finished article in terms of process theories. Nevertheless it is suggestive of further research into social movements and their constituent organisations. To what extent has an ecocentric orientation has permeated environmental organisations and the wider public? In what ways is the internationalisation phase altering established local and national environmental organisations? What is the current extent of overlap among environmental organisation members? What evidence is there of dissatisfaction with the lack of democratic participation in the organisations? Could the international orientation develop into a more properly 'global' one?

My general intention has been to start to clear the ground for a more adequate understanding of nature politics, and to show that a social process perspective which takes the longer-term seriously in relation to social movements, can highlight some of the lines of continuity and direction of development which are easily missed in theories which concentrate attention only on contemporary manifestations.

Notes

1 These attempts would also include those of academics working both within and outside the Green Party itself.
2 In more sociological conceptualisations of the society/nature relationship it is possible to identify both 'weak' and 'strong' forms of social constructionism. An example of the former is as follows:

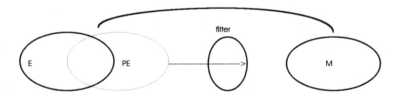

Key: E   Environment [Nature]
      PE Perceived Environment
      M   Man

Source: Pepper 1996: 6 (after Jeans, D, 'Changing Formulations of the man-environment relationship in Anglo-American Geography' in *Journal of Geography*, 73(3), 36-40).

Figure 7.4 Man / environment relationship

Here, Pepper argues that societies only come to know nature via specific cultural filters, such as religions or science, which means that the 'perceived environment' is what counts in policy proposals and decision - making. Nevertheless, there is an awareness that a real world of nature exists in itself, outside of the way that humans construct it. However, 'strong' constructionism goes further than this to argue that, because the real environment is only knowable through the filter of a particular culture, analysis should focus on the way that different societies' cultural filters effectively construct different natural worlds (as in Tester 1991). We can represent this different perspective as follows:

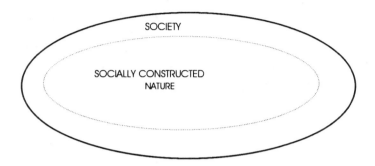

Figure 7.5 Social construction of nature

There is no recognition here of a real natural world with its own properties, or which exists in itself. These differing conceptualisations are of course one part of current disputes between realism and social constructionism in sociology (Delanty 1996).

3   Jamison's use of the term environmentalism does not run directly parallel with my own. He uses the term to describe both environmentalism and radical ecology, as I use these terms. This misses the interplay between reformist and radical approaches to society/nature relations.

4   Offe (1990) has also attempted to show the development of social movements towards more established and professional forms of organisation.

5   The thesis of movements as cognitive praxis is explored in detail in Eyerman, R & Jamison, A, 1989, 1991.

6   In the discussion of knowledge interests here, there is more than a hint of the influence of Habermas's (1972) thesis in, *Knowledge and Human Interests*, London, Heinemann.

7   Kelsen argues that 'primitive man' (sic) does not treat the natural world respectfully due to a kind of ecological consciousness, rather, the dualism of nature/society does not exist. This does not mean that all is 'natural' however, but that all is 'social'. "Nature' for him is not, as for civilized man, a sphere different from society. Such a dualism does not exist for primitive man. Still less does he conceive society, as do modern sociologists, as a part of nature; rather, nature for him is a part of society' (Kelsen 1944: 44). In short, non-modern cultures often interpret all phenomena in terms of and in relation to the social relations and practices in which they live.

8   It is possible to subdivide this period into 1900-47, and 1948-60 based on the shift towards a more international environmentalism with the creation of the I.U.C.N. I have chosen not to do so because consolidation at the national level carried on with the

formation of the Nature Conservancy in 1948, the beginning of explicit state involvement in conservation.

9   In relation to the student counter-culture, Shils (1972: 297) astutely noted that 'Widespread enthusiasm has never persisted before in human history, and it is not likely to do so in the future'.

Bibliography

Adam, B. (1996), 'Re-vision: The Centrality of Time for an Ecological Social Science Perspective', in Lash, S. Szerszynski, B. and Wynne, B. (eds) *Risk, Environment and Modernity: Towards a New Ecology*, London, Sage, pp.84-103.

Albrow, M. (1992), 'Globalization', in Bottomore, T. and Outhwaite, W. (eds), *The Blackwell Dictionary of Twentieth Century Social Thought*, Oxford, Basil Blackwell.

Allen, D.E. (1978), *The Naturalist in Britain: A Social History*, Harmondsworth, Penguin Books Ltd.

Allen, R. (1992), *Waste Not, Want Not: The Production and Dumping of Toxic Waste*, London, Earthscan Publications.

Atkinson, A. (1991), *Principles of Political Ecology*, London, Bellhaven Press.

Aveling, E. B. (1883), *God Dies: Nature Remains*, London, Freethought Publishing Co.

Bagguley, P. (1992), 'Social Change, the Middle Class and the Emergence of New Social Movements: A Critical Analysis' in *The Sociological Review*, Vol.40, No.1, February, pp.26-48.

Bahro, R. (1979), *The Alternative in Eastern Europe*, London, Verso.

Bahro, R. (1982), *Socialism and Survival*, London, Heretic Books.

Bahro, R. (1984), *From Red to Green: Interviews with New Left Review*, London, Verso.

Bahro, R. (1986), *Building the Green Movement*, London, GMP.

Barr, J. (ed) (1971), *The Environmental Handbook: Action Guide for the UK*, London, Ballantine/Friends of the Earth in association with Pan Books Ltd.

Baudrillard, J. (1975), *The Mirror of Production*, St. Louis, Telos Press.

Baudrillard, J. (1983), *Simulations*, New York, Semiotext(e).

Bauman, Z. (1982), *Memories of Class*, London, Routledge and Kegan Paul.

Bauman, Z. (1992), *Intimations of Postmodernity*, London, Routledge.

Beck, U. (1992), *Risk Society : Towards a New Modernity*, London, Sage Publications.

Beck, U. (1994), 'The Reinvention of Politics: Towards a Theory of Reflexive Modernization', in Beck, U. Giddens, A. and Lash, S. (1994), *Reflexive Modernization: Politics, Tradition and Aesthetics in the Modern Social Order*, Cambridge, Polity Press. pp.1-55.

Beck, U. Giddens, A. and Lash, S. (1994), *Reflexive Modernization: Politics, Tradition and Aesthetics in the Modern Social Order*, Cambridge, Polity.

Bédarida, F. (1979), *A Social History of England 1851-75*, London, Methuen.

Bell, D. (1974), *The Coming of Post-Industrial Society: A Venture in Social Forecasting*, Harmondsworth, Penguin Books.

Bell, D. (1980), *The Cultural Contradictions of Capitalism*, New York, Basic Books.

Bence Jones, W. (1882), 'Landowning as a Business', in *The Nineteenth Century*, No.XI, pp.346-368.

Bennie, L. G., et al (1995), 'Green Dimensions: The Ideology of the British Greens', in Rüdig, W. (ed), *Green Politics Three*, Edinburgh, Edinburgh University Press, pp. 217-39.

Benton, T. (1991), 'Biology and Social Science - Why the Return of the Repressed Should be Given a Cautious Welcome', in *Sociology*, 25, pp.1-29.

Benton, T. (1994), *Natural Relations: Ecology, Animal Rights and Social Justice*, London, Verso.

Berman, M. (1981), *The Re-enchantment of the World*, Ithaca, Cornell University Press.

Berman, M. (1985), *All That is Solid Melts Into Air: The Experience of Modernity*, London, Verso Press.

Best, G. (1985), *Mid-Victorian Britain 1851-75*, London, Fontana Press.

Bodeman, Y. M. (1985/86), 'The Green Party and the New Nationalism in the Federal Republic of Germany', in *The Socialist Register*, pp.137-157.

Boggs, C. (1986a), 'The Green Alternative and the Struggle for a Post-Marxist Discourse' in *Theory and Society*, Vol.15, No.6, pp.869-900.

Boggs, C. (1986b), *Social Movements and Political Power: Emerging Forms of Radicalism in the West*, Philadelphia, Temple University Press.

Bookchin, M. (1980), *Towards an Ecological Society*, Montreal, Black Rose Books.

Bookchin, M. (1982), *The Ecology of Freedom: The Emergence and Dissolution of Hierarchy*, Palo Alto, Cheshire Books.

Bookchin, M. (1986), *The Modern Crisis*, Philadelphia, New Society Publishers.

Bookchin, M. (1987), 'Social Ecology Versus Deep Ecology. A Challenge for the Ecology Movement', in *Green Perspectives*, No.s 4 and 5.

Borgstrom, G. (1969), *Too Many*, New York, Macmillan Press.

Bottomore, T. and Rubel, M. (eds) (1990), *Karl Marx: Selected Writings in Sociology and Social Philosophy*, London, Penguin Books.

Lord Brabazon. (1881), 'Health and Physique of our City Populations', in *The Nineteenth Century*, No.10, pp.80-89.

Lord Brabazon. (1887), 'The Decay of Bodily Strength in Towns', in *The Nineteenth Century*, May, pp.673-676.

Bramwell, A. (1989), *Ecology in the Twentieth Century, A History*, London, Yale University Press.

Brand, K.W. (1990), 'Cyclical Aspects of New Social Movements' in Dalton, R.J and Kuechler, M (eds) (1990), *Challenging the Political Order: New Social and Political Movements in Western Democracies*, Cambridge, Polity Press, pp.23-42.

Brantlinger, P. (1975), '"News From Nowhere": Morris's Socialist Anti-Novel', in *Victorian Studies*, XIX, pp.35-49.

Briggs, A. (1984), *A Social History of England*, London, Book Club Associates.

Briggs, A. (ed) (1986), *William Morris: News From Nowhere and Selected Writings and Designs*, Harmondsworth, Penguin Books.

Bryce, J. (1882), *SPAB Report and General Meeting*, SPAB No.24, London.

Brzezinski, Z. (1970), *Between Two Ages: America's Role in the Technotronic Era*, New York, Viking Press.

Bunyard, P. and Morgan - Grenville, F. (eds) (1987), *The Green Alternative*, London, Methuen.

Bunyard, P., Morgan-Grenville, F. and Goldsmith, E. (eds) (1988), *Gaia: The Thesis, the Mechanisms and the Implications*, Wadebridge Ecological Centre, Camelford.

Burke, T. (1982), 'Friends of the Earth and the Conservation of Resources', in Willets, P. (ed), *Pressure Groups in the Global System*, London, Frances Pinter, pp.105-124.

Bürklin, W. P. (1984), 'Governing Left Parties Frustrating the Radical Non-Established Left: The Rise and Inevitable Decline of the Greens', in *European Sociological Review*, No.3, pp.109-26.

Burningham, K. and Cooper, G. (1999), 'Being Constructive: Social Constructionism and the Environment' in *Sociology*, Vol.33, No.2, May, pp.297-316.

Bury, P. (1985), *Agriculture and Countryside Conservation*, Farm Business Unit, Wye College, University of London, FBU Occasional Paper, No.10.

Calhoun, C. (1993), 'Postmodernism as Pseudohistory' in *Theory, Culture and Society*, Vol.10, No.1, February, pp.75-96.

Calhoun, C. (1995), *Critical Social Theory: Culture, History and the Challenge of Difference*, Oxford, Blackwell.

Callenbach, E. (1978), *Ecotopia: A Novel About Ecology, People and Politics in 1999*, London, Pluto Press.

Callinicos, A. (1989), *Against Postmodernism: A Marxist Critique*, Cambridge, Polity Press.

Campbell, C. (1987), *The Romantic Ethic and the Spirit of Modern Consumerism*, Oxford, Blackwell.

Capra, F. (1975), *The Tao of Physics*, London, Fontana.

Capra, F. (1983), *The Turning Point: Science, Society and the Rising Culture*, London, Fontana.

Carpenter, E. (1913), *England's Ideal and Other Papers on Social Subjects*, London, George Allen and Unwin Ltd.

Carpenter, E. (1917), *Towards Democracy* (2nd Edition), Manchester, George Allen and Unwin Ltd.

Carpenter, E. (1917), *Civilization: Its Cause and Cure, and Other Essays*, London, George Allen and Unwin Ltd.

Carson, R. (1962), *Silent Spring*, Boston, Massachusetts, Houghton Mifflin.

Chandler, W.M. and Siaroff, A. (1986), 'Postindustrial Politics in Germany and the Origins of the Greens', in *Comparative Politics*, Vol.18, No.3, April, pp.303-325.

Chisholm, A. (1972), *Philosophers of the Earth: Conversations with Ecologists*, London, Sidgwick and Jackson.

Church, C. (1988), 'Great Chief Sends Modified Word', in *ECOS*, 4, pp.40-1.

Ciba Foundation Symposium (1972), *Civilization and Science: in Conflict or Collaboration?*, Associated Scientific Publishers, Elsevier, Excerpta Medica, North Holland.

Cipolla, C. M. (1967), *The Economic History of World Population*, Harmondsworth, Penguin Books.

Clapp, B. W. (1994), *An Environmental History of Britain Since the Industrial Revolution*, London, Longman Group UK Ltd.

Clayre, A. (ed) (1979), *Nature and Industrialization*, Oxford, Oxford University Press.

Cohen, J. L. (1985), 'Strategy or Identity: New Theoretical Paradigms and Contemporary Social Movements', in *Social Research*, Vol.52, No.4, pp.663-716.

Collingwood, R. G. (1945), *The Idea of Nature*, Oxford, Oxford University Press.

Collins English Dictionary (1991), Glasgow, HarperCollins Publishers.

Conford, P. (ed) (1988), *The Organic Tradition: an Anthology of Writings on Organic Farming 1900-1950*, Bideford, Devon, Green Books.

Conwentz, H. W. (1909), *The Care of Natural Monuments*, Cambridge, Cambridge University Press.

Cornish, V. (1937), *The Preservation of Our Scenery*, Cambridge, Cambridge University Press.

Cotgrove, S. (1982), *Catastrophe or Cornucopia: The Environment, Politics and the Future*, Chichester, John Wiley and Sons.

Cotgrove, S. and Duff, A. (1980), 'Environmentalism, Middle Class Radicalism and Politics' in *The Sociological Review*, No.28i, pp.333-351.

Cotgrove, S. and Duff, A. (1981), 'Environmentalism, Values and Social Change' in *The British Journal of Sociology*, Vol.32, No.1, pp.92-110.

Cramer, J, Eyerman, R. and Jamison, A. (1987), 'The Knowledge Interests of the Environmental Movement and its Potential for Influencing the Development of Science' in Blume, S., et al (eds), *The Social Direction of the Public Sciences*, Dordrecht, Reidel.

Dalton, R.J. and Kuechler, M. (eds) (1990), *Challenging the Political Order: New Social and Political Movements in Western Democracies*, Cambridge, Polity Press.

D'Anieri, P., Ernst, C. and Kier, E. (1990), 'New Social Movements in Historical Perspective', in *Comparative Politics*, Vol.22, No.4, pp.445-456.

Devall, B. (1990), *Simple in Means, Rich in Ends: Practising Deep Ecology*, London, Green Print.

Devall, B. and Sessions, G. (1985), *Deep Ecology: Living as if Nature Mattered*, Salt Lake City, Peregrine Smith.

Diani, M. (1992), 'The Concept of Social Movement', in *The Sociological Review*, No.40, Vol.1, pp.1-19.

Dicken, P. (1992), *Global Shift: The Internationalization of Economic Activity* (Second Edition), London, Paul Chapman Publishing.

Dickens, P. (1992), *Society and Nature: Towards a Green Social Theory*, Hemel Hempstead, Harvester Wheatsheaf.

Dobson, A. (1990), *Green Political Thought: An Introduction*, London, Unwin Hyman Ltd.

Dobson, A. (ed) (1991), *The Green Reader*, London, André Deutsch Ltd.

Doughty, R. W. (1975), *Feather Fashions and Bird Preservation: A Study in Nature Protection*, Berkeley, University of California Press.

Douglas, M. (1984), *Purity and Danger*, London, Routledge.

Dryzek, J. (1987), *Rational Ecology: Environment and Political Economy*, Oxford, Blackwell.

Dwyer, J.C. and Hodge, I.D. (1996), *Countryside in Trust: Land Management by Conservation, Recreation and Amenity Organisations*, Chichester, John Wiley and Sons.

Dyos, H.J. and Wolff, M. (eds) (1973), *The Victorian City: Images and Realities*, London, Routledge and Kegan Paul.

Eckersley, R. (1989), 'Green Politics and the New Class: Selfishness or Virtue?', in *Political Studies*, Vol.xxxvii, No.2, pp.205-223.

Eckersley, R. (1990), 'Habermas and Green Political Thought: Two Roads Diverging', in *Theory and Society*, Vol.19, No.6, December, pp.739-776.

Eckersley, R. (1992), *Environmentalism and Political Theory: Toward an Ecocentric Approach*, London, University College London Press.

Ecology Party. (1983), *Politics for Life: General Election Manifesto*, London, UK Ecology Party.

Eder, K. (1982), 'A New Social Movement?', in *Telos*, No.52, Summer, pp.5-20.

Eder, K. (1985), 'The "New Social Movements", Moral Crusades, Political

Pressure Groups, or Social Movements?', in *Social Research*, No.52, pp.869-890.

Eder, K. (1990), 'The Rise of Counter-Culture Movements Against Modernity: Nature as a New Field of Class Struggle', in *Theory, Culture and Society*, Vol.7, No.4, November, pp.21-48.

Eder, K. (1993), *The New Politics of Class: Social Movements and Cultural Dynamics in Advanced Societies*, London, Sage Publications.

Ehrenfield, D. (1981), *The Arrogance of Humanism*, Oxford, Oxford University Press.

Ehrlich, P. (1962), *The Population Bomb*, New York, Ballantine Books.

Elias, N. (1970), *What is Sociology?*, London, Hutchinson.

Elias, N. (1987a), 'The Retreat of Sociologists into the Present', in *Theory, Culture and Society*, No.4 (2-3), pp.223-48.

Elias, N. (1987b), *Involvement and Detachment*, Oxford, Basil Blackwell.

Elias, N. (1994), *The Civilizing Process: The History of Manners and State Formation and Civilization*, Oxford, Blackwell Publishers.

Enloe, C. (1975), *The Politics of Pollution in a Comparative Perspective*, New York, Davis Mackay.

Enzensberger, H.M. (1974), 'Critique of Political Ecology', in *New Left Review*, Vol.84, pp.3-31.

Evans, D. (1992), *A History of Nature Conservation in Britain*, London, Routledge.

Evans, R. (1893), *The Age of Disfigurement*, London, Remington.

Evans, R. (1926), *An Account of the SCAPA Society*, London, Constable.

Evernden, N. (1985), *The Natural Alien: Humankind and Environment*, Toronto, University of Toronto Press.

Evernden, N. (1992), *The Social Creation of Nature*, Baltimore, John Hopkins University Press.

Eyerman, R. (1984), 'Social Movements and Social Theory', in *Sociology*, Vol.18, No.1, pp.71-82.

Eyerman, R. (1989), 'Social Movements: Between History and Sociology', in *Theory and Society*, Vol.18, No.4, July, pp.531-545.

Eyerman, R. and Jamison, A. (1991), *Social Movements: A Cognitive Approach*, Cambridge, Polity Press in association with Basil Blackwell.

Featherstone, M. (ed) (1990), *Global Culture: Nationalism, Globalization and Modernity*, London, Sage Publications.

Fedden, R. (1968), *The Continuing Purpose*, London, Longman Press.

Fedden, R. (1974), *The National Trust: Past and Present*, London, Jonathon Cape Ltd.

Fleischman, J. (1969), 'Conservation, the Biological Fallacy', in *Landscape*, No.18, pp.23-7.

Fogt, H. (1989), 'The Greens and the New Left: Influences of Left Extremism on Green Party Organization and Policies', in Kolinsky, E (ed) (1989), *The Greens in West Germany: Organization and Policy-Making*, Oxford, Berg Publishing, pp.89-121.

Foreman, D. and Haywood, B. (eds) (1989), *Ecodefense: A Field Guide to Monkeywrenching*, Tucson, Ned Ludd Books.

Foucault, M. (1975), *Discipline and Punish*, London, Tavistock.

Fox, W. (1984), 'Deep Ecology: A New Philosophy of Our Time?', in *The Ecologist*, Vol.14, No.'s 5 and 6, pp.194-200.

Fox, W. (1990), *Towards a Transpersonal Ecology*, London, Shambala Publications.

Frankel, B. (1987), *The Post-Industrial Utopians*, Cambridge, Polity Press.

Frankland, G. E. (1990), 'Does Green Politics Have a Future in Britain? An American Perspective', in *Green Politics One*, Edinburgh, Edinburgh University Press.

Fraser, D. (1976), *Urban Politics in Victorian England: The Structure of Politics in Victorian Cities*, Leicester, Leicester University Press.

Fraser-Darling, F. (1971), *Wilderness and Plenty*, New York, Ballantine.

Freiberg, J. W. (1973), 'Review of A. Touraine, "Production de la Societé"', in *Theory and Society*, No. 2, Vol. 2.

Galbraith, J. K. (1969), *The New Industrial State*, Harmondsworth, Penguin Books.

Galtung, J. (1986), 'The Green Movement: A Socio-Historical Explanation', in *International Sociology*, No.1.

Gamson, W. (1975), *The Strategy of Social Protest*, Illinois, Dorsey Press.

Gane, M. (1991), *Baudrillard: Critical and Fatal Theory*, London, Routledge.

Gaze, J. (1988), *Figures in a Landscape: A History of the National Trust*, Barrie and Jenkins in association with The National Trust.

Gellner, E. (1986), *Nations and Nationalism*, Oxford, Blackwell.

Gershuny, J. I. (1978), *After Industrial Society? The Emerging Self-Service Economy*, London, Macmillan Press.

Giddens, A. (1971), *Capitalism and Modern Social Theory: An Analysis of the Writings of Marx, Durkheim and Max Weber*, Cambridge, Cambridge University Press.

Giddens, A. (1990), *The Consequences of Modernity*, Cambridge, Polity Press.

Giddens, A. (1991), *Modernity and Self Identity: Self and Society in the Late Modern Age*, Cambridge, Polity Press.

Giddens, A. (1994), 'Living in a Post-Traditional Society', in Beck, U, Giddens, A and Lash, S. (1994), *Reflexive Modernization: Politics, Tradition and Aesthetics in the Modern Social Order*, Cambridge, Polity Press, pp.56-109.

Gilig, A. W. (1981), 'Planning for Nature Conservation: a Struggle for Survival and Political Responsibility' in Kain, R. (ed), *Planning for Conservation*, New York, St. Martin's Press, pp.97-116.

Glasier, J. B. (1921a), *William Morris and the Early Days of the Socialist Movement*, London, Longmans.

Glasier, J.B. (1921b), *The Meaning of Socialism*, Manchester, National Labour Press Ltd.

Golby, J.M. (1986), *Culture and Society in Britain 1850-1890*, Open University Press.

Goldsmith, E., Allen, R., Allaby, M., Davoll, J. and Lawrence, S. (1972), 'A Blueprint for Survival', in *The Ecologist*, Vol.2, No.1, January. pp.1-43.

Goldsmith, E. (1988), *The Great U - Turn: De - Industrializing Society*, Hartland, Devon, Green Books.

Goodin, R.E. (1992), *Green Political Theory*, Oxford, Polity Press.

Gorz, A. (1980), *Ecology as Politics*, London, Pluto Press.

Gorz, A. (1985), *Paths to Paradise: On the Liberation form Work*, London, Pluto Press.

Goudsblom, J. (1989), 'Human History and Long-Term Social Processes', in Goudsblom, J., Jones, E. and Mennell, S. *Human History and Social Process*, Exeter, University of Exeter Press, pp.11-26.

Gould, P. (1988), *Early Green Politics: Back to Nature, Back to the Land and Socialism in Great Britain 1880-1900*, Brighton, Harvester Press.

Green Party. (1986), *Manifesto for a Sustainable Society*, London, Green Party.

Green Party. (1992), *General Election Campaign Manifesto - New Directions: The Path to a Green Britain Now*, London, Green Party.

Gregory, R. (1976), 'The Voluntary Amenity Movement', in Macewan, M. (ed), *Future Landscapes*, London, Chatto and Windus, pp.119-217.

Griffin, S. (1978), *Woman and Nature: the Roaring Inside Her*, New York, Harper and Row.

Grundmann, R. (1991), 'The Ecological Challenge to Marxism', in *New Left Review*, Vol.187, May/June, pp.103-120.

Habermas, J. (1981), 'New Social Movements', in *Telos*, No.49, Fall, pp.33-37.

Hajer, M.A. (1996), 'Ecological Modernisation as Cultural Politics', in Lash, S., Szerszynski, B. and Wynne, B. (eds), (1996), *Risk, Environment and Modernity: Towards a New Ecology*, London, Sage. pp.246-268.

Hall, P. et al (eds) (1973), *The Containment of Urban England*, London, George Allen and Unwin Ltd.

Hall, S and Jacques, M. (eds)(1989), *New Times*, London, Lawrence and Wishart.

Hannigan, J. A. (1995), *Environmental Sociology: A Social Constructionist Perspective*, London, Routledge.

Hardin, G. (1968), 'The Tragedy of the Commons', in *Science*, 162. pp.1243-1248.

Hardin, G. (1977), *The Limits to Altruism*, Indianapolis, Indiana University Press.

Hardy, D. (1979), *Alternative Communities in Nineteenth Century England*, London, Longman Press.

Harries-Jones, P. (1995), *Recursive Visions: Ecological Understanding and Gregory Bateson*, Toronto, University of Toronto Press.

Harrison, B. (1967), 'Religion and Recreation in Nineteenth Century England', in *Past and Present*, Vol.36-38, pp.98-137.

Harrison, B. (1973), 'Animals and the State in Nineteenth Century England', in *English Historical Review*, Vol.88, pp.786-820.

Harvey, D. (1990), *The Condition of Postmodernity*, Oxford, Blackwell.

Harvey, D. (1993), 'The Nature of Environment: The Dialectics of Social and Environmental Change', in *The Socialist Register 1993*, pp.1-51.

Hays, S. (1987), *Beauty, Health and Permanence: Environmental Politics in the U.S., 1955-85*, Cambridge, Cambridge University Press.

Heberle, R. (1951), *Social Movement: An Introduction to Political Sociology*, New York, Appleton Century and Crofts.

Heller, A. and Feher, F. (1988), *The Postmodern Political Condition*, Cambridge, Polity Press.

Hetherington, K. 1993: 'Review of Pakulski, J. (1991), *Social Movements: The Politics of Moral Protest*, Longman Press', in *The Sociological Review*, Vol.41, No.4, pp:766-768.

Hill, H. (1980), *Freedom to Roam: The Struggle for Access to Britain's Moors and Mountains*, Ashbourne, Moorland Publishing.

Hill, O. (1884), 'Colour, Space, and Music for the People', in *The Nineteenth Century*, May, pp.741-752.

Hill, O. (1888), 'More Air for London', in *The Nineteenth Century*, February, pp.181-188.

Hill, O. (1899), 'The Open Spaces of the Future', in *The Nineteenth Century*, No.46, July/December, pp.26-35.

Hobsbawm, E.J. (1968), *Industry and Empire*, Harmondsworth, Penguin Books.

Hobsbawm, E. J. (1974), *Labour's Turning Point 1880-1900: Extracts from Contemporary Sources*, Hassocks, Harvester Press.

Hollis, P. (ed). (1974), *Pressure From Without in Early Victorian England*, London, Edward Arnold.

Horigan, S. (1989), *Nature and Culture in Western Discourses*, London, Routledge.

Howard, E. (1898), *Tomorrow: A Peaceful Path to Real Reform*, London, Faber.

Hulsberg, W. (1985), 'The Greens at the Crossroads', in *New Left Review*, No.152, July/August, pp.5-29.

Hulsberg, W. (1987), *The West German Greens*, London, Verso Press.

Hunter, R. (1898), 'Places and Things of Interest and Beauty', in *The Nineteenth Century*, No.XLIII, January/June, pp.570-589.

Hunter, R. (1980), *The Greenpeace Chronicle*, London, Pan Books Ltd.

Inglehart, R. (1977), *The Silent Revolution: Changing Values and Political Styles Among Western Publics*, Princeton, Princeton University Press.

Inglehart, R. (1990), 'Values, Ideology, and Cognitive Mobilization', in Dalton, R. J. and Kuechler, M. (eds) (1990), *Challenging the Political Order: New Social and Political Movements in Western Democracies*, Basil Blackwell. pp.43-66.

Irvine, S. and Ponton, A. (1988), *A Green Manifesto: Policies for a Green Future*, London, Macdonald Optima.

Jamison, A. (1996), 'The Shaping of the Global Agenda: The Role of Non-Governmental Organisations', in Lash, S, Szerszynski, B. and Wynne, B. (eds) (1996), *Risk, Environment & Modernity: Towards a New Ecology*, London, Sage Publications, pp.224-245.

Jamison, A. and Eyerman, R. (1989), 'Environmental Knowledge as an Organizational Weapon: The Case of Greenpeace', in *Social Science Information* (2).

Jones, A. (1987), 'The Violence of Materialism in Advanced Industrial Society: An Eco-Sociological Approach', in *The Sociological Review*, Vol.35, No.1, pp.19-47.

Joseph, L.E. (1990), *Gaia: The Growth of an Idea*, London, Penguin Books.

Kain, R. (ed) (1981), *Planning for Conservation*, New York, St. Martin's Press.

Kelley, K. (ed) (1988), *The Home Planet: Images and Reflections of Earth from Space Explorers*, London, Macdonald, Queen Anne Press.

Kelsen, H. (1944), *Society and Nature: A Sociological Inquiry*, London, K.Paul, Trench, Trubner.

Kelvin, N. (1984), *The Collected Letters of William Morris: Vol.1, 1848-1880*, Princeton, Guildford, Princeton University Press.

Kilminster, R. (1991), 'Structuration Theory as a World-View', in Bryant, C.G.A. and Jary, D. (eds) (1991), *Giddens' Theory of Structuration: A Critical Appreciation*, London, Routledge.

Kilminster, R. (1997), 'Globalization as an Emergent Concept', in Scott, A. (ed) (1997), *The Limits of Globalization*, London, Routledge, pp.257-283.

Kimber, R. and Richardson, J.J. (eds) (1974), *Campaigning for the Environment*, London, Routledge and Kegan Paul.

King, Y. (1990), 'Healing the Wounds: Feminism, Ecology and the Nature / Culture Dualism', in Diamond, I. and Orenstein, G. F. (eds), *Reweaving the World: The Emergence of Eco-feminism*, San Francisco, Sierra Club Books.

Kitschelt, H. P. (1986), 'Political Opportunity Structures and Political Protest: Anti - Nuclear Movements in Four Democracies', in *The British Journal of Political Science*, Vol.16, January, pp.57-85.

Kitschelt, H.P. (1989), *The Logics of Party Formation: Ecological Politics in Belgium and West Germany*, Cornell University Press.

Kitschelt, H. P. (1990), 'New Social Movements and Party Organization', in Dalton, R.J., Kuechler, M (eds) (1990), *Challenging the Political Order: New Social and Political Movements in Western Democracies*, Cambridge, Polity Press.

Kitschelt, H. P. (1991), 'Resource Mobilization Theory: A Critique', in Rucht, D. (ed), *Research on Social Movements: The State of the Art in Western Europe and the USA*, Frankfurt, Frankfurt University Press. pp.323-347.

Kitson Clark, G. (1970), *The Making of Victorian England: Being the Lectures Delivered Before the University of Oxford*, London, Methuen and Co. Ltd.

Klandermans, P. B., Kriesi, H. and Tarrow, S. (eds) (1988), *International Social Movement Research. Vol. 1: From Structure to Action*, Greenwich, London: JAI Press.

Klandermans, P. B. (1990), 'Linking "Old" and "New" Movement Networks in the Netherlands', in Dalton, R.J. and Kuechler, M. (eds), *Challenging the Political Order: New Social and Political Movements in Western Democracies*, Cambridge, Polity Press, pp.122-136.

Klandermans, P. B. (1991), 'New Social Movements and Resource Mobilization: The European and the American Approach Revisited', in Rucht, D. (ed) (1991), *Research on Social Movements: The State of the Art in Western Europe and the USA*, Frankfurt, Frankfurt University Press, pp.17-44.

Kolinsky, E. (1988), 'The German Greens - A Womens' Party?', in *Parliamentary Affairs*, No.1, a, pp.129-148.

Kolinsky, E. (ed) (1989), *The Greens in West Germany: Organization and Policy-Making*, Oxford, Berg Publishing.

Kostede, N. (1989), 'The Greens and the Intellectuals', in Kolinsky, E. (ed), *The Greens in West Germany: Organization and Policy-Making*, Oxford, Berg Publishing, pp.123-139.

Kropotkin, P. (1899), *Fields, Factories and Workshops Tomorrow*, London, Freedom Press.

Kumar, K. (1986), *Prophecy and Progress: The Sociology of Industrial and Post-Industrial Society*, Harmondswoth, Penguin Books Ltd.

Kumar, K. (1995), *From Post-Industrial to Post-Modern Society: New Theories of the Contemporary World*, Oxford, Blackwell Publishers Ltd.

Kvistad, G.O. (1987), 'Between State and Society: Green Political Ideology in the Mid-1980s', in *West European Politics*, Vol.10, No.2, pp.221-228.

Kynaston, D. (1976), *King Labour: The British Working Class 1850-1914*, London, Allen and Unwin.

Landes, D. S. (1969), *The Unbound Prometheus: Technological Change and Industrial Development in Western Europe from 1750 to the Present*, London, Cambridge University Press.

Langguth, G. (1986), *The Green Factor in German Politics*, Boulder, Westview.

Lash, S., Szerszynski, B. and Wynne, B. (eds), (1996), *Risk, Environment and Modernity: Towards a New Ecology*, London, Sage.

Lash, S. and Urry, J. (1987), *The End of Organized Capitalism*, Cambridge, Polity Press.

Lash, S. and Wynne, B. (1992), 'Introduction' in Beck, U, Risk Society: *Towards a New Modernity*, London, Sage Publications, pp.1-8.

Lewes, C.L. (1887), 'How to Ensure Breathing Spaces' in *The Nineteenth Century* No.21, May, pp: 677-82.

Lewis, E. (1915), *Edward Carpenter: An Exposition and Appreciation* (2nd Edition), London, Methuen and Co. Ltd.

Lewis, M.W. (1994), *Green Delusions: An Environmentalist Critique of Radical Environmentalism*, Durham and London, Duke University Press.

Lively, J. (1966), *The Enlightenment*, London, Longmans.

Lovelock, J. E. (1979), *Gaia: A new look at life on Earth*, Oxford, Oxford University Press.

Lovelock, J. E. (1986), 'Gaia: The World as a Living Organism', in *New Scientist*, December 18th.

Lovelock, J.E. (1988), *The Ages of Gaia: A Biography of our Living Earth*, New York, Norton.

Low, S. (1891), 'The Rise of the Suburbs' in *The Contemporary Review*, October, pp.545-58.

Lowe, P. D. and Goyder, J. (1983), *Environmental Groups in Politics*, London, Allen and Unwin.

Loyd, R.W. (1924), *The Protection of Birds: An Indictment*, London, Longman.

Lubasz, H. (1970), 'Marx's Conception of the Revolutionary Proletariat', in *Praxis*, Vol.5, pp.288-90.

Luke, T. (1983), 'Informationalism and Ecology', in *Telos*, No.56, Summer, pp.59-73.

Luke, T. (1988), 'The Dreams of Deep Ecology', in *Telos*, No.76, Summer, pp.65-92.

Luke, T. and White, S.K. (1985), 'Critical Theory and an Ecological Path to Modernity', in Forester, J. (ed) (1985), *Critical Theory and Public Life*, Cambridge, MIT Press.

Lynd, H.M. (1968), *England in the 1880s*, London, Oxford University Press.

Lyotard, J. F. (1984), *The Postmodern Condition: A Report on Knowledge*, Manchester, Manchester University Press.

MacCarthy, F. (1996), *William Morris*, London, Faber and Faber.

MacFadyen, D. (1933), *Sir Ebeneezer Howard and the Town Planning Movement*, Manchester, Manchester University Press.

Macnaghten, P. and Urry, J. (1995), 'Towards a Sociology of Nature', in *Sociology*, Vol.29, No.2, pp.203-220.

Malthus, T. R. (1970), *An Essay on the Principles of Population*, Harmondsworth, Penguin.

Manes, C. (1990), *Green Rage: Radical Environmentalism and the Unmaking of Civilization*, Boston, Little, Brown.

Mannheim, K. (1953) (translation, Kecskemeti, P.), *Essays on Sociology and Social Psychology*, London, Routledge and Kegan Paul Ltd.

Marcuse, H. (1964), *One Dimensional Man: Studies in the Ideology of Advanced Industrial Society*, London, Sphere.

Margulis, L. and Lovelock, J. (1974), 'Biological Modulation of the Earth's Atmosphere', in *Icarus*, Vol.21, pp.471-489.

Marien, M. (1977), 'The Two Visions of Post-Industrial Society', in *Futures*, October.

Marsh, A. (1959), *The Story of the National Society for Clean Air*, London, N.S.C.A.

Marsh, G. P. (1864), *Man and Nature*, Cambridge, Massachusetts, Harvard University Press.

Marsh, J. (1982), *Back to the Land: The Pastoral Impulse in England From 1880-1914*, London, Quartet Books.

Martell, L. (1994), *Ecology and Society: An Introduction*, Cambridge, Polity Press.

Marx, L. (1964), *The Machine in the Garden: Technology and the Pastoral Ideal in America*, New York, Oxford University Press.

Maslow, A.H. (1954), *Motivation and Personality*, New York, Harper.

Mattausch, J. (1989), *A Commitment to Campaign: A Sociological Study of CND*, Manchester, Manchester University Press.

Maurice, C. E. (ed) (1914), *Life of Octavia Hill as Told in Her Letters*, London, Macmillan.

McCormick, J. (1991), *British Politics and the Environment*, London, Earthscan Publishers Ltd.

McKibben, B. (1990), *The End of Nature*, London, Viking, Penguin.

McNeill, W.H. (1979), *A World History*, Oxford, Oxford University Press.

Meadows, D. H., Meadows, D. L., Randers, J. and Behrens III, W. (1974), *The Limits to Growth*, London, Pan Books.

Medawar, P.B. and J.S. (1972), 'Some Reflections on the Theme of Science and Civilization', in Ciba Foundation Symposium: *Civilization and Science: in Conflict or Collaboration?*, Associated Scientific Publishers, Elsevier, Excerpta Medica, North Holland.

Meier, P. (1978), *William Morris: The Marxist Dreamer*, Hassocks, Harvester Press Ltd.

Mellos, K. (1990), *Perspective on Ecology: A Critical Essay*, London, Macmillan Press.

Melucci, A. (1980), 'The New Social Movements: A Theoretical Approach', in *Social Science Information*, Vol.19, No.2.

Melucci, A. (1985), 'The Symbolic Challenge of Contemporary Movements', in *Social Research*, No.52, pp.789-816.

Melucci, A. (1988), 'Social Movements and the Democratization of Everyday Life', in Keane, J. (ed), *Civil Society and the State*, London, Verso Press.

Melucci, A. (1989), *Nomads of the Present: Social Movements and Individual Needs in Contemporary Society*, London, Hutchinson Radius.

Melucci, A. (1995), 'The New Social Movements Revisited: Reflections on a Sociological Misunderstanding', in Maheu, L. (ed), *Social Movements and Social Classes: The Future of Collective Action*, London, Sage Publications in association with the International Sociological Association, pp.107-19.

Mennell, S. (1992), *Norbert Elias: An Introduction*, Oxford, Blackwell Publishers.

Merchant, C. (1982), *The Death of Nature: Women, Ecology and the Scientific Revolution*, London, Wildwood House.

Merchant, C. (1992), *Radical Ecology: The Search for a Liveable World*, London, Routledge.

Mill, J. S. (1979), 'Nature' from 'Nature, the Utility of Religion, and Theism', written 1850-8, in Clayre, A (ed), *Nature and Industrialization*, Oxford University Press. pp.303-312.

Mingay, G.E. (1977), *Rural Life in Victorian England*, London, Heinemann.

Mingay, G.E. (1986), *The Transformation of Britain 1830 - 1939*, London, Routledge and Kegan Paul.

Morris, R.J. (1983), 'Voluntary Societies and British Urban Elites 1780-1850: An Analysis', in *Historical Journal*, Vol.26, No.1, pp.95-118.

Morris, R.J. (1990), *Class, Sect and Party: The Making of the British Middle Class, Leeds 1820-1850*, Manchester, Manchester University Press.

Morris, W. (1908), *News From Nowhere or An Epoch of Rest, Being Some Chapters From A Utopian Romance*, London, Longmans, Green, and Co.

Moscovici, S. (1976), *Society Against Nature: The Emergence of Human Societies*, Hassocks, Harvester Press.

Moscovici, S. (1977), 'The Reenchantment of the World' in Birnbaum, N. (ed), *Beyond the Crisis*, Oxford, Oxford University Press, pp: 133-168.

Moscovici, S. (1990), 'Questions for the 21st Century', in *Theory, Culture and Society*, Vol.7, No.4, November, pp.1-19.

Müller - Rommel, F. (1982), 'Ecology Parties in Western Europe', in *West European Politics*, Vol.5, No.1, January, pp.68-74.

Müller - Rommel, F. (1989a), 'The German Greens in the 1980s: Short-term Cyclical Protest or Indicator of Transformation?', in *Political Studies*, Vol.xxxvii, No.1, March, pp.114-122.

Müller - Rommel, F. (1989b), *New Politics in Western Europe: The Rise and Success of Green Parties and Alternative Lists*, Boulder, Westview.

Müller - Rommel, F. and Poguntke, T. (1989), 'The Unharmonious Family: Green Parties in Western Europe', in Kolinsky, E. (ed), *The Greens in West Germany: Organization and Policy - Making*, Oxford, Berg Publishing, pp.11-29.

Musgrove, F. (1974), *Ecstasy and Holiness: Counter Culture and the Open Society*, London, Methuen and Co. Ltd.

Naess, A. (1973), 'The Shallow and the Deep, Long-Range Ecology Movement, A Summary', in *Inquiry*, Vol.16, pp.95-100.

Naess, A. (1984), 'Intuition, Intrinsic Value and Deep Ecology', in *The Ecologist*, Vol.14, No.'s 5 and 6, pp.201-203.

Naess, A. (1988), 'The Basics of Deep Ecology', in *Resurgence*, 126, 4-7.

Naess, A. (1989), *Ecology, Community and Lifestyle*, Cambridge, Cambridge University Press.

Neuhaus, R.J. (1971), *In Defence of People: Ecology and the Seduction of Radicalism*, New York, Macmillan.

Nicholson, M. (1972), *The Environmental Revolution*, Harmondsworth, Penguin.

Nicholson, M. (1987), *The New Environmental Age*, Cambridge, Cambridge University Press.

Oberschall, A. (1973), *Social Conflict and Social Movements*, Englewood Cliffs, N.J., Prentice Hall.

Offe, C. (1985), 'New Social Movements: Challenging the Boundaries of Institutional Politics', in *Social Research*, No.52, Winter, pp.817-868.

Offe, C. (1990), 'Reflections on the Institutional Self - Transformation of Movement Politics: A Tentative Stage Model', in Dalton, R.J and Kuechler, M. (eds), *Challenging the Political Order: New Social and Political Movements in Western Democracies*, Cambridge, Polity Press.

Olofsson, G. (1987), 'After the Working Class Movement? An Essay on What's "New" and What's "Social" in the New Social Movements', in *Acta Sociologica*, Vol.31, No.1, pp.15-34.

Olson, M. (1965), *The Logic of Collective Action*, Harvard University Press.

O'Neil, J. (1994), 'Humanism and Nature', in *Radical Philosophy*, No. 66, pp.21-9.

Ophuls, W. (1977), *Ecology and the Politics of Scarcity: Prologue to a Theory of the Steady State*, San Francisco, California, W.H. Freeman.

O'Riordan, T. (1981), *Environmentalism*, London, Pion.

Paehlke, R. (1989), *Environmentalism and the Future of Progressive Politics*, New Haven: London, Yale University Press.

Pakulski, J. (1991), *Social Movements: The Politics of Moral Protest*, Cheshire, Longman Press.

Papadakis, E. (1984), *The Green Movement in West Germany*, London, Croom Helm.

Papadakis, E. (1988), 'Social Movements, Self - Limiting Radicalism and the Green Party in West Germany', in *Sociology*, Vol.22, No.3, August, pp.433-454.

Parkin, F. (1968), *Middle Class Radicalism*, Manchester, Manchester University Press.

Parkin, S. (1989), *Green Parties: An International Guide*, London, Heretic Books.

Pearce, F. (1991), *Green Warriors: the People and the Politics Behind the Environmental Revolution*, London, Bodley Head.

Peek, F. and Hall, E. T. (1892), 'The Unhealthiness of Cities', in *The Contemporary Review*, February, pp.221-37.

Pelling, H. (1965), *Origins of the Labour Party 1880-1900*, Oxford University Press.

Pepper, D. (1984), *The Roots of Modern Environmentalism*, London, Croom Helm.

Pepper, D. (1986), 'Radical Environmentalism and the Labour Movement', in Weston, J. (ed), *Red and Green: The New Politics of the Environment*, pp, 115-39.

Pepper, D. (1991), *Communes and the Green Vision: Counterculture, Lifestyle and the New Age*, London, Green Print.

Pepper, D. (1996), *Modern Environmentalism: an Introduction*, London, Routledge.

Plumwood, V. (1993), *Feminism and the Mastery of Nature*, London, Routledge.

Poguntke, T. (1987), 'New Politics and Party Systems: The Emergence of a New Type of Party?', in *West European Politics*, Vol.10, No.1, January, pp.76-88.

Polanyi, K. (1967), *The Great Transformation*, Boston, Beacon Press.

Pollert, A. (1990), 'Conceptions of British Employment Restructuring in the 1980s', in Varcoe, I., McNeil, M. and Yearley, S. (eds), *Deciphering Science and Technology: The Social Relations of Expertise*, London, Macmillan Press.

Porritt, J. (1984), *Seeing Green: The Politics of Ecology Explained*, Oxford, Basil Blackwell.

Porritt, J. (1988), 'Let the Green Spirit Live', (Schumacher Lecture 1987), in *Resurgence*, No.127.

Porritt, J., Winner, D. (1988), *The Coming of the Greens*, London, Fontana Paperbacks.

Prigogine, I. and Stengers, I. (1984), *Order Out of Chaos: Man's New Dialogue with Nature*, Boulder: Colorado, Random House.

Princen, T. and Finger, M. (1994), *Environmental NGOs in World Politics: Linking the Local and the Global*, London and New York, Routledge.

Prochaska, F.K. (1980), *Women and Philanthropy in Nineteenth Century England*, Oxford, Oxford University Press.

Prynn, D. (1976), 'The Clarion Clubs, Rambling and the Holiday Associations in Britain Since the 1880s', in *Journal of Contemporary History*, No. XI, pp.65-77.

Przeworski, A. (1986), *Capitalism and Social Democracy*, Cambridge, Cambridge University Press.

Purdue, B. (1987), *Town and Country*, Milton Keynes, Open University Press.

Ranlett, J. (1981), 'The Smoke Abatement Exhibition of 1881', in *History Today*, No.31, November, pp.10-13.

Ranlett, J. (1983), 'Checking Nature's Desecration: Late Victorian Environmental Organization', in *Victorian Studies*, Winter, pp.197-222.

Rawnsley, H. D. (1890), 'Sunlight or Smoke', in *The Contemporary Review*, No.57, April, pp.512-524.

Read, D. (1979), *England 1868-1914*, London, Longman Group Ltd.

Redclift, M. and Benton, T. (eds) (1994), *Social Theory and the Global Environment*, London, Routledge.

Richards, T. (1990), *The Commodity Culture of Victorian England: Advertising and Spectacle 1851-1914*, California, Stanford University Press.

Roberts, H. (ed). (1915), *The Simplification of Life (From the Writings of Edward Carpenter)*, London, Allen and Unwin.

Rose, M. (1991), *The Postmodern and the Postindustrial: A Critical Analysis*, Cambridge, Cambridge University Press.

Roszak, T. (1969), *The Making of a Counter Culture: Reflections on the Technocratic Society and its Youthful Opposition*, New York, Anchor Books.

Roszak, T. (1973), *Where the Wasteland Ends: Politics and Transcendence in Post-Industrial Society*, London, Faber and Faber.

Roszak, T. (1981), *Person/Planet: The Creative Disintegration of Industrial Society*, St. Albans, Granada.

Rowbotham, S. and Weeks, J. (1977), *Socialism and the New Life: The Personal and Sexual Politics of Edward Carpenter and Havelock Ellis*, London, Pluto Press.

Rubenstein, D. (1977), 'Cycling in the 1890s', in *Victorian Studies*, Vol.XXI, pp.47-71.

Rucht, D. (1990), 'The Strategies and Action Repertoires of New Movements' in Dalton, R.J. and Kuechler, M. (eds) (1990), *Challenging the Political Order: New Social and Political Movements in Western Democracies*, Cambridge, Polity Press, pp.156-175.

Rucht, D. (ed) (1991), *Research on Social Movements: The State of the Art in Western Europe and the USA*, Frankfurt, Frankfurt University Press.

Rucht, D. (1995), 'Ecological Protest as Calculated Law-Breaking: Greenpeace and Earth First! in Comparative Perspective', in Rüdig, W. (ed), *Green Politics Three*, Edinburgh, Edinburgh University Press.

Rüdig, W. (1988), 'Peace and Ecology Movements in Western Europe', in *West European Politics*, No.11, January, pp.26-39.

Rüdig, W. (ed) (1990), *Green Politics One*, Edinburgh, Edinburgh University Press.

Rüdig, W. (ed) (1995), *Green Politics Three*, Edinburgh, Edinburgh University Press.

Rüdig, W., Bennie, L.G. and Franklin, M.N. (1991), *Green Party Members: A Profile*, Glasgow, Delta Publications.

Rüdig, W. and Lowe, P. (1986), 'The Withered Greening of British Politics: A Study of the Ecology Party', in *Political Studies*, Vol.xxxiv, pp.262-284.

Ruskin, J. (1905), *The Stones of Venice*, London, George Allen and Sons.

Russell, R. (1902), 'The Reduction of Town Fogs', in *The Nineteenth Century*, No.51, pp.131-43.

Ryle, M. (1988), *Ecology and Socialism*, London, Century Hutchinson.

Sale, K. (1984), 'Bioregionalism, A New Way to Treat the Land', in *The Ecologist*, Vol.14, No.4, pp.167-73.

Sale, K. (1985), *Dwellers in the Land: The Bioregional Vision*, San Francisco, Sierra Club Books.

Schell, J. (1982), *The Fate of the Earth*, London, Pan Books Ltd.

Schmitt, P.J. (1969), *Back to Nature: The Arcadian Myth in Urban America*, New York, Oxford University Press.

Schumacher, E.F. (1973), *Small is Beautiful: A Study of Economics as if People Mattered*, London, Abacus Books.

Scott, A. (1990), *Ideology and the New Social Movements*, London, Unwin Hyman.

Scott, A. (ed) (1997), *The Limits of Globalization*, London, Routledge.

Shannon, R. (1974), *The Crisis of Imperialism 1865-1915*, London, Hart-Davis, MacGibbon.

Shaw-Lefevre, G. (1894), *English Commons and Forests: The Story of the Battle During the Last 30 Years for Public Rights Over the Commons and Forests of England and Wales*, London, Cassell.

Sheail, J. (1976), *Nature in Trust: The History of Nature Conservation in Britain*, Glasgow, Blackie and Son Ltd..

Sheail, J. (1981), *Rural Conservation in Inter - War Britain*, Oxford, Oxford University Press.

Shepard, P. (1969), 'Introduction - Ecology and Man - A Viewpoint', in Shepard, P. and McKinley, D. (eds), *The Subversive Science: Essays Toward an Ecology of Man*, Boston, Houghton Mifflin, pp.1-10.

Shils, E. (1972), *The Intellectuals and the Powers and Other Essays*, Chicago and London, University of Chicago Press.

Shiva, V. (1988), *Staying Alive: Women, Ecology and Survival in India*, London, Zed Books.

Sklair, L. (1991), *Sociology of the Global System*, Hemel Hempstead, Harvester Wheatsheaf.

Sklair, L. (1994), 'Global Sociology and Environmental Change' in Redclift, M. and Benton, T. (eds), *Social Theory and the Global Environment*, London, Routledge, pp.205-227.

Smith, D. (1982), *Conflict and Compromise: Class Formation in English Society 1830-1914*, London, Routledge and Kegan Paul Ltd.

Spretnak, C. (1986), *The Spiritual Dimension of Green Politics*, Santa Fe, NM, Bear and Co.

Spretnak, C. (1993), *States of Grace: The Recovery of Meaning in the Postmodern Age*, New York, HarperCollins Publishers.

Spretnak, C. and Capra, F., in collaboration with Rüdiger Lutz. (1984), *Green Politics: The Global Promise*, London, Hutchinson and Co. Ltd.

Spring, D. (1960), 'The Role of the Aristocracy in the Late Nineteenth Century', in *Victorian Studies*, No.IV, pp.55-64.

Stansky, P. (1985), *Redesigning the World: William Morris, the 1880s and the Arts and Crafts*, Princeton, N.J, Princeton University Press.

Steward, F. (1985), 'Growing Greens', in *Marxism Today*, November, pp.17-19.

Steward, F. (1985), 'Rainbow Warriors', in *Marxism Today*, November, pp.20-22.

Sutton, P. (1999), 'Genetics and the Future of Nature Politics' in *Sociological Research Online*, vol.1995, no.1,<http://www.socresonline.org.uk/socresonline/-1995/1/sutton.html>

Swidler, A. (1986), 'Culture in Action: Symbols and strategies' in *American Sociological Review*, 51, pp.273-86.

Szerszynski, B. (1996), 'On Knowing What to Do: Environmentalism and the Modern Problematic', in Lash, S, Szerszynski, B and Wynne, B (eds), *Risk, Environment and Modernity: Towards a New Ecology*, London, Sage, pp.104-137.

Tarrow, S. (1991), 'Comparing Social Movement Participation in Western Europe and the United States: Problems, Uses and a Proposal for Synthesis', in Rucht, D. (ed), *Research on Social Movements: The State of the Art in Western Europe and the USA*, Frankfurt, Frankfurt University Press, pp.392-420.

Tarrow, S. (1994), *Power in Movement: Social movements, Collective Action and Politics*, Cambridge, Cambridge University Press.

Taylor, R. K. S. (1985), 'Green Politics and the Peace Movement', in Coates, D.,

Johnston, G. and Bush, R. (eds), *A Socialist Anatomy of Britain*, Cambridge, Polity Press, pp.160-70.

Tester, K. (1991), *Animals and Society: The Humanity of Animal Rights*, London, Routledge.

Thomas, K. (1984), *Man and the Natural World: Changing Attitudes in England 1500-1800*, London, Penguin Books.

Thompson, E.P. (1976), *William Morris: Romantic to Revolutionary*, New York, Pantheon.

Toffler, A. (1981), *The Third Wave*, London, Pan Books.

Toulmin, S. (1972), 'The Historical Background to the Anti-Science Movement', in Ciba Foundation Symposium: *Civilization and Science: in Conflict or Collaboration?*, Associated Scientific Publishers, Elsevier, Excerpta Medica, North Holland.

Toulmin, S. (1982), *The Return to Cosmology: Postmodern Science and the Theology of Nature*, Berkeley, University of California Press.

Touraine, A. (1969), *The May Movement: Revolt and Reform: May 1968 - The Student Rebellion and Workers' Strikes - The Birth of a Social Movement*, New York, Random House.

Touraine, A. (1971), *The Post-Industrial Society: Tomorrow's Social History: Classes, Conflict and Culture in the Programmed Society*, New York, Random House Inc.

Touraine, A. (1981), *The Voice and the Eye: An Analysis of Social Movements*, Cambridge, Cambridge University Press.

Touraine, A. in collaboration with Gesicka, G. (1986), *Solidarity: The Analysis of a Social Movement, Poland 1980-81*, Cambridge, Cambridge University Press.

Touraine, A. (1983), *Anti-Nuclear Protest: The Opposition to Nuclear Energy in France*, Cambridge, Cambridge University Press.

Tsuzuki, C. (1980), *Edward Carpenter 1844 - 1929: Prophet of Human Fellowship*, Cambridge, Cambridge University Press.

Turner, T. (1899), *The Society for the Protection of Ancient Buildings: A Chapter of its Early History*, London, SPAB.

Varcoe, I. (1995), 'Technocracy and Democratic Politics', in Kilminster, R. and Varcoe, I. (eds), *Culture, Modernity and Revolution: Essays in Honour of Zygmunt Bauman*, London, Routledge, pp.66-102.

Vidal, J. (1997), 'Gone to Ground', in *The Guardian*, February 22nd, pp.30-7.

Walby, S. (1990), *Theorizing Patriarchy*, Oxford, Basil Blackwell.

Walker, K.J. (1989), 'The State in Environmental Management: The Ecological Dimension', in *Political Studies*, Vol.xxxvii, No.1, March, pp.25-38.

Wallerstein, I. (1979), *The Capitalist World-Economy*, Cambridge, Cambridge University Press.

Wallerstein, I. (1983), *Historical Capitalism*, London, Verso Press.

Webb, S. (1890), *Socialism in England*, London, S.Sonnenchein.

Weber, M. (edited by Shils, A. and Finch, H.A.) (1949), *The Methodology of the Social Sciences*, Glencoe, Free Press.

Wellmer, A. (1991), *The Persistence of Modernity: Essays on Aesthetics, Ethics and Postmodernism*, Cambridge, Polity Press in association with Basil Blackwell.

West German Green Party. (1983), *Election Manifesto*, London, Heretic Books.

Weston, J. (ed) (1986), *Red and Green: The New Politics of the Environment*, London, Pluto Press.

White, Lynn Jr. (1967), 'The Historical Roots of Our Ecological Crisis', in *Science*, 155, March, pp.1203-1207.

Wiener, M. (1981), *English Culture and the Decline of the Industrial Spirit 1850-1980*, Cambridge University Press.

Wilkinson, P. (1971), *Social Movement*, London, Pall Mall Press Ltd.

Williams, R. (1973), *The Country and the City*, Oxford, Oxford University Press.

Williams, R. (1987), *Keywords: A Vocabulary of Culture and Society*, London, Fontana Paperbacks.

Wolf, F. O. (1986), 'Eco - Socialist Transition on the Threshold of the Twenty-First Century', in *New Left Review*, No. 158, pp, 32-42.

Worster, D. (1985), *Nature's Economy: A History of Ecological Ideas*, Cambridge, Cambridge University Press.

Wynne, B. (1996), 'May the Sheep Safely Graze? A Reflexive View of the Expert - Lay Knowledge Divide' in Lash, S, Szerszynski, B and Wynne, B (eds), (1996), *Risk, Environment and Modernity: Towards a New Ecology*, London, Sage, pp.44-83.

Yearley, S. (1991), *The Green Case: A Sociology of Environmental Issues, Arguments and Politics*, London, HarperCollins Academic.

Yearley, S. (1994), 'Social Movements and Environmental Change' in Redclift, M. and Benton, T. (eds), *Social Theory and the Global Environment*, London and New York, Routledge. pp.150-168.

Yeo, S. (1976), *Religion and Voluntary Organizations in Crisis*, London, Croom Helm.

Yeo, S. (1977), 'A New Life: The Religion of Socialism 1883-1896', in *History Workshop Journal*, Autumn, pp.5-56.

Young, J. (1990), *Post Environmentalism*, London, Bellhaven Press.

Young, S.C. (1993), *The Politics of the Environment*, Manchester, Baseline Book Company.

Zald, M. and Ash, R. (1966), 'Social Movement Organizations: Growth, Decay and Change', in *Social Forces*, Vol.44, pp.327-340.

Zald, M. and McCarthy, J. (1987), *Social Movements in an Organizational Society: Collected Essays*, New Brunswick, Transaction.

Zukav, G. (1980), *The Dancing Wu Li Masters: An Overview of the New Physics*, London, Fontana.

Index

Allen, D.E. 65-6, 135
Atkinson, A. 106, 147

back-to-nature ideas 68, 109-10
Bagguley, P. 13, 25, 125, 139
Bahro, R. 130, 138
Beck, U. 36, 43, 68-76, 118, 145, 173
Bell, D. 8, 18, 23, 169
Berman, M. 170, 183-4
Boggs, C. 19, 22, 146,
Bookchin, M. 92-3, 115n, 135, 192
Brand, K.W. 43, 52, 56-61, 65, 75, 77, 78-9n
Briggs, A. 98, 180-2
Bryce, J. 91, 95-8

Calhoun, C. 62, 68, 167
Capra, F. 6, 62-4, 138, 148-9, 173, 204
Carpenter, E. 109, 112, 116n, 138, 193, 205
Commons Preservation Society (CPS) 89-90, 93-105, 115n
Cotgrove, S. 11, 25, 79n, 121, 191

Dalton, R.J. 120-1, 137-8, 157
deep ecology 7-8, 128, 134, 138
Devall, B. 7, 128, 135, 138, 192
Dobson, A. 1-2, 127-9, 133, 140, 146-8, 160n

Earth First! 26, 117, 124-5, 129, 133-4, 151, 157
Eckersley, R. 1-2, 25, 86, 115n, 131, 135, 139, 143-5, 160-1n, 177, 192
ecological self 135-6, 192-3, 210
Ecology Party 119, 149-50
Eder, K. 8-9, 19, 43, 61-9, 71, 77, 124, 129, 134, 137, 159n, 169, 173, 194, 199, 204, 210
Elias, N. 71, 87-9, 118, 175, 204

Evans, D. 57, 59, 90, 99, 104, 114n, 120, 123-4, 206

Fox, W. 86, 135-8, 192
Friends of the Earth (FoE) 17, 26, 103, 105, 117, 119-21, 127, 155, 157, 172, 195-6, 201

Giddens, A. 69, 72-3, 76, 78n, 118, 166, 168, 171-5, 186-7
Goldsmith, E. 11, 133, 141-2, 147, 162, 166
Goodin, R.E. 4, 8, 113n, 193
Goudsblom, J. 71, 165, 175, 199
Gould, P. 83-4, 91-2, 95-6, 107, 109, 113n, 129, 145
Green Party 22, 24, 47, 49, 78n, 119, 121, 128, 142-3, 147-57, 162n, 172, 195, 202, 209
Greenpeace 17, 25-6, 38, 98, 100, 103, 105, 117, 119, 121-7, 151, 154, 157, 163, 196-7, 201, 208-9

Habermas, J. 22-3, 32
Hannigan, J.A. 46, 72, 141
Harvey, D. 76, 86, 113n
Hetherington, K. 34, 197
Hill, O. 92, 96, 100, 205
Hobsbawm, E.J. 110, 184-5
Hunter, R. 92, 96, 100-1

Industrial Revolution 11, 93, 163-5, 167
Inglehart, R. 24, 44-5, 168-70

Jamison, A. 18, 48, 194-8

Kitschelt, H.P. 19, 46, 176
Klandermans, P.B. 18, 22, 40n
Kumar, K. 8, 39, 176, 178-80, 182, 187n
Landes, D.S. 164-5, 176

Lash, S. 13, 69-70, 72, 76, 210
Lovelock, J. 140-1, 160n
Lowe, P.D. 59, 121-3, 125, 152, 159n

Mannheim, K. 129, 199
Marsh, J. 83-4, 95, 97, 101, 102, 107
Martell, L. 43, 45, 47-9, 130, 146
Marx, K. 27-8, 62, 179, 184
McCormick, J. 26, 89-90, 114n, 121-2,
    156, 158n
Melucci, A. 16, 18-19, 22, 26, 29, 33-7,
    39, 47, 122, 176, 198
Merchant, C. 62, 204
Morris, W. 86, 96, 107, 108-9, 112,
    115n, 130, 135, 186, 205
Müller-Rommel, F. 117, 189
Musgrove, F. 134, 171, 208, 209

Naess, A. 7-8, 86, 135, 137
National Parks 57, 206-7
National Trust 2, 17, 90, 92, 94, 96-100,
    104-5, 121-4, 177, 205-6, 210
new social movements 10, 17, 19, 23,
    27, 30-1, 37, 84, 103, 117, 124, 128,
    137-8, 156, 168-70, 194

Offe, C. 19, 22, 25, 125, 212n
O'Riordan, T. 5, 12n, 79n, 135, 141, 191

Pakulski, J. 15, 41n, 175
Pepper, D. 4, 63, 107, 123, 129, 132, ,
    134, 136, 139-40, 173, 188n, 211n
phases (of environmentalism) 26-7, 57,
    90, 99, 118, 120-1, 124, 126, 133,
    157, 194-210 *passim*
Polanyi, K. 167, 182, 185,
Porritt, J. 1, 10, 67, 107, 152, 155, 158n,
    162n, 172-3
post-industrial theory 8-11, 12-14, 18-
    23, 26-7, 31-33, 35-6, 39-40, 71, 73,
    84, 118, 156, 163-4, 167, 169, 170,
    173-4, 181, 185-6, 187n, 210
postmaterialism 21, 24, 44-7, 164-70,
    209
process theories 37, 40, 71, 84, 139,

171, 174-5, 194, 199-203, 210
radical ecology 2, 4-8, 43, 50, 56, 59,
    61-2, 68-77 *passim*, 83-5, 92, 107,
    112, 118, 128-9, 130, 132, 134, 138,
    140-1, 142, 146-8, 151, 156-8, 164,
    186-7, 189-94, 197, 209-10
Ranlett, J. 95, 97-9, 105
romanticism 56, 62-4, 67-8, 77, 129,
    134-7, 145, 199-200, 204, 209
Roszak, T. 10, 171
R.S.P.B. 2-3, 17, 104, 206
Rucht, D. 19, 26-9, 32
Ruskin, J. 92, 96, 106, 135, 138, 205

Scott, A. 14-15, 19, 34, 47
Shaw-Lefevre, G. 93, 95, 97, 102-3
Shils, E. 170, 209, 213n
Sklair, L. 71, 126, 157, 194
social constructionism 49, 71-2
Spretnak, C. 138, 148-9
symbolic protest 20, 26, 35, 53, 94, 102-
    3, 113, 121, 125, 154
Szerszynski, B. 134-5, 142

Tarrow, S. 19, 51-5, 202
Tester, K. 12n, 72, 212n
Thomas, K. 65, 87, 89, 96, 104, 136,
    204
Thompson, E.P. 130, 160n
Toulmin, S. 8, 62-4, 75, 199
Touraine, A. 8-9, 18-19, 23, 26-33, 34,
    35, 37, 41n, 48, 55, 124, 128, 169,
    173, 188n, 198, 210

U.N.C.E.D process 202, 209

Weston, J. 107, 131-2
Williams, R. 85, 92, 150, 186
Worldwide Fund for Nature 17, 197,
    208-9
Worster, D. 129, 134-6
Wynne, B. 69-70, 73, 81n

Yearley, S. 26, 48, 72, 155
Zald, M. 17-18, 37, 139